Athene Series
Feminist Scholarship on
Culture and Education

General Editors
Gloria Bowles
Renate Klein
Janice Raymond

Consulting Editor
Dale Spender

(continued)

THE
Feminist Teacher
Anthology

PEDAGOGIES
AND
CLASSROOM STRATEGIES

Gail E. Cohee
Elisabeth Däumer
Theresa D. Kemp
Paula M. Krebs
Sue Lafky
Sandra Runzo
EDITORS

FOREWORD by *Bernice R. Sandler*

Teachers College, Columbia University
New York and London

Published by Teachers College Press, 1234 Amsterdam Avenue, New York, NY 10027

"Montreal, December '89" words and music by Judy Small. From the album "Snapshot," © Crafty Maid Music 1990.

"Prior Restraint," by Pauline Bart, in Pauline Bart and Eileen Moran (Eds.), *Violence Against Women: The Bloody Footprints*, p. 4, © 1993. Reprinted by permission of Sage Publications, Inc.

Library of Congress Cataloging-in-Publication Data

The Feminist teacher anthology : pedagogies and classroom strategy /
    Gail Cohee . . . [et al.] ; foreword by Bernice Sandler.
        p.   cm.
    Includes bibilographical references and index.
    ISBN 0-8077-6296-2.—ISBN 0-8077-6295-4 (pbk.)
        1. Feminism and educatlon—United States.   2. Women teachers—
United States.   3. Sexism in education—United States.
    4. Discrimination in education—United States.   I. Cohee, Gail.
    LC197.F478   1998
    370'.82—dc21   98-4870

ISBN 0-8077-6295-4 (paper)
ISBN 0-8077-6296-2 (cloth)

Printed on acid-free paper

Manufactured in the United States of America

05   04   03   02   01   00   99   98   8   7   6   5   4   3   2   1

Contents

PART II   BRINGING THE WORLD INTO THE FEMINIST CLASSROOM

Foreword

For many years, *Feminist Teacher* has been providing schoolteachers and college/university faculty members with information and classroom teaching strategies. Choosing from their wealth of impressive articles to make up this collection could not have been an easy task. This anthology of the "greatest hits" from *Feminist Teacher*'s first 10 volumes will be an inspiration to educators and thinkers in all sectors of education.

Feminist Teacher grew out of the need to examine the classroom and how gender affected it. Recognizing that the classroom does not sit in isolation but is an expression and outgrowth of the general culture, *Feminist Teacher* has covered a wide range of ideas such as the chilly classroom climate, mentoring, women in administration, and alternative classroom pedagogies from grade school to graduate school. It has also examined the intersection of race and gender in the classroom, as well as issues involving ethnicity, age, sexuality, and other factors.

One of the major strengths of *Feminist Teacher* over the years has been the translation of the knowledge produced by scholars into strategies, techniques, and tactics that teachers could use in the classroom. It is the only publication aimed at *those who teach*, whether they are teaching an introductory course in history, a high school math class, a graduate seminar, or a course in women's studies. Always on the cutting edge, it now examines new technologies, such as learning and video teaching, as well as the theoretical issues that arise with any new pedagogy. Collaborative learning has been at the heart of not only mainstream pedagogy, but also feminist pedagogy. Often overlooked by mainstream pedagogical thinkers, feminist pedagogy expands the notion of collaborative learning, especially as it applies to women and girls. One can read many of the leading theorists in pedagogical thinking, from John Dewey to Carl Rogers to Paolo Freire and Jonathan Kozol; none mentions gender in his discussions of teachers and students. *Feminist Teacher* remedies that omission by focusing on how gender affects the classroom and learning. In conclusion:

Feminist theory and pedagogy have been developed by communication among female faculty, students, and learners who were experiencing similar theoretical, political, and pedagogical "dissonance" with what the "founding fathers" had conceptualized as pedagogy for self and social empowerment. Feminists begin to ask the question: What difference does it make if the students you empower are women? Feminist theory and pedagogy are distinct in their focus on women and women's diversity of experience, how these experiences contextualize and inform knowledge, and how the classroom can be constructed to involve students as teacher-learner and invite them to be active participants in their own education (Sandler, Silverberg, & Hall, 1996, p. 38).

Bernice R. Sandler
Senior Scholar in Residence
National Association for Women in Education

REFERENCE

Sandler, Bernice R., Silverberg, Lisa A., and Hall, Roberta M. (1996). *The chilly classroom climate: A guide to improve the education of women*. Washington National Association of Women in Education.

Acknowledgments

No feminist project survives without the assistance of volunteers. *Feminist Teacher* is no different, and we would like to thank the friends, colleagues, student workers, and institutions that have helped the journal during its existence thus far. First of all, we are grateful to those who helped the journal during its early days at Indiana University. The journal received much needed assistance from friends Karen Frane, John Clower, and Alice Falk, as well as student workers Erika Schwindt, Judith Martin, Lisa Jung, and Cairril Mills. The Department of English at Indiana University, under chairs Mary Burgan and Patrick Brantlinger, provided crucial help in the form of office space, telephone access, and graduate assistance.

Likewise, Wheaton College in Norton, Massachusetts also made it possible for *Feminist Teacher* to have an office and student help while the journal was housed there. We would like to acknowledge the invaluable aid provided by Marilyn Todesco, Beverly Lyon Clark, the Department of English, the Office of the Provost, and the Madeline Clark Wallace Library. We also owe gratitude to editorial assistants Lauren Jenks, Angie Moorman, Rene Letourneau, Angie Pierce, Marcie Michaud, Anne Lewis, and Jess Vaile.

The College of Liberal Arts and Sciences and the Ethnic/Gender Studies Program at Emporia State University have made it possible most recently to house the business/production office of *Feminist Teacher* there. We would like to thank Leslie Lewis, the Director of the Ethnic/Gender Studies Program, graduate assistant Melody Stutzman, and office worker Jennifer Pope, for making the transition as smooth as possible. We are also grateful to the Department of English at the University of Alabama, Birmingham, for making it possible to move the journal's editorial office there.

In addition, we would like to thank Kristel Van Buskirk and Margaret Greathouse, who have served as editorial assistants at Denison University, as well as Carolyn Dyer and John Solski of the University of Iowa, Ernest M. Lafky, Carl J. Lafky, James O. Lafky, Dorothy M. Krebs, Caryn McTighe Musil, Claire Buck, Leslie Lewis, Mike Kemp, and Sylvia Brown, who have given invaluable help and support to the journal and to the members of the collective. We particularly want to thank former collective members Jane Hilberry and Diane Ledger for their tireless work on the journal, as well as Jeanne Kerl, the co-editor of book reviews.

The work involved in pulling together the collection of essays that form this book necessitates a separate list of acknowledgments. We want to thank Faye Zucker in particular, who believed in this book and who provided us with cogent advice on a number of decisions. Lori Tate, our production editor at Teachers College Press, has been a patient and skillful reader. The collection would not exist without our authors, of course, and we owe a debt of gratitude to them for taking the time to express their classroom experiences and strategies, observations, and theories in writing. We also would like to thank Eloise Buker, who offered cogent suggestions when we were developing the proposal for this project, and Katie Perry, Angie Pfeiffer, and the reference librarians at Eastern Michigan University, who provided essential help, often at the last minute.

While compiling this anthology has been a truly collective effort, we would like especially to acknowledge Sue Lafky for first promoting the idea of putting together a collection of *Feminist Teacher*'s "greatest hits," and Gail Cohee and Sandy Runzo for taking on the project. Without them the book would not have become a reality.

Collectively Speaking

As a group of graduate students at Indiana University in the early 1980s, we began to think about ways to combine feminist politics and perspectives with our classroom work as teachers. Dissatisfied with the departmentally mandated syllabi for the courses we were teaching (in the department of English and in the schools of journalism and education), we sought strategies for incorporating issues of gender, race, and class into the classroom. What started out as a project to subvert the traditional curriculum turned into something larger: *Feminist Teacher*. Beginning with the first issue in 1985, we at *Feminist Teacher* strove to make connections between theory and practice in the classroom and to provide a forum for teachers committed to fighting sexism, racism, classism, homophobia, and other forms of social injustice.

We decided early on to work as an editorial collective, modeling ourselves on the nonhierarchical organizational structure used by the radical feminist publication *off our backs*, published monthly out of Washington, D.C. As members of the collective, we share a vision of feminism as a political strategy as well as a theoretical position. The phrase *politics and teaching do mix* is something of an informal motto for us, serving not only as a reminder of *Feminist Teacher*'s goal of promoting a pedagogy that challenges dominant ideological, cultural, and political structures, but also as an acknowledgment that teaching within the dominant paradigm is inevitably a political act.

Although the commitment to examine the interlocking dynamics of gender, race, class, and power may be lauded in some academic circles, the labeling of this endeavor as *feminist* has never generated as many conflicting responses as now. Feminist theory continues to be identified with a narrow focus on gender, and this despite a growing number of works that explore the integral role of feminism to liberation movements, critical pedagogies, and ethnic/multicultural studies.[1] In addition, postmodernism—the most influential theoretical movement in academe in the past decade—is frequently yoked to "postfeminism," so that increasingly open and comprehensive views of sexuality, race, women, and culture would seem to judge feminism passé, the whining of special interests.[2]

In regard to teaching, it has become apparent that students are reluctant to name themselves feminist, even when their own behaviors, stands, and choices would seem to identify them as such. Feminist teachers, in turn, find their work trivialized or judged as inadequate by evaluation committees. This at the same time that many educational institutions have begun to embrace pedagogical practices first advanced by feminist teachers and to establish courses explicitly focused on women's issues and feminist theory (a process referred to by some as the institutionalization of feminism).[3]

Coincident with these changes, feminist teachers have come under increasing attacks from the Right. Most surprising, perhaps, is what Elaine Ginsberg and Sara Lennox (1996) name the "newest wave of antifeminism," which "cloaks itself in the vestments of feminism." These "new antifeminists are women who, claiming to be feminists themselves, now maintain that they are rescuing the women's movement from those who led it astray" (p. 170). As seen in recently published books, some scholars and teachers have voiced their reservations about central tenets of feminist pedagogy and the role of feminism in educating young women and men.[4] Clearly, speaking feminism and pursuing a feminist pedagogy are fraught with contention from both within and without.

Because of these recurring and shifting challenges to feminist education, because of the "backlash" to feminism, and because of the many distorting pictures presented of feminist pedagogy, this collection of essays addresses a vital need: Teachers and administrators—wherever they may live and work—urgently need more thoughtful theorizing and strategizing about feminism and education. Our own thinking about feminist education has been furthered by many fine books and essays published over the past 20 years: Berenice Fisher's 1981 essay in *Radical Teacher*, "What Is Feminist Pedagogy?"; Roberta Hall and Bernice Sandler's *The Classroom Climate: A Chilly One for Women?* (1982); Charlotte Bunch and Sandra Pollack's *Learning Our Way: Essays in Feminist Education* (1983); Margo Culley and Catherine Portuges's *Gendered Subjects: The Dynamics of Feminist Education* (1985); Kathleen Weiler's *Women Teaching for Change* (1988); Jennifer Gore's *The Struggle for Pedagogies* (1993); Carmen Luke and Gore's edited collection *Feminisms and Critical Pedagogy* (1992). The writers of the essays in this volume carry on the work of these educators and thinkers.

What issues garnered attention 10 years ago in *Feminist Teacher*? The first year of publishing included articles that addressed the interplay of race and gender, harassment in academe, equity in the classroom, girls' science anxiety, the self-esteem of girl and women students. Tellingly, these same issues have persistently demanded our attention over the decade. One of the most exciting aspects of assembling this collection has been the confirmation of the continuing interest and value of these essays; the evidence of their enduring relevance has also been discouraging. As several of the authors note in their newly written introductions, "Nothing has changed."

In an essay written in 1978, Adrienne Rich posited two choices for educators: "to lend our weight to the forces that indoctrinate women to passivity, self-depreciation, and a sense of powerlessness . . . or to consider what we have to work against, as well as with, in ourselves, in our students, in the content of the curriculum, in the structure of the institution, in society at large" (1979, p. 240). As editors, we witness the dedication and creativity of feminist teachers who fight this indoctrination and deliberate the very same choices and conflicts that Rich describes. The 19 essays in this volume reflect the practice of feminist teaching in its diversity and complexity. The authors profess both theory and practice; they exhibit the interdisciplinarity so common in the feminist classroom; they examine the means to use and shift the dynamics of power and powerlessness inherent in the classroom.

In these essays feminist teachers describe what they do in their classrooms and theorize what happens. Moreover, the authors' accounts of pedagogical practices reveal the many meanings of feminist education—its aims, its shapes, its difficulties, paradoxes, and possibilities. The essayists propose several tenets as prominent in feminist pedagogy:

1. Feminist pedagogy evolves from feminist social practice. It is therefore oriented toward social transformation, consciousness-raising, and social activism, that is, the translation of thought into action.

2. Feminist pedagogy emphasizes the development of epistemological frameworks that stress both the subjective and communal reality of knowing. It asks whose interests are served by knowledge and requires "knowers" and "learners" to be accountable to the uses of knowledge.

3. Feminist pedagogy is concerned for women students, both within and outside the classroom, and is committed to improving the lives of women.

4. Feminist pedagogy addresses race, class, and gender as crucial categories for analyzing experience and institutions. It also explores the complex and frequently ignored intersections of these categories.

5. Feminist pedagogy addresses the undeniable force of sexism and heterosexism in society.

6. Feminist pedagogy is concerned with exploring issues of sexuality honestly with students and with aiding students in discovering a language with which to discuss sexualities.

This collection of essays allows readers to review or familiarize themselves with feminist pedagogy as it evolves in the teaching practices of
educators in a variety of disciplines and circumstances. In addition to implicitly or expressly theorizing feminist pedagogy, the authors in this collection put forth practical classroom strategies: readings and resources,
writing assignments, classroom exercises, "field exercises" (Deay and
Stitzel's phrase), "active engagement assignments" (James's phrase), and
guidance for using journals, multimedia workshops, and new technologies. Drawing on examples from their own experiences in classrooms,
workshops, or administrative offices, the authors provide specific suggestions for generating students' (or other participants') involvement, for
preventing students from distancing themselves from feminist research
or dismissing it, and for helping students and teachers alike cope with
the often daunting task of examining women's lives as they are actually
lived.

The collection is divided into two parts: "Encountering the Classroom:
Developing Feminist Strategies" and "Bringing the World into the Feminist Classroom." In each part, the essays are arranged chronologically, so
that those in Part I originally appeared from 1985 through 1995, and those
in Part II from 1988 through 1994. Each essay contains a new introduction,
which either updates resources or information or offers the author's reflections on her/his original essay. In addition, each essay includes a brief
author biography.

The essayists in Part I look at various manifestations of feminist pedagogy—theoretical as well as practical. They offer guidelines for confronting very real problems often faced by feminist teachers, students, and administrators. Although it should go without saying that teaching is the most
important work of educators, Carla Golden examines the reality that di-
minishes the centrality of teaching for those who work in colleges and
universities. She stresses that despite the lack of encouragement proffered
for good teaching, placing a high value on teaching can be important feminist work. Even a commitment to so-called small gestures, such as learning students' names, is deemed important to her work as a feminist educator. Frances A. Maher recalls teaching an early introduction to women's
studies class, and, through that recollection, examines assumptions regarding our authority as teachers, goals we set for what students learn, and
attitudes about the epistemological basis for knowledge. Sue V. Rosser's
"Warming Up the Classroom Climate for Women" takes as its starting point
the series of "Chilly Climate" papers produced by the Project on the Status and Education of Women of the Association of American Colleges (Hall
& Sandler, 1982, 1984; Sandler & Hall, 1986). Rosser offers concrete exercises to help faculty, students, and administrators recognize and diffuse

the various forms of sexism too often present in educational settings. Karen J. Warren addresses yet another important aspect of the manifestation of feminism in the academy—through challenging the mainstream ("malesteam") curriculum. Warren states that the "feminist challenge is to make the curriculum inclusive of women" and proposes multiple aims of feminist pedagogy.

Every feminist teacher who has ever entered a classroom has heard about the "exception to the rule"—the examples that students cite to disprove statistics and other general statements about women and men, and thus to dismiss whatever the teacher might have to say. This is exactly the topic that Susanne Bohmer examines in her essay. She provides welcome suggestions for keeping these "exceptions" from disrupting or derailing a class. As Martha E. Thompson reminds us, telling and hearing the truth of women's lives is often painful and anxiety producing for students as well as teachers. In "The Power of No," Thompson transfers a technique used by IMPACT self-defense instructors into the classroom to help channel those emotions into something constructive. In her description of a first-year required course on gender, race, and class, Joy James offers compelling classroom strategies designed to raise students' consciousness and to enable students to understand their own place and role in larger structures of oppression and domination. Ardeth Deay and Judith Stitzel confront, head-on, the sometimes unsettling emotions—their own and their students'—elicited by teaching as feminists, and offer 10 field exercises aimed at addressing resistance in the classroom. Recounting her experiences teaching in a community educational program, Berenice Fisher explains how she used a variety of pedagogical media, including drama, movement, and visual art, to enable students' exploration of their relation to the newspaper and to their notions of home. Implicit in the use of such varied pedagogical media, Fisher argues, is an important feminist critique of "received distinctions about what is 'educational.'" Distance learning initiatives often grow out of schools' desires to serve more students with fewer teachers, but Ellen Cronan Rose points out the feminist potential of video and E-mail technologies as well as the pitfalls. Cronan Rose is self-critical in her discussion of her own teaching, a characteristic she shares with many other authors in this collection.

The essayists in Part II share a vision of the classroom (and other sites of learning or knowledge production within educational institutions) as inevitably gendered and racialized places in which larger social and cultural conflicts are reproduced. The classroom perhaps cannot fully become a haven in which no one is silenced or marginalized; the authors nevertheless contend that by alerting students to the powerful role of gender, race, class, and sexuality in understanding self and others, the classroom can become an important, if never entirely comfortable or conflict-free, site of critical consciousness-raising and social transformation. Paula Rothenberg examines her difficulties in persuading students that racism and sexism continue to be fundamental, identity-shaping forces. She insists that unless we talk about gender, race, and class in integrated ways, we will obscure, rather than illuminate, these forces. David Bleich draws on first-year student essays on homosexuality to demonstrate that "sexism underlies homophobia." In addressing the virulent hostility against homosexuals in students' writing, Bleich theorizes on males' social anxieties regarding both women's equality and males' loss of power. The essay composed by Allison Berg, Jean Kowaleski, Caroline Le Guin, Ellen Weinauer, and Eric A. Wolfe continues the examination of students' difficulties discussing sexual preference and extends that investigation to teachers' difficulties. The authors assess the heterosexist bias in a specific assignment of their design and contemplate the conflict generated from students' "silence" and "honesty" in reacting to that assignment.

Lynette Carpenter's essay highlights the crosscurrent that feminist administrators must navigate between the desire to make an institution more humane and more feminist and the university's status quo. She reminds us of the sometimes untenable position of daily compromise faced by the feminist administrator, cautioning us to not hold her to impossibly idealistic principles and urging us to choose our fights carefully—to be wary of creating the kind of divisiveness that antifeminists can use against us. In "The Hand and the Hammer" Eloise Knowlton takes on the most mundane of topics—classroom equipment—in order to query classroom semiotics. In her elegant deconstruction of the overhead projector, Knowlton ponders the power structure and gendered significations of a specific classroom "scene." In her analysis of the importance of an "authentic" classroom atmosphere, Janet Wright proposes that coming out as a lesbian or gay man not only models honesty and acceptance, but also puts forward for examination issues of oppression, identity, silencing, and power. Suzanne K. Damarin reminds us of the ever increasing role of technology in our teaching and research. She takes off from the pioneering work of primatologist and historian of science Donna Haraway to ask feminist teachers, "Would you rather be a cyborg or a goddess?" We can and should be a bit of both, she argues. In her essay on the 1989 Montreal massacre, Jennifer Scanlon emphasizes that the emotional and political climates outside the classroom directly affect women's ability to participate fully as fruitful producers of culture and society. She advocates that we situate the massacre along a continuum of harassment, violence, and hatred against women, insisting that "until we name the connections, little will change." The final essay of this collection calls us to reflect upon the meanings of radicalism at a time when radical thought is rejected, depoliticized, or commodified as trendy. Recalling her experience teaching a course called Gender, Race, and Radicalism, Joy James explores students' troubled responses to the antiracist analyses of structural violence and genocide embedded in the autobiographies of Native American and African American women who were also activists engaged in liberation movements.

The special usefulness of these essays, taken together, is that they move beyond analysis of the obstacles and the frustrations of feminist teaching and feminist administrating to proposing detailed strategies and resources for raising students' (and teachers') consciousness about gender, race, class, and sexuality; for responding, in sensitive and respectful ways, to student resistance; for introducing students to—or constructing with them—epistemological frameworks that allow them/us to understand our own place and role in larger structures of domination and oppression; for transforming larger institutional environments to make them physically safe for women students; for transforming larger institutional environments to make them more equitable, democratic places for the collective construction of knowledge; for creating a classroom atmosphere of acceptance and openness for gay and lesbian students and teachers; for addressing students' fears and prejudices regarding difference.

Although we have organized the essays into two main sections, these writings may be grouped in other provocative and productive ways. For instructors wishing to use the anthology as a textbook for courses in education or women's studies, but who may not have time to cover all the essays in their syllabus, we suggest some potential categories and alternative groupings. "Pedagogy and the Role of Media and Technology": Cronan Rose, Fisher, Knowlton, Damarin, Scanlon. "Teaching about Gender, Race, and Class": one or both essays by James, Rothenberg, Warren. "Teaching about Sexualities": Bleich, Berg et al., Wright. "The Transformative Power of Feminist Teachers and Administrators": Golden, Maher, Warren, Wright, Damarin, Carpenter. "The Classroom Climate": Rosser, Bohmer, Thompson, Deay and Stitzel, Bleich, Berg et al. These groupings are by no means definitive, and readers certainly will devise other ways of linking the essays.

Despite the richness of this collection, one volume cannot cover every issue pertaining to feminist pedagogy. None of the essays discusses the hiring or tenuring of feminist teachers, for example, although stories with which all of us are personally familiar, or a glance through the programs of the yearly conferences of the National Women's Studies Association, remind us that these concerns remain salient. The collection also does not address the new challenges created by the dismantling of public assistance at the federal level and the consequent hindrances to earning a college degree that many women encounter. While we wish that this volume could address all the issues confronting feminist teachers, administrators, and scholars, the gaps reinforce the multiple concerns of feminists within the academy and outside of it. This collection testifies to the central, abiding role of feminist educators in creating and maintaining equitable learning, teaching, and research environments in which women, and men, can reach their full intellectual and emotional potential.

The *Feminist Teacher Collective*
Gail E. Cohee, Emporia State University
Elisabeth Däumer, Eastern Michigan University
Theresa D. Kemp, University of Alabama at Birmingham
Paula M. Krebs, Wheaton College
Sue Lafky, University of Iowa
Sandra Runzo, Denison University

NOTES

1. See, for example, bell hooks's *Talking Back* and her *Teaching to Transgress*; Henry A. Giroux; Paula Rothenberg; Patricia Hill Collins; Liza Fiol-Matta and Miriam K. Chamberlain.
2. For critiques of postmodernism's creation of a postfeminism, see Somer Brodribb and Tania Modleski. See Susan Faludi for analysis of declarations of postfeminism by the media.
3. For commentary on this phenomenon, see Jane Gallop's introduction to her *Around 1981: Academic Feminist Literary Theory*.
4. See, for example, Daphne Patai and Noretta Koertge, and Christine Hoff Sommers.

REFERENCES

Brodribb, Somer. (1992). *Nothing mat(t)ers: A feminist critique of postmodernism*. North Melbourne, Australia: Spinifex Press.

Bunch, Charlotte, and Pollack, Sandra. (1983). *Learning our way: Essays in feminist education*. Trumansburg: Crossing Press.

Collins, Patricia Hill. (1991). *Black feminist thought: Knowledge, consciousness, and the politics of empowerment*. New York: Routledge.

Culley, Margo, and Portuges, Catherine. (1985). *Gendered subjects: The dynamics of feminist education*. Boston: Routledge & Kegan Paul.

Faludi, Susan. (1992). *Backlash: The undeclared war against American women*. New York: Doubleday.

Fiol-Matta, Liza, and Chamberlain, Miriam K. (Eds.). (1994). *Women of color and the multicultural curriculum: Transforming the college classroom.* New York: Feminist Press.

Fisher, Berenice. (1981). What is feminist pedagogy? *Radical Teacher, 18,* 24–29.

Gallop, Jane. (1992). Introduction. In *Around 1981: Academic feminist literary theory* (pp. 1–10). New York: Routledge.

Ginsberg, Elaine, and Lennox, Sara. (1996). Antifeminism in scholarship and publishing. In V. Clark, S. N. Garner, M. Higonnet, and K. H. Katrak (Eds.) (pp. 169–199). *Antifeminism in the academy.* New York: Routledge.

Giroux, Henry. (Ed.). (1991). *Postmodernism, feminism, and cultural politics: Redrawing educational boundaries.* Albany: State University of New York Press.

Gore, Jennifer. (1993). *The struggle for pedagogies: Critical and feminist discourses as regimes of truth.* New York: Routledge.

Hall, Roberta M., and Sandler, Bernice R. (1982). *The classroom climate: A chilly one for women?* Washington, DC: Project on the Status and Education of Women, Association of American Colleges.

hooks, bell. (1989). *Talking back: Thinking feminist, thinking black.* Boston: South End Press.

hooks, bell. (1994). *Teaching to transgress: Education as the practice of freedom.* New York: Routledge.

Luke, Carmen, & Gore, Jennifer. (Eds.). (1992). *Feminisms and critical pedagogy.* New York: Routledge.

Modleski, Tania. (1991). *Feminism without women: Culture and criticism in a "postfeminist" age.* New York: Routledge.

Patai, Daphne, and Koertge, Noretta. (1994). *Professing feminism: Cautionary tales from the strange world of women's studies.* New York: Basic Books.

Rich, Adrienne. (1979). Taking women students seriously. In *On lies, secrets, and silence* (pp. 237–245). New York: Norton.

Rothenberg, Paula S. (Ed.). (1995). *Race, class, and gender in the United States: An integrated study.* New York: St. Martin's Press.

Sommers, Christine Hoff. (1994). *Who stole feminism?* New York: Touchstone.

Weiler, Kathleen. (1988). *Women teaching for change: Gender, class and power.* South Hadley, MA: Bergin & Garvey.

ABOUT THE EDITORS

Gail E. Cohee currently teaches English and is a member of the steering committee of the Ethnic/Gender Studies Program at Emporia State University. Her work focuses on early modern British literature, literature by women, and feminist pedagogy. She has been the co-editor of book reviews for *Feminist Teacher* for several years and is now managing the business/production office for the journal. She is also active in the National Women's Studies Association.

A founding member of the *Feminist Teacher* editorial collective, **Elisabeth Däumer** is an associate professor of English at Eastern Michigan University. She teaches introductions to literature, twentieth-century poetry, and literary theory. Born and raised in what was then West Berlin, she became interested in feminism long before joining the doctoral program in English at Indiana University. Her work in feminist theory and poetry has appeared in such journals as *Hypatia* and *English Literary History*.

Theresa D. Kemp is an assistant professor of English at the University of Alabama at Birmingham, where she teaches early modern British literature and English women writers before 1700. She has written on teaching Elizabeth Carey's *Tragedy of Mariam* and *Othello* for *Shakespeare Quarterly*, and has contributed to *The Bloomsbury Guide to Women's Literature*. She is now managing the editorial office for *Feminist Teacher*.

Paula M. Krebs, another founding member of the *Feminist Teacher* collective, teaches Victorian literature and cultural studies at Wheaton College in Norton, Massachusetts. Her research focuses on questions of gender and race in Victorian imperial discourse.

Sue Lafky is an associate professor of journalism and mass communication at the University of Iowa. She received her undergraduate degree from the University of Oregon and her M.A. and Ph.D. from Indiana University. She teaches gender and mass media. She also will teach the first course on feminist pedagogy to be offered for the new doctoral program in women's studies, which will begin at the University of Iowa in 1998.

Sandra Runzo is an associate professor of English and women's studies at Denison University in Granville, Ohio. She writes about women poets of nineteenth- and twentieth-century America, as well as about feminist pedagogy. She, too, is a founding member of the *Feminist Teacher* editorial collective.

Part I

Encountering the Classroom: Developing Feminist Strategies

CHAPTER I

The Radicalization of a Teacher

Carla Golden

I wrote this article when I had been teaching for 7 full years, which in my youthful view was a long time. What amazes me now is how much of what I expressed in the original article still holds true after 20 full years of teaching, though I use the word *full* here in a very different sense than one of time, to mean both rich and laden. I am still a radical college teacher and continue to regard teaching as the most important work I do. Although I experience more support than previously for this stance, I also feel challenged in that priority, in ways that are more subtle and by people I wouldn't have expected it from (some feminist academics). As for the practice, noted in my article, of learning the names of all my students, I'm as committed as ever and more than willing to share my strategy.

As I reflect on what I wrote, I realize that my concept of what constitutes teaching has broadened; no longer is it simply what I do in the classrooms of my home campus or on other campuses where I am invited to speak. I welcome the opportunity to teach at community sites, from Rotary clubs to public schools, where I interact with teachers, parents, and interested citizens. I consider such teaching political.

Probably the most remarkable change is that I have completely altered my *style* of teaching, while remaining committed to the seven components I earlier identified as essential to a liberal arts education. At the time I wrote the accompanying article, my teaching consisted almost entirely of lecturing, regardless of class size. Currently, I teach classes of about 30 students, but I no longer lecture at all.

This chapter originally appeared in *Feminist Teacher*, 1985, *1*(3), 22–25.

The Feminist Teacher *Anthology: Pedagogies and Classroom Strategies.* Copyright © 1998 by Teachers College, Columbia University. All rights reserved. ISBN 0-8077-3741-0 (paper), ISBN 0-8077-3742-9 (cloth). Prior to photocopying items for classroom use, please contact the Copyright Clearance Center, Customer Service, 222 Rosewood Drive, Danvers, MA 01923, USA, telephone (508) 750-8400.

As I read over the seven goals I had outlined as critical to my teaching, I was struck by the degree to which they are still integral. I wouldn't change the gist of any of them, though I might present them differently. For example, I still very much stand by my sixth and seventh goals (examining one's own life, and developing and acting on a sense of social responsibility), though if I were to write it now I would probably be more specific in referring to ethnicity, "race," class, gender, sexuality, and so on, and most crucially, to the interconnectedness of these in understanding people and addressing oppression.

After 20 years of teaching, I can securely say, and without internalized devaluation, that teaching continues to be my most important work. This position has not gone unquestioned by certain of my feminist academic peers who have built their professional lives on their scholarship, more than on their teaching. They convey in subtle ways that they can't imagine why I don't do the same, especially since I have been increasingly recognized for my scholarly work over the years. How could I be so satisfied with teaching, they wonder? In the end, I think we do what really engages us. And through 20 years of teaching what has most engaged me is the young people who come into my care, whose lives I affect and who affect mine. As their minds are opened to new ideas, so is mine; as they envision and strive to create a different kind of world, so do I. They inspire me and give me hope for the future.

I went to graduate school in psychology because I wanted to be a university professor. Ten years later I am proud to identify myself as a radical college teacher. In the intervening years, I completed my graduate training in life span developmental psychology, secured an academic position at an elite women's college, and became totally immersed in women's studies and feminist psychology. After 6 years, I lost that first academic position and found another. In the context of these and related experiences I evolved from aspiring university professor to radical college teacher.

Even though I had chosen to go to graduate school because I wanted to teach, my development as a teacher was profoundly affected by the devaluation of teaching so pervasive in institutions of higher learning. The subtle ways in which I had internalized this devaluation made me unaware of how important teaching was to me. Although my behavior and active commitment to teaching suggested otherwise, I could not, until recently, feel comfortable and confident about the priority I placed on teaching in my work as an academic psychologist.

LEARNING TO DEVALUE

What I would like to do in this chapter is to describe two critical incidents from my life as a teacher. These incidents raised my consciousness about the extent to which even I, whose dream was to be a university professor, had internalized the devaluation of teaching. First, I will discuss why I pursued graduate study and what my early professional socialization was like.

I chose to go to graduate school in psychology because as an under-graduate I felt absorbed and challenged by psychological issues. I thought that as a graduate student, and then as a professor, I would be able to continue doing what I found so stimulating—reading books and discussing ideas with intelligent people who were interested in learning. But most of all, I really wanted to teach in a college or university.

The discipline of psychology is just over 100 years old, and it is a dis-cipline whose nonclinical practitioners, for historical reasons as well as those related to status and prestige, pride themselves on being scientists. So what I learned in graduate school was to become a researcher. This meant thinking in terms of testing and verifying hypotheses about human behavior. It meant learning to think quantitatively and to do experiments. I took, along with content-based psychology courses, those in experimen-tal design and statistics. I learned how to read and critically evaluate writ-ings about quantitative research, to conduct my own research, and to write about it.

The work was absorbing, and I hardly noticed what was absent in my professional training. What is very clear to me now is that although I was taught how to evaluate research and to do my own, I was never taught to be a teacher. In fact, teaching was almost never discussed.

Nevertheless, I had the opportunity to teach during my fourth year in graduate school. Before that year, nothing was ever said to me about teach-ing and its place in one's work as an academic psychologist. In fact, my advisers discussed teaching with me in more than superficial terms only twice that year. One of those discussions is worth mentioning: The chair of my graduate program asked me to come into his office to discuss the com-puterized course evaluations from the courses I was teaching. He told me that mine were the best ratings he had ever seen for a graduate student in the department and suggested that they could only mean that I was de-voting too much time to my teaching and that I wasn't putting as much energy as I should into my dissertation research. He said that in getting and keeping an academic position, my research credentials would be far more important than positive teaching evaluations. From experience, I have now learned that he was absolutely correct.

The sad truth is that I did not receive any support for teaching during my graduate school years. After having conversations with peers, I don't believe that my experience was at all uncommon. I at least had the opportunity to teach while in graduate school; some of my academic colleagues didn't even have that. But still, having the opportunity to teach is not in itself sufficient. It is important to learn how to teach in an environment where teaching is taken seriously and where there is recognition that teaching is as critical to our training as academic psychologists as is learning to do research.

I would have benefited from the opportunity to discuss the process of teaching with others who were engaged in it. Among other things, this would have served as an acknowledgment that teaching is a complex process that requires both skill and effort. I can think of no other kind of professional work for which there is a training period, in which the trainees are so often uninstructed in the theory and process of what is clearly to become a major part of their work after they have established employment in the field for which they have been trained.

During my last year in graduate school, I began to look for an academic position, and I discovered that there was one in the psychology department at Smith College, which I knew to be an undergraduate liberal arts college for women. Like other private liberal arts colleges, it was (supposed to be) devoted to excellence in teaching. I was excited by the prospect of teaching in such a place, and in my rather naive state, I was sure that I had found the perfect teaching environment.

I applied, I got the job, and I was terrified. Despite my success in teaching in graduate school, I was sure I would fail miserably at Smith. I was afraid that I was really an impostor, that I wasn't as good as my previous students thought, and that in coming to Smith I would be found out. I was later to learn that such feelings are not at all uncommon among professional, high-achieving women. I learned from reading the literature that some psychologists had identified a "phenomenon" (psychologists have a tendency to call interesting behavioral quirks phenomena) that they characterized as the imposter phenomenon. This refers to the tendency among high-achieving women who are quite successful by objective criteria (e.g., as demonstrated in the winning of awards, receiving of promotions, etc.) to feel as if they are imposters.

I found, however, that I was good at teaching at Smith. And during my years there I found the process of teaching more and more demanding and at the same time more and more stimulating, challenging, and rewarding. Teaching let me learn about areas of my discipline that were different from the very specialized area of my research. And teaching let me interact with students and participate in their intellectual and social development.

ATTITUDE PROBLEM

I can say now, unequivocally and after 7 years of doing it, that I consider teaching to be the most important work I do. But I haven't always been able to say that because I haven't always known it. Or perhaps it would be more accurate to say that even when I did realize it I couldn't feel good about it because I thought there was something wrong with my attitude. Teaching is devalued in academe, and even at an institution that claimed to be devoted to teaching, there was never much support for my commitment to teaching, so I thought there was something wrong with my attitude.

For me to so thoroughly enjoy teaching, and to view it as central in my professional life, was odd. Not only did I believe that it was important, but I wanted to direct my primary energies to teaching, and this kind of priority was both unusual and different. As so often happens when we feel different, we begin to wonder whether there is something wrong with us. And other people tend to treat us as if we are peculiar, which serves to confirm our own sense of deviance.

One experience stands out in my memory. During my first year at Smith, a professor from another department asked me how I liked teaching at Smith. I answered honestly and enthusiastically that I found it challenging and that I enjoyed it immensely. He appeared shocked, and then he asked me how long I had been teaching. When I said that it was my first year, his surprise was much abated, and he said something like "That explains it," and said that he would be interested in my response to the same question 2 years hence. His attitude was clearly that teaching is a burden, a view repeatedly confirmed by other academicians who refer to the courses they teach as their "teaching load."

I have often been the recipient of similarly negative attitudes whenever I have expressed such positive sentiments about teaching. I can't recount the number of times my colleagues have told me that my love of teaching would wear off with time, and that while they too loved it when they were younger, they had come to tire of it and find it dull. At first I was quite distressed by those remarks because I took them to be true, and I began to dread that day when teaching would cease to be exciting and challenging.

But my love of teaching remains strong after 7 full years, and although there are those who would still have me believe that I have yet to pass the magic age beyond which even the greatest of teachers lose their excitement about the process, I no longer believe them. I suspect that their need to convince me otherwise says more about them and their experiences of teaching than it does about me and mine. I have only recently come to understand the extent to which people who have long since lost excitement about what they are doing find another person's vitality threatening and almost intolerable.

I have recounted here some experiences concerning what certain academics have said to me. I was fully aware of the devaluation of teaching inherent in their words. The two critical incidents to which I alluded at the beginning of this paper reveal the extent to which I had internalized the devaluation of teaching in spite of my sensitivity to devaluing the attitudes of others.

The first such experience occurred 3 years ago when I was teaching a course on the psychology of women. With its 13-page syllabus, 5-hour-a-week time commitment, and the amount of written work required, it is what was known as a heavy-duty course. On the first day of the class, I wanted to impress upon the students that I was very serious about my teaching and that I expected them to be serious about the course. I said to them—and this is a direct quote—"I take teaching very seriously; it's one of the most important things I do professionally." I was aware as I spoke those words that I wasn't being exactly truthful. Teaching was *the* most important thing I did professionally, not one of the most important. I was conscious of the fact that at the last moment before the words came out of my mouth I added *one of the* because I didn't want to admit that I felt that teaching was the most important aspect of my work as an academic psychologist.

When the class ended, I thought about why I had done that, and it was then that I realized that I didn't want to admit my real feelings because I had internalized the devaluation of teaching. I didn't know anyone among my colleagues who would say that being a teacher was more important than being a scholar. Some rated teaching and scholarship as equally important, and some, in keeping with their professional socialization, considered scholarship more important than teaching. But never had I encountered an academic who felt that teaching was more important and more rewarding than his or her scholarly activities.

This incident revealed to me that although I experienced teaching as the most important part of my work, I was reluctant to admit this, even to the people who would be the most likely to appreciate it—the students. At some deeper level I felt that it somehow reflected a flaw in my professional character.

WHAT'S YOUR NAME?

The second experience I'd like to describe demonstrates that my consciousness continues to be raised about the importance of teaching in my life and the extent to which I have been unconsciously resistant to acknowledging its importance. I believe that it is important and worthwhile to learn the names of the students in my classes. In small classes (those with 25 to 35 students), I learn names in 3 or 4 days, and in large classes of about 100 students, it takes me about 6 days, or 2 weeks of class. This is a matter of amazement to my students, and I've gone through an interesting three-stage progression in understanding why I do it. At first, I was simply pleased with the students' reaction. They were impressed with what they could only view as an awesome memory, and in response I was pleased with what I uncritically thought of as my impressive memory.

As each semester brought new batches of students who were impressed with the power of my memory, I became somewhat bored by it. My second reaction to students' amazement and their continued query, "How do you do it?" was to develop a specific response to the question. It started out as a spontaneous answer given in class to a student who asked the question. Over the course of several years, it developed into a fairly polished account that I offered when, early in the semester, the question was inevitably posed. I contended that if one is really motivated, one can do almost anything, at least something as simple as learning names. I speculated that if the college administration were to offer $5,000 to those faculty members who learned the names of their students in the first or second week of classes, many more professors would undoubtedly learn their students' names. After all, I noted with sarcasm, the college administration often called attention to its distinguished faculty. Surely they could accomplish a task involving simple memorization. Finally, I pointed out to my students that perhaps what should amaze them more than the fact that I learned their names was that in their other, often smaller, classes they remained nameless. You can see why certain of my colleagues were not overly pleased with my views.[1]

THROUGH THE GRAPEVINE

Eventually, I reached a third level of awareness about what is involved in learning students' names. This awareness was triggered by a phone call from a member of the faculty at a prominent southern university. The woman who called had been teaching for about 8 years, and she had decided it was not too late to begin learning her students' names. She had heard through the professional grapevine that I had a strategy for doing this and was calling to see if I would share it with her. I was flattered that my powers of memory were known beyond Smith, and, as I was in the habit of doing whenever I was asked about my ability to remember names, I launched into my motivational account. This somewhat distinguished psychologist listened politely as I spoke about how she could do it as long as she was motivated to do so, and then she said, quite emphatically, "I am already motivated. The reason I called was to learn your strategy." Somewhat impatiently she repeated the purpose of her call, "I want to know exactly how you do it."

I had never been asked so pointedly, and by such an "important" person to explain my strategy. But I proceeded to do so, articulating for the first time exactly how I did it. It took me about 25 minutes to describe to her in precise detail what I did to learn the names of my students. Without my ever having been consciously aware of it, I had developed a rather sophisticated strategy for this practice. The psychologist with whom I spoke expressed amazement, not at my ability to remember names, but at my willingness to invest the time and energy that it took to use the strategy I had described to her. As I reflected on the phone conversation, I realized that I had minimized the process of learning students' names because I didn't want to admit (to myself or others) that I put so much effort into it. Although I had made conscious efforts to challenge the hierarchical nature of the educational process (and learning students' names was one such challenge), I hadn't completely rejected all aspects of it. At some level, I had internalized that I was more important than the students. For me, a professor, to spend 2 important hours of my time each day for the first week of class learning the names of people as "unimportant" as students was a challenge to the hierarchy of the system as well as to my own sense of importance. I wanted to convey the impression that, although it certainly was important to me, it didn't take very much effort. Once again, I was shocked to realize the extent to which I had been affected by hierarchical values and negative attitudes toward teaching.

Thinking about why (and not simply how) I learn students' names led me to another important insight about teaching and what it means to me. I learn the names of my students because I couldn't imagine doing otherwise. I learn names because it is absolutely critical, if what one is doing is teaching students. Whereas some professors see themselves as primarily teaching a subject or a discipline, others like myself consider themselves to be teaching students. And there's an enormous difference. If one is teaching subject matter, knowing students' names might not be critical. But if one is teaching students, learning their names constitutes an essential first step in the teaching/learning process.

I do, of course, teach a specific subject. I teach introductory psychology, developmental psychology, and the psychology of women. My major concern, however, is with students' intellectual and social growth in the broadest sense. I try to teach my students things that I consider essential to a liberal arts education, and I use psychology as the medium for that kind of teaching.

A SEVEN-POINT PLAN

I have identified at least seven aspects of a liberal arts education that I consider essential and that I strive to incorporate in my teaching. First of all, I want my students to experience learning and thinking as exciting and challenging and to know that reading and discussing issues and ideas can enrich their lives. I hope that they will leave my classes wanting to read more and to discuss the issues raised in class with their friends and with others. I try to convey this excitement through my own enthusiasm and through lecture and readings. This sometimes means choosing to teach about issues that are not necessarily in the mainstream of the discipline. I have found that the theoretical and empirical issues that are of most significance to the experts in the field are not necessarily so to students.

Second, I want my students to learn that to write well is both necessary and important. I require a lot of written work, and I comment extensively on student papers. I want students to recognize their weaknesses in writing and to realize that good writing requires hard work. I'm not sure where so many of them picked up the notion that one either is or isn't a good writer and that effort has little to do with it. When they seem unappreciative of my urging more effort in writing papers, I point out to them that there will be no other period in their lives when someone else will take the time and energy to supervise and comment extensively on their written work. I encourage them to take advantage of this opportunity to work on their writing.

Third, I want my students to feel comfortable when speaking. I provide as many opportunities as I can for them to speak and express their views to the rest of the class. One kind of assignment that I have found works well in facilitating oral expression is to have students engage in discussion sessions, one with a classmate who has been exposed to the same new ideas they have, and one with a person who is not in the class. This provides the opportunity for them to articulate what they have learned as well as to think it through more thoroughly and to build on their knowledge with peers.

My fourth goal is that my students learn that thinking for themselves is crucial. I encourage them to think through issues and to form and express their own opinions. I am more pleased when a student says that after much thought and consideration of an issue that I raised in a lecture, she doesn't quite agree with me than I am by a student who comes up right after class and says that she agrees with everything I have said.

My fifth goal is to have my students learn that discipline is important. Too many of the things that students learn these days in college cannot be generalized to apply to their lives beyond college, but learning how to discipline oneself is one skill that will continue to have relevance. I try to emphasize the importance of discipline by expecting students to be in class on time and to hand in work on time. Unfortunately, I have found procrastination a serious problem among the students I have taught.

A sixth aim in my teaching philosophy is that students, in their classes as well as in extracurricular activities, examine their own lives. I want them to give serious thought to how they have lived and how they would like to live. Further, I would like them to consider the ways in which their own lives connect with or impinge on those of others on this earth. Toward this end, I present material (in readings and lectures) that will facilitate their thinking about such issues.

Along the same lines, but of separate importance, I want my students to be socially responsible and concerned as a result of their having taken my classes. I want them to understand the importance of learning about other people, about other cultures, and about what is going on in the world. I hope to help them develop a sense of social responsibility and to see ways that they can express that sense. I want them to know and to feel that they can make a difference in whatever way seems right for them. To foster such commitment, I integrate material about persons who have resisted oppression and have been engaged in social change movements. In addition, I do not hesitate to make announcements in class about campus, community, and national groups with which they might become involved.

I think that what these seven goals amount to is teaching students to take themselves and their education seriously. In Adrienne Rich's terms, I want to create a climate in which my students can claim their education, and my role in the classroom and my course structure are designed to facilitate that. From all that I have said, the difference between teaching students and teaching subject matter should be clear. I hope that my students will be excited by the subject matter that I present in class and that they will remember some of it. But when they forget the facts, I must admit that I don't really care. What I do care deeply about are those seven goals, which I believe are independent of subject matter yet can be taught as part of any subject.

In my evolution from aspiring university professor to radical college teacher, I have come to identify teaching as of primary importance in my work. This was not without some periods of subtle and insidious self-doubt. But through reflecting on several fairly ordinary experiences, my repressed consciousness was awakened, and I was able to give clear expression to my teaching philosophy. I am a teacher of students, and I want my students to learn to take their education, themselves, other people, and their social responsibilities seriously. In educational institutions where teaching wasn't so devalued, there wouldn't be anything particularly radical about that.

NOTE

1. In fairness to my colleagues, however, let me note that many of them do not learn their students' names not because they don't care but because they think they can't, or, even more sadly, it hasn't even occurred to them that they should try. And this is related to the fact that many graduate students receive no training and supervision in teaching skills. If I were to teach a course to graduate students or to teachers about how to create an environment in the classroom that was hospitable to learning, I would emphasize as a critical starting point the learning of students' names. I have found that students feel alive and present in the classroom when their teacher knows they are there and knows something as simple, yet as personal, as their names. I, too, feel totally different about walking into a classroom of named, as opposed to nameless, faces.

ABOUT THE AUTHOR

Carla Golden is associate professor of psychology at Ithaca College. She has taught courses in developmental psychology, the psychology of women, and women's studies at Smith College (1977–1983), Ithaca College (1983–present), and the University of Pittsburgh's Semester at Sea program (Fall 1984, Spring 1988). Dr. Golden was a Danforth Associate (1981–1986), recognized for her excellence in teaching, and a Beatrice Bain Scholar at the University of California, Berkeley (1990–1991). She has lectured widely and written on feminist psychoanalytic theories of gender, as well as on the development of women's sexuality. She is coeditor of *Lectures on the Psychology of Women* (McGraw-Hill, 1996).

CHAPTER 2

My Introduction to "Introduction to Women's Studies"

THE ROLE OF THE TEACHER'S AUTHORITY IN THE FEMINIST CLASSROOM

Frances A. Maher

.

This article was written in 1987, 10 years ago by now! In 1987, the main issue preoccupying students and faculty at Wheaton College was the upcoming transition to coeducation, anticipated in the fall of 1988. Whereas classrooms and the broader environment at Wheaton have changed a great deal since then in a variety of ways, most of the faculty and students, even the males, remain comfortable with a "gender-sensitive" model of coeducation that promotes consciousness of all forms of diversity as a central value. Class discussions seem to me to be not better or worse, but different, with a new range of viewpoints supplanting intimacy gained in all-female environments. A few males now appear in Introduction to Women's Studies, and although several have been hostile and threatened at times, the majority are interested and helpful.

Also when this article was written in 1987, I had started research on a book about feminist pedagogies, an ethnography of gender, race, and class at the center of both their content and their approaches to teaching. *The Feminist Classroom, An Inside Look at How Professors and Students are Transforming Higher Education in a Diverse Society*, was coauthored with Mary Kay Tetreault, and was published by Basic Books

This chapter originally appeared in *Feminist Teacher*, 1987, 3(1), 9–11.

The Feminist Teacher *Anthology: Pedagogies and Classroom Strategies*. Copyright © 1998 by Teachers College, Columbia University. All rights reserved. ISBN 0-8077-3741-0 (paper), ISBN 0-8077-3742-9 (cloth). Prior to photocopying items for classroom use, please contact the Copyright Clearance Center, Customer Service, 222 Rosewood Drive, Danvers, MA 01923, USA, telephone (508) 750-8400.

in 1994. We examined many teachers' struggles with the issues I raise in this article in terms of my own teaching.

We used four themes of analysis in the book. *Mastery* looks at the ways that substantive knowledge is acquired when "truth" emerges from multiple perspectives. *Authority*, which is explored in the article below, concerns how teachers conceptualize the grounds for their expertise with students. *Voice* examines how students fashion identities and perspectives for themselves in different classrooms, and, finally, *positionality* explores the interactions and relationships between the different social positions reflected in each class. Gender, race, class, and culture are not fixed identities, but rather shifting relationships, and classrooms are arenas for both reflecting and critiquing these relations. More recently, we have used our insights about the societal relationships of power in the classroom to look at the enactments of intellectual dominance in our data, asking how assumptions of Whiteness and heterosexuality as the norm organize classroom discourse. Rereading this article, I am struck by how our challenges remain the same, even as we interpret them differently over time and in different contexts. Feminist pedagogies are a series of processes, never "done" and always evolving.

It was my first semester teaching the introductory course in women's studies at Wheaton College, and in fact was the first time the course had been offered. We have a minor, which includes courses in most disciplines except for the sciences, and a feminist theory course, which I also teach. But until this particular spring there was no "intro" course. I am in the education department at Wheaton, and my research is in feminist pedagogy, so I was eager to use this course as an experiment in new (for me) pedagogical techniques. As I evaluate and assess the strengths and weaknesses of the course, I want again to concentrate on pedagogy, although of course the choice of content is crucial to pedagogical choices and classroom events. I want to focus particularly on what I learned about the ways in which our pedagogy reflects our assumptions about our authority as teachers, our goals for what students learn, and our attitudes toward authority over knowledge itself.

I knew in advance that the students in this class, partially because it was the first time it was offered, would span the full range between committed and knowledgeable feminist juniors and seniors, and first-year students who had never considered women's experiences as worthy of study or gender as a category of analysis. I wanted them all to have access to readings and issues that would engage them on personal terms, and give them questions and answers appropriate to their own stage of development. In addition, I wanted the course to be built on their questions. I believed that their concerns would have enough in common with one another and with my own so that we could build connections, while at the same time attending to variations in our own and other women's experiences. I also wanted them to actively engage with the materials, articulating their personal responses as well as their interpretations of what they were reading in such a way that they could share these with one another.

To this end, I set the course up to include more than 200 pages a week for each topic (such as mothering, working, sexuality, feminism, and so on) out of which they were to pick 60 pages each to read and respond to in their journals. They were asked to summarize the main points of the article, story, or book chapter, and then give their own response to or interpretation of it. At least one journal entry a week was to be on one or more of these readings; the other could be about one of the class discussions. The readings included chapters in a women's studies textbook, fictional accounts (particularly *Black-Eyed Susans*, edited by Mary Helen Washington), essays by Gloria Steinem, and two books of readings, one representing various materials on images of women's lives from the 19th century through to the present, and the other a book of analytical articles on women's societal roles.[1] Quite a smorgasbord; we discussed in the beginning of the course the type of material that each one was, and what kinds of knowledge could be gained from each. (For example, we discussed how textbooks could best be approached by seeing them as reference and background sources for answering certain types of general questions.)

In addition, the students had an assignment to interview a woman who was significantly different from themselves in terms of race, class, gender, culture, age, or sexual orientation. Finally, they wrote a term paper on an aspect of women's lives that had been affected by the contemporary women's movement (i.e., almost any topic they wanted).

Overall, the response to this format was very positive and productive. The students did choose a range of materials, and their journal entries were thoughtful and engaged. The tone of the class, which was very intense and increasingly trustful, was set very early by a stunning event at Wheaton. I had begun the course by asking the students to come up with a statement that could be made about "all women," and as you might suspect, we found very little that we could generalize about.

I had then, as part of this first week's readings, assigned (to everyone) a short story by Joanna Russ, called "When It Changed." This story is about a utopian world populated only of women, in which the characters play every human role and have a full range of interests and concerns, thus illustrating the difficulties of generalizing about all women. Their society is suddenly invaded by three male visitors, who confidently assert that they are there to bring Earth and this society back together. The narrator mourns the sudden loss of self-confidence that she feels. The day following this assignment, we learned that the trustees had voted to make Wheaton coeducational in the fall of 1988. We all felt that the story was an emblem and a prediction of the way we would feel, and it became a vehicle for expressing our shock and our mourning. (It also was a way of beginning to talk about the distortions of women's varieties and differences by the impositions of male views of us over time and cross-culturally.)

Another powerful discussion, again benefiting from a rich comparison of our own and others' experiences, occurred in our discussion of mothering. Many students had read stories about mothers' sacrifices for their children, including two stories in *Black-Eyed Susans* about Black mothers who had lost touch with their daughters when the latter became activists in the civil rights movement and then looked down on their mothers' old-fashioned ways. We used these stories and others like them to explore the tensions between generations, tensions from which mothers often suffer the most. My students themselves were adamant that *they* were not going to invest their whole lives in their children's welfare. And yet when I asked what kind of mothers they themselves had, they described paragons of self-sacrifice, saying, for example, "Even though my Mom always worked, she was always there for us first." The tensions between their expectations of their mothers and for themselves as mothers opened a very fruitful discussion on the costs and benefits of this central role for women.

CROSS-FERTILIZED

However, this cross-fertilization had its limits, three of which I would like to explore here. All of these limitations, or mistakes, if you will, stemmed from the same source, namely my reluctance to use (and therefore explicitly name and describe) the roots and nature of my own power and authority in the classroom. The first was in the realm of the inclusion of Black and Third World female experiences within each topic. I decided, I think rightly, that for each topic I would include Third World, working-class, and Black women's experiences, rather than make a separate topic. The advantage of this approach was that every topic was multifocal, in that each was seen through the lenses of a variety of women's lives. The disadvantage was that we treated issues such as racism and class exploitation as subtopics of others such as work, rather than giving them a central focus as issues on their own. The real weakness in this regard, however, lay with me. Because the class was (with one exception) all White, it was easy for the students not to choose the readings about women who were not White. So in the beginning of the course, for a few topics, we all colluded in not spending much time on Third World women.

The point here is that I could have insisted that we all read a full range of the materials (something I eventually did), even if everyone did not read the same material every week. When I did so I was forced to confront the contradictions in my approach to the course, which was set up as a "democracy" in terms of readings and knowledge. I had to use my authority, my experience, and my wider knowledge of the field to tell the students that if we didn't make all women's experiences the arena of our concerns, we would be missing out on a large part of the truth, about other women as well as about ourselves. A powerful example is an article many of them read about the two-career family's reliance on working-class assistance to make the balance work. It is true that the burdens of responsibility for these lifestyles rest disproportionately on the women; it is also true that they in turn get by with help from other women whom they hire.

There was one Japanese student in the class, and I was particularly conscious of her silent presence when we were discussing material on women in Japan or elsewhere in Asia. I never solved this problem of her ongoing silence, except by using small groups, which was a little uncomfortable for all of us because general discussions were usually more productive and engaging. I made up my mind very early not to push her to talk, and none of the other students did either. However, she and I met in private to discuss her journal and her reactions to the material; I was able to weave some of her insights into things I later said. Not a good solution, but the best I could come up with.

WHERE ARE THEY?

The second major problem that pinpointed the limitations of the way I had conceived my authority was in attendance. Several of the feminist activists, the juniors and seniors, became very active in the sos (Save Our School) group, the student organization committed to preventing coeducation at Wheaton. They cut all their classes frequently, with the excuse that these real events were more important in their lives as women than any course could be. The other students complained to me about this, saying that one student in particular had taken advantage of me by pretending not to understand the interview assignment and thus gaining an unfair extension. (In the event, this complaint was absolutely justified; the paper was 2 weeks later even than the extension.)

It is clear now (and was clear at the time) that I had been manipulated into behaving unfairly to the whole class. But more than that, I had allowed these feminists to avoid confronting the responsibilities (not to mention the consciousness-raising and learning opportunities for them) entailed in active participation in the class. Toward the end of the semester, I took several of them aside, and told them that they had missed some great opportunities and some great discussions. I said that for them to cut women's studies in order to organize against coeducation was like cutting a class full of Russian students in order to work for global understanding and peace. They got the point, but it was too late. Again, I needed to make more explicit to all of them, not just the feminists, the political and ideological nature of the course and the topics we were discussing, as a critique of the dominant ideologies reflected in other courses. Making women's experiences visible and using them to make meaning of our own lives as students (and teachers) is valuable enough to insist that people be there.

The third mistake I made was one of omission. In one section of the syllabus, there were some articles on women's cognitive development, and on women and students. In another course the previous fall, I had assigned an article I had written on female students and feminist pedagogy—and then been unable to run a discussion on it because I was too shy to ask students what they thought. In the introductory course I did not even assign the article. I include this problem because I realize now that whatever its merits, my fear of becoming visible as an authority figure (and as someone who knew something) prevented me from allowing my students to read it. This fear made me think about how I usually teach an article I have assigned. I would ask the students to summarize what they thought the writer's meaning and intentions were. Then I could guide them into "the right interpretation" by my clever questions. But here I couldn't ask them what they thought the writer's intentions might be when the writer would be right there in front of them. So I would have to ask them what they thought, as students, of what I was saying (about them as students). It would have been scary, but we all would have learned a lot about classroom dynamics and about ourselves, and I would have shown them, again, something about both the extent and the limits of my authority.

What all these examples have in common, I think, is a reluctance on my part to fully engage with the students as a learner and knower, as someone who is struggling with the same issues they are facing and who at the same time has a different—and differently useful—perspective. Often, I think teachers set up a pseudodemocracy in the classroom even as we are setting up a pseudoview of knowledge. We introduce students to old debates in the field (where we know the compromise version) instead of to the issues we are grappling with in our research and in our discussions with colleagues. Or, we pretend that everyone gets to choose what to read (or discuss) and then resort to manipulation to make sure that our own

CHAPTER 3

Warming Up the Classroom Climate for Women

Sue V. Rosser

These exercises for "Warming Up the Classroom Climate for Women"
originally appeared in the spring 1989 issue of *Feminist Teacher*; I
conceived of them and wrote them in 1988. The foundation for these
exercises was laid in the groundbreaking 1982 paper "Chilly Climate in
the Classroom for Women" by Bernice Sandler and Roberta Hall.
Although they based their paper on the implications of several research
studies carried out in the 1970s and on considerable qualitative data
gathered from visits to college and university campuses, at that time, the
notion of a chilly climate seemed revolutionary and new. Since then,
numerous additional studies and meta-analyses (Girls Incorporated, 1993;
Sadker and Sadker, 1994; American Association of University Women,
1992) have demonstrated that males interact more with faculty and
adult leaders, are praised more, are called on more, and tend to
dominate group discussions. Simultaneously, in these coeducational
situations, the females tend to change their behavior and hold back in
participation and performance in the presence of males.

   Despite, or perhaps because of, a growing number of gender equity
projects that use these and other exercises and studies to teach faculty
to be more equitable in their treatment of girls and women in the
classroom, a strong backlash movement questions the need for, and
even the research that undergirds, such exercises. Even some individuals
who call themselves feminists and identify as women's studies faculty

This chapter originally appeared in *Feminist Teacher*, 1989, 4(1), 8–12.

have attacked notions of gender equity in curriculum and pedagogy (Sommers, 1994; Patai and Koertge, 1994). Unfortunately, then, the need for exercises such as these still exists, more than 7 years after they were written and well more than a decade after the research on which they are based was carried out. In this highly polarized political environment of the 1990s, these exercises may provide a relatively unthreatening mechanism with which to begin discussions with faculty, both liberal and conservative, about gender equity in the classroom.

On campuses across the country, faculty, students, and administrators are showing renewed interest in eliminating sexism in its various forms from their institutions. A beginning step taken in many classes and development workshops for faculty and administrators is providing information about the diverse ways in which women experience sexism daily on the campus. The series of "Chilly Climate" papers produced by the Project on the Status and Education of Women of the Association of American Colleges (Hall & Sandler, 1982, 1984; Sandler & Hall, 1986) serve as a resource guide for extensive material about sexism in language, nonverbal behavior, and teaching approaches—the sexism that creates, for female students, a chilly climate in the classroom. The series also documents the more subtle sexist problem of the absence of women's roles, experiences, and achievements from curricular content and the overt problem of sexual harassment as factors that prevent women students from enjoying full equality of educational opportunity.

Lectures and discussions based on the information from the "Chilly Climate" series provide excellent avenues for educating administrators, students, and faculty. Active participation in exercises may reinforce the ideas presented in lectures and discussion. The aim in the following group of five exercises is to stimulate the active participation of a group of individuals learning about sexism. Each exercise focuses on a particular aspect of sexism developed in the "Chilly Climate" series. All five exercises may be used together in a workshop that introduces the diverse forms of sexism. Each exercise may also be used separately and without others to reinforce information presented in depth in a workshop on a particular topic such as gender and language or curricular reform.

DEFINING SEXISM

Purpose. This exercise allows participants to express definitions of sexism and suggest interpretations of how sexism may contribute to a chilly climate in the classroom for women.

Who. Students, faculty, and administrative staff may all benefit from defining and hearing the definitions and interpretations of the others in the group.

When. This is an ideal exercise with which to open a workshop or discussion on the chilly climate topic. Although the exercise is particularly effective in crystallizing the thoughts of participants who have read the "Chilly Climate" papers in preparation for the session, the exercise may be modified slightly for participants who have not read the papers in advance.

Why. The exercise provides the group with a common basis—to which everyone has had an opportunity to contribute—with which to begin a discussion of chilly climate issues. After hearing the definitions of others, participants are likely to recognize that members of the group hold diverse views.

Where. No particular setting is necessary for the exercise.

How. The exercise can be used as an activity for participants as they arrive and are waiting for the session to begin. Give each participant an index card upon their entering the room.

1. Ask each participant to write a definition of sexism and a statement of how sexism is related to creating a chilly climate in the classroom for women. (If participants have not read the "Chilly Climate" papers before the session, ask them how they think that sexism might create a chilly climate in the classroom for women.)
2. Collect the cards.
3. Read all the cards aloud to the group without comment. If the group is particularly large or if time is short, every second or third card might be read. However, it is important that the group realize that cards read were not preselected.
4. Ask the group for their comments about the definition of sexism and its relationship to chilly climate issues.

Outcome: For most groups, this exercise becomes an avenue for breaking the ice, uniting the group, and providing a common ground for beginning the session.

PRONOUNS AS POWER

Purpose. This exercise emphasizes the point that male pronouns, even when used generically, evoke a mental image that is male, thereby excluding women.

Who. Students, faculty, and administrators can benefit from this exercise.

When. "Pronouns As Power" may be used to initiate a discussion or lecture on the importance of language in conveying sexism. Alternatively, it may be used as a closing statement after such a discussion or in response to the question, Why do women feel excluded by terms such as *mankind* and *he,* which are used generically to include all individuals?

Where. No special equipment or settings are necessary for the exercise.

Why. Many individuals, particularly men, fail to understand the exclusion that women feel when so-called generic terms (*man*) and pronouns (*he, his*) are used (Martyna, 1978). If generic pronouns are truly inclusive, then, in a passage containing them, the same message and feeling should be conveyed when such generic pronouns are switched to female pronouns. After reading a familiar passage in which feminine pronouns have been substituted for generic pronouns, most people begin to comprehend that generic language is not really inclusive.

How. The following information may be helpful in completing the exercise:

1. Select a passage that is familiar and that conveys a message of power or impact. People may not care if they are included in passages conveying little of significance or import. A passage from the Bible, the Constitution, or some other famous document carries the necessary significance and familiarity for most people.
2. Read the passage aloud to the group, changing the original language from masculine nouns and pronouns to feminine nouns and pronouns. Then change supposed generic terms such as *mankind* to truly generic words such as *humanity* that convey the same meaning. A sample passage:

> Genesis 2:18–25.
>   Then the Lord God said, "It is not good that the woman should be alone; I will make her a helper fit for her." So out of the ground the Lord God formed every beast of the field and every bird of the air, and brought them to the woman to see what she would call them; and whatever the woman called every living creature, that was its name. The woman gave names to all cattle, and to the birds of the air, and to every beast of the field; but for the woman there was not found a helper fit for her. So the Lord God caused a deep sleep to fall upon the woman, and while she slept took one of her ribs and closed

up its place with flesh; and the rib which the Lord God had taken from the woman she made into a man and brought him to the woman. Then the woman said, "This at last is bone of my bones and flesh of my flesh; he shall be called Man, because he was taken out of Woman."

Therefore a woman leaves her mother and her father and cleaves to her husband, and they become one flesh. And the woman and her husband were both naked, and were not ashamed.

3. After the participants have listened to the passage, ask them to describe their reactions to hearing the passage with the reversed nouns and pronouns.

Outcome. Most people say that the familiar passage contains a slightly different meaning for them when the pronouns have been reversed. Women often express feelings of empowerment, inclusion, and authority after hearing the passage. Men may feel distanced and excluded.

GENDER DIFFERENCES IN EXPERIENCES WITH SEXISM

Purpose. The purpose of this exercise is to provide participants with a physical representation of how chilly climate issues and sexism may have affected their education or career.

Who. This exercise is useful in raising the awareness of students, faculty, or administrators to sexism and chilly climate issues that differentially affect women and men. Although it may be most effective when used with a faculty department, class of students, or unit, it may be modified slightly (see modifications that follow) to be used with groups consisting of faculty, staff, and students from throughout the institution. The exercise can be used only in a group containing both males and females.

Why. Individuals who hear the information about chilly climate issues and sexism may not clearly understand that these incidents occur much more frequently in women's lives than in men's. This exercise causes each person to see that sexism more frequently affects women than men.

When. This exercise is most effective when used after a presentation about chilly climate issues and sexism; it is a particularly effective response to the question, Do sexism and chilly climate issues really affect women more than men?

Where. A rectangular room or hallway free of chairs or other obstructions is the ideal space for the free movement of the number of people in the group.

How. The following instructions will help to orient the group to the exercise:

1. Ask the group to imagine that an imaginary line runs from one end of the room to the other. They should imagine that one end of the line corresponds with the answers "agree strongly," "always," or 10; the other end of the line corresponds with "disagree strongly," "never," or 0. In between the two ends are the points 1 through 9, which correspond to the gradations between "always" and "never" (i.e., the midpoint between the two ends of the room corresponds to "sometimes" or "neither agree nor disagree").
2. Ask the individuals in the group to stand and to place themselves arbitrarily along the imaginary line.
3. Tell the group that you will read a series of 12 statements. After each statement, each individual should move to the position on the imaginary line that corresponds with her/his experience in light of that statement.
4. Each person is asked to notice not only her/his position after each statement but also to be aware of the gender distribution along the imaginary line after each statement.

Statements: The following statements should be read for a group of faculty. Remind the individuals to be aware of the position of males compared to females, as well as of their own position after each statement.

1. I find that I have trouble picturing or including myself when I hear terms such as *mankind*.
2. I think that males are superior to females in mathematical or visual-spatial ability.
3. I often find myself being interrupted or ignored by my colleagues.
4. I have been sexually harassed by an employer or professor.
5. A professor or colleague has questioned whether I am serious about my chosen career.
6. I worry a considerable amount about how well my career plans will fit in with my plans for a relationship or family.
7. I have been questioned by my department chair or dean about my plans for marriage or family.

8. All of my classes include information about contributions made by famous people of my sex.
9. Several times when I was in college, a professor made comments to me about my clothes or physical appearance.
10. I find that I learn the names of the individuals of the opposite sex in my classes better than the names of the people of my own sex.
11. A factor in the choice of my major was that it is an appropriate (traditional) field for a person of my sex.
12. At least half of the faculty members in my department are of the same sex that I am.

Modifications. The statements may be modified in varying ways to more appropriately fit the backgrounds of individuals in the group. For example, statement 7 might be changed to the following for a group consisting solely of students: "I have been questioned by my advisor or a professor about my plans for marriage or family." Statement 12 might be modified to the following for a group consisting entirely of staff: "At least half of the employees in my department or division are of the same sex that I am."

Outcome. After all the statements have been read, the group can be asked about the differences in gender distributions they observed after each statement. This exercise provides most groups with a physical demonstration that although some individuals of both genders may have similar experiences that correspond to particular statements, gender differences in experiences are usually revealed by these statements. Sexism and chilly climate issues occur more frequently in the lives of women than of men.

Exceptions. In certain fields such as nursing, which are more traditionally dominated by females, statements 8 and 12 in particular may show the reverse of the usual chilly climate pattern (i.e., women will strongly agree with these statements and men will strongly disagree with them). If participants in the group come from diverse fields that include some women from male-dominated disciplines and some men from female-dominated disciplines, gender differences on some statements may be obscured even though sexism exists in the disciplines. These exceptions and others resulting from the particularities of the group, such as wide variation in age or deviation of an individual department from the national norm in terms of gender distribution, should be discussed when assessing the outcome of the exercise.

INCORPORATING SCHOLARSHIP ON WOMEN
INTO A TRADITIONAL DISCIPLINARY COURSE

Purpose. This exercise facilitates discussion of course revision to include new scholarship on women in traditional disciplinary (i.e., non–women's studies) course offerings.

Who. Faculty who are familiar with recent feminist research and who are open to revising their traditional introductory or advanced course to include the new scholarship are the most likely group to profit from this exercise by changing their course syllabi. The exercise permits students to review courses they have taken and to recognize how those courses might be improved and changed. This realization may lead students to demand such information in future courses.

When. Faculty in institutions that have adopted curricular reforms requiring inclusion in general education courses of information on women's studies and ethnic studies will have compelling interest in the exercise. Faculty who have recently been exposed through faculty development seminars, presentations at professional meetings, or personal reading to recent feminist research may also be eager to consider syllabus revision. However, the exercise can also be successfully used to introduce the new scholarship to faculty and students.

Why. Feminist research represents the cutting edge of scholarship in many disciplines. In addition to being incorporated in women's studies courses, this research must be integrated into traditional departmental courses. Even faculty who are knowledgeable about the new scholarship and eager to integrate it into their courses may not know how to begin the transformation. This exercise provides an avenue to initiate that process.

Where. No particular setting is necessary for the exercise. A chalkboard or flip chart for the facilitator and a table on which the participants may write are useful.

How. In anticipation of this exercise, each participant is asked to bring a course syllabus. The facilitator presents the McIntosh (1984), Schuster and Van Dyne (1985), or Tetreault (1985) scheme as a model representing phases of curricular development. Each participant then evaluates her/his course syllabus against the phase model to determine the extent to which the course transformation has occurred. Then participants consider what might be done to further transform this course to the next stage.

Model. I prefer to use the McIntosh model developed for phases of curricular integration in history to illustrate transformation. This model is less complex and is therefore more easily comprehended after an oral presentation:

Phase I. *Womanless History:* This is the very traditional approach to the discipline, which is exclusive in that only great events and men in history are deemed worthy of consideration.

Phase II. *Women in History:* Heroines, exceptional women, or an elite few who are seen to have been of benefit to culture as defined by the traditional standards of the disciplines are included in the study.

Phase III. *Women as a Problem, Anomaly, or Absence in History:* Women are studied as victims, as deprived or defective variants of men, or as protestors, with "issues." Women are at least viewed in a systematic context, since class, race, and gender are seen as interlocking political phenomena. Categories of historical analysis are still derived from those who had the most power.

Phase IV. *Women as History:* The categories for analysis shift and become racially inclusive, multifaceted, and filled with variety; they demonstrate and validate plural versions of reality. This phase takes account of the fact that since women have had half of the world's lived experience, we need to ask what that experience has been and to consider it as half of history. This causes faculty to use evidence and source materials that academics are not in the habit of using.

Phase V. *History Redefined and Reconstructed to Include Us All:* Although this history will be a long time in the making, it will help students to sense that women are both part of and alien to the dominant culture and the dominant version of history. It will create more usable and inclusive constructs that validate a wider sample of life.

Examples for art, literature, psychology, and biology may be used to illustrate the use of the model in diverse disciplines (Rosser, 1987).

Outcome. Few participants will leave the room with a revised course syllabus. However, the exercise provides most with ideas for beginning course transformation.

STEREOTYPES AFFECT DISCUSSIONS
OF SEXUAL HARASSMENT POLICY

Purpose. This exercise demonstrates that stereotypes surrounding factors such as gender, position or rank, and known previous sexual history may influence discussion of sexual harassment policy. Specifically, the stereotypic "labels" worn by individuals affect their contributions to the discussion, the perceptions of their remarks by other group members, and the extent to which the group permits them to influence the discussion.

Who. Groups containing individuals of both sexes who hold different positions within the institution are appropriate for this exercise. Probably more learning occurs when individuals representing both sexes and a wide diversity of positions (students, faculty, administrative staff) comprise the group. However, the exercise may be used with single-sex groups containing participants of similar institutional status.

When. Modifications in the question given to the group for discussion make the exercise appropriate for use at different points in a sexual harassment discussion. For an institution that is developing its official policy on sexual harassment, it may provide an effective mechanism with which to initiate discussion among various groups throughout the institution about the policy. For institutions that have already adopted an official policy, the exercise provides a means for educating various constituencies within the college or university about the policy and about some of the difficulties that may arise in its implementation. The exercise may also be used during a general discussion of sexism and its connection with sexual harassment without reference to a specific policy of sexual harassment.

Where. The ideal setting for this exercise is a room in which a small circle of chairs to hold six to eight group members can be surrounded by another circle of chairs that is large enough to accommodate the remaining participants in the group. The inner circle should be easily visible to everyone in the outer circle. Although no particular limit need be placed on the size of the group, the exercise is likely to be more effective for groups containing between 20 and 30 people.

Why. Stereotypic labels resulting from gender status within the organization, and knowledge of personal information, including history, may affect the influence that an individual has in discussions of most topics. Controversial subjects such as sexual harassment, however, may particularly evoke stereotypical responses because of lack of information about the topic and embarrassment over discussing sexual issues. This exercise provides an avenue in which to raise awareness about the role that stereotypical labeling may be playing in the dynamics of group discussion.

How. The group role play may be carried out in the following way:

1. Select six or eight people from the larger group to participate in the role play. Choose an approximately equal number of individuals of each sex. If the positions of individuals within the institution are known, try to choose small group participants who represent a variety of ranks.
2. Ask the six or eight small-group participants to sit in a circle, with the remainder of the larger group sitting in a surrounding circle.
3. Select a previously prepared label to place on the forehead of each small-group participant. The label should be as different as possible from the true gender, rank, and known sexual history of the individual on whom the label is being placed. (For example, a male department chair might receive the label *Female untenured professor. Ignore me.*) No small-group participant is permitted to see her/his own label. However, each participant must show the label to all participants in both the smaller and larger groups.

Labels. Labels may be mailing labels or any other suitable material that may be temporarily affixed to the forehead. Write the following sorts of descriptors in magic marker on the labels.

Male department head. Tell me I'm right.
Female sorority member. Tell me I'm cute.
Male professor who harasses students sexually.
Female student who has been sexually harassed.
Male student accused of acquaintance rape.
Female untenured professor. Ignore me.
Male football coach. Tell me I'm a good old boy.
Female director of women's studies. Tell me I'm radical.

Instructions. Give the following instructions to the members of the smaller group:

1. The topic for discussion is, What should be the sexual harassment policy for our institution? (If a sexual harassment policy has already been developed for the institution, then the question might be, What is our sexual harassment policy and how does it affect the different campus constituencies?)
2. Everyone in the group must participate in the discussion.
3. Since this is a role play, you must react and respond to other participants according to each one's label, not to what you know about her/his true gender, rank, or history.

4. Try to guess what your own label says by observing the reaction of other participants to you. At the end of the discussion you will be asked what you think your label is.
5. You will have 15 minutes for the role play/discussion.

Give the participants in the surrounding larger group the following instructions:

- Observe the group dynamics in the smaller group during the discussion.
- After the discussion you will be asked to comment on what the exercise revealed regarding the way that stereotypic labels affect discussions of sexual harassment policy.

Outcome. If everyone in the small group does participate according to the instructions, most individuals are able to guess fairly accurately what their label might be. Some men who hold powerful positions are surprised by how differently their responses are treated when they are wearing a label such as *Female untenured professor. Ignore me.* Students and women are similarly amazed at the positive reinforcement they receive when wearing a label such as *Male department head. Tell me I'm right.* Larger group observers normally have insightful comments about the impact of these stereotypic labels on the discussion of the topic.

CONCLUSION

Sexism in language and classroom behaviors, combined with the absence from the curriculum of information about the achievements, roles, and experiences of women, leaves many female students feeling somewhat distant, different, and alienated from what they are learning. Sexism may be particularly severe in cases where women are attempting to enter fields such as science and engineering, which are not perceived as traditional arenas for women. Small inequities that occur in the classroom have a cumulative negative effect on women students' self-esteem, choice of major, and career plans. If these inequities are aggravated by an overt form of sexism such as sexual harassment, the effects on the women are likely to be more severe: dropping the course, changing majors, or dropping out of postsecondary school entirely.

These exercises sensitize faculty and staff to providing a comfortable learning environment for female students. Overcoming sexism as a barrier to learning and including more information about women in curricular content are ways to begin to warm up the classroom climate.

REFERENCES

American Association of University Women. (1992). *How schools shortchange girls: The AAUW report.* Washington, DC: American Association of University Women Educational Foundation; National Education Association.

Girls Incorporated. (1993). *Girls Incorporated program planning guide.* New York: Author.

Hall, Roberta M., & Sandler, Bernice R. (1982). The classroom climate: A chilly one for women? Washington, DC: Project on the Status and Education of Women, Association of American Colleges.

Hall, Roberta M., & Sandler, Bernice R. (1984). Out of the classroom: A chilly campus climate for women? Washington, DC: Project on the Status and Education of Women, Association of American Colleges.

Martyna, W. (1978). What does 'he' mean? Use of the generic masculine. *Journal of Communication, 28,* 131–138.

McIntosh, Peggy. (1984). The study of women: Processes of personal and curricular re-vision. *The Forum for Liberal Education, 6,* 2–4.

Patai, Daphne, & Koertge, Noretta. (1994). *Professing feminism: Cautionary tales from the strange world of women's studies.* New York: New Republic, Basic Books.

Rosser, Sue V. (1987). Gender balancing the curriculum. *Carolina View, 111,* 17–20.

Sadker, Myra, & Sadker, David. (1994). *Failing at fairness.* New York: Scribner.

Sandler, Bernice R., & Hall, Roberta M. (1986). The campus climate revisited: Chilly for women faculty, administrators, and graduate students. Washington, DC: Project on the Status and Education of Women, Association of American Colleges.

Schuster, Marilyn R., & Van Dyne, Susan. (1985). *Women's place in the academy: Transforming the liberal arts curriculum,* Totowa, NJ: Rowman and Allanheld.

Sommers, Christina. (1994). *Who stole feminism?* New York: Touchstone.

Tetreault, Mary K. (1985). Stages of thinking of about women: An experience-derived evaluation model. *The Journal of Higher Education, 15*(4), 368–384.

ABOUT THE AUTHOR

Sue Rosser received her PhD in zoology from the University of Wisconsin-Madison in 1973. Since January 1996, she has served as director for the Center for Women's Studies and Gender Research at the University of Florida-Gainesville, where she is also a professor of anthropology. In 1995, she was senior program officer for women's programs at the National Science Foundation. From 1986 to 1995 she served as director of women's studies at the University of South Carolina, where she also was a professor of family and preventive medicine in the medical schools. She has edited collections and written approximately 70 journal articles on the theoretical and applied problems of women and science and women's health. Her books include *Teaching Science and Health from a Feminist Perspective: A Practical Guide* (Pergamon Press, 1986), *Female Friendly Science* (Pergamon Press, 1990), and *Re-Engineering Female Friendly Science* (Teachers College Press, 1997), among others.

CHAPTER 4

Rewriting the Future

THE FEMINIST CHALLENGE TO THE MALESTREAM CURRICULUM

Karen J. Warren

All feminists in the academy agree that the virtual exclusion of women from the mainstream Western curriculum (or, "canon") has resulted in a male-biased—or "malestream"—curriculum. What feminist academics disagree about is the nature of that bias and strategies for making the curriculum genuinely inclusive of the experiences and contributions of women.

   In this paper I explore the nature and desirability of feminist challenges to the malestream curriculum. I argue that a transformation of the curriculum to make it inclusive of women should be reconceived in terms of goals, rather than in terms of content; otherwise, feminist curricular transformation projects will not be especially useful to gender-resistant subject matter fields such as mathematics, physics, and chemistry. I discuss these goals in terms of six domains, each involving interrelated issues of gender, race/ethnicity, class, age, and affectional orientation: (1) primary content subject areas; (2) secondary content areas (e.g., illustrations and examples); (3) methodology; (4) pedagogy; (5) teachers as professional role models; and (6) world views (or, conceptual frameworks). Throughout the essay, I describe the advantages of a multidimensional, goal-oriented model of feminist curricular transformation efforts.

Since its early emergence as a political movement over three hundred years ago, feminism has been involved in re-visioning the future. "Contemporary feminism" is really an umbrella concept, an elliptical way of speaking about a variety of competing and alternative feminisms. Despite important differences among us, *all* feminists agree that sexism (or, the oppression of women) exists, is wrong, and must be changed. A minimal conditional conception of feminism that captures the claims on which all feminists agree, then, is that feminism is the movement to end sexist oppression.

Over the past decade, feminists in academia have begun to explore ways of ending sexist oppression in the mainstream curriculum. The focus of this paper is twofold: to reveal the nature and to demonstrate the desirability of the feminist challenge to the mainstream—or, perhaps more appropriately, "malestream"—curriculum. I argue that, if taken seriously, the feminist challenge to the mainstream curriculum re-visions and rewrites the future in ways that promise or threaten, depending on how one looks at it, the mainstream curriculum in fundamental, and not merely incidental or tangential, ways.

FEMINIST ISSUES

Any issue is and should be a feminist issue insofar as an understanding of it contributes to understanding and eliminating the oppression of women. Day care centers, comparable pay for comparable work, and poverty are feminist issues wherever and whenever understanding them contributes to understanding and eliminating the oppression of women. What counts as a feminist issue, then, will depend largely on context.

Feminists argue that the mainstream curriculum is a feminist issue because an understanding of it can and should contribute to an understanding of the oppression of women. With regard to mainstream scholarship, feminists continually press the questions, For whom? According to whom? This penchant for contextualizing discourse in this way has led feminists to insist on marking traditional academic disciplines with their appropriate prefixes. For instance, feminists ask of the disciplines of classics, philosophy, and art, Classics for whom? Philosophy according to whom? Art by whom and for whom? Without the appropriate prefixes, a discipline such as philosophy masquerades as "just philosophy," inclusive philosophy, when it is not. It is Western philosophy, or dominant Western philosophy, or philosophy as authored by White heterosexual bourgeois men of the Western world. With the appropriate prefixes, it becomes at least an open question whether that philosophy is truly representative or inclusive of the realities of workers, women and men of color, non-Westerners, of the multiple realities of diverse groups of people.

This insistence on "prefixing" or "marking" traditions has two very important and related functions: It makes visible ways in which privilege and power are invisible in the mainstream curriculum, and it raises questions about gender, race, class, and other sorts of bias in traditional scholarship. For many feminists, the ultimate roots of this bias will be found in the worldviews or "conceptual frameworks" inside which traditional scholarship is housed.

A conceptual framework is a set of basic beliefs, values, attitudes, and assumptions that constitute the "lens" through which we see ourselves and our world (Warren, 1986). An oppressive conceptual framework is one in which the basic beliefs, values, attitudes, and assumptions are used to justify and maintain the subordination of one group by another. Such a framework typically is characterized by "up-down?" thinking, whereby what is "up" is assumed to be superior to what is "down" by virtue of some characteristic it has that what is down lacks, and by virtue of a "logic of domination," a moral premise that assumes that superiority justifies subordination. In an oppressive conceptual framework, simply having an up characteristic justifies the dominance of what is up and the subordination of what is down.

Feminists are particularly interested in patriarchal conceptual frameworks, conceptual frameworks in which the basic beliefs, values, attitudes, and assumptions give higher value, prestige status, or weight to what is traditionally identified as male than to what is traditionally identified as female. Patriarchal conceptual frameworks put men up and women down, minds up and bodies down, reason up and emotions down. Many feminists have argued that the conceptual roots of sexist oppression are located in an oppressive patriarchal conceptual framework characterized by up–down thinking and a logic of domination.

THE CHALLENGE

The basic feminist challenge to the malestream curriculum is to reveal how it is oppressive to women and to eliminate that oppression. Stated differently, the feminist challenge is to make the curriculum inclusive of women.

Feminists have suggested various transformation projects to make the curriculum inclusive of women. In the remainder of this article, I build upon what I take to be the strengths of these projects and suggest ways to overcome their weaknesses. I do so by suggesting ways to reconceive feminist curriculum transformation projects as goal-oriented projects, rather than as curriculum revision projects in primary content areas.

The most popular curricular transformation model is Peggy McIntosh's (1983) theory of five interactive phases. McIntosh identifies "five phases of perception" as one moves toward a more inclusive body of knowledge. With history and biology as examples, these follow:

McIntosh's Five Interactive Phases

Phase 1 Womanless _____ (history, biology)
Phase 2 Woman in _____ (history, biology)
Phase 3 Women as a problem, anomaly, or absence in _____ (history, biology)
Phase 4 Woman as _____ (history, biology)
Phase 5 _____ (history, biology) redefined/reconstructed to include us all.

Consider biology. In Phase 1, womanless biology, women simply are not present. Phase 2, women in biology, is about exceptional, not ordinary, women; it is about what Gerda Lerner calls the "woman worthies." As McIntosh (1983) states, "Phase 2 tends to be about a few of the few who had access to lab equipment, a handful of women still remembered for their work" (p. 3). Phase 3 biology analyzes women as problems or absences or anomalies. Phase 4 biology is about women doing science differently. Biologist Evelyn Fox Keller engages in Phase 4 biology by challenging different assumptions and ways of doing science in her books *Reflections on Gender and Science* (1983b) and *A Feeling for the Organism: The Life and Work of Barbara McClintock* (1983a). Phase 5 biology has not yet been developed. It would be biology reconstructed to include us all.

Several salient features of these five interactive phases are worth noting. Phase 3 has come to be called the "add-women-and-stir" approach to curricular revision. But feminists are quick to point out that there are some serious difficulties with this approach to including women in the curriculum. Some ideas cannot be added, because they are logically contradictory to claims of the mainstream canon. One example would be a feminist's claim that traditional philosophy is gender biased. Where the "addition of women" leads to the view that at least some of traditional philosophy is gender biased, then the addition of women to traditional philosophy courses does, indeed, become a problem.[1]

It is at this juncture that Phase 4 becomes so attractive and vital to feminists interested in transforming the curriculum. Frustrated by the problems posed by attempts to integrate or assimilate women into traditional courses, many feminists turn to teaching Phase 4 courses exclusively, such as feminist philosophy, women's art, women's history, the psychology of women, the biology of women, women's politics.

But Phase 4 curriculum development poses its own special challenges. Once one begins to rethink a discipline or a subject area from a Phase 4 "women as _____" perspective, many of the traditional assumptions and claims, even those that are taken as definitive of the discipline or subject, have to be called into serious question, if not simply abandoned. Whereas in Phase 3 thinking *women* are a problem, in Phase 4 thinking the traditional discipline—philosophy or biology—becomes the problem. This is because

> curriculum work in Phase 4 . . . breaks all the rules of ordinary research or teaching. One studies American literature of the nineteenth century not by asking, "Did the women write anything good?" but by asking "What did the women write?" One asks not "What great work by a woman can I include in my reading list?" but "How have women used the written word?" In Phase 4 one asks, "How have women of color in many cultures told their stories?" not "Is there any good third world literature?" (McIntosh, 1983, p. 17)

Phase 5 curriculum revision will be the hardest to accomplish; we aren't there yet. Its content may even currently be unthinkable. Until oppressive, socially constructed categories of gender, race, and class (for starters) are eliminated such that sameness and difference are just that—sameness and difference, rather than what is better and what is worse—we will not have a Phase 5, genuinely inclusive, curriculum.

LIMITATIONS OF THE MODEL

Despite its importance as a way of revealing the exclusivity of the mainstream curriculum, the five-phase model has limitations. Two are worth noting here—one major and one minor.

The minor weakness of the McIntosh model is that it is incomplete. By labeling the *ideal* Phase 5, the McIntosh model implies that a move from a Phase 4 curriculum, "Woman as _____" to a Phase 5 curriculum, "_____ to include us all" does not require any intermediary phases. But this is mistaken. Having recently begun to ask gender-differentiated questions about women qua women, we now know something about women in their diversities—enough to articulate, where appropriate, the first four phases of a feminist curriculum transformation project. But we know very little about men qua men. What the traditional curriculum has inherited and transmitted about males is mistakenly taken to be representative of what humanness is—males qua human and human qua males, rather than males *qua* men (or, men *qua* men). That is, the traditional malestream curriculum was built predominantly, if not exclusively, on male examples of what it was to be a human being engaged in so-called human activities—whether those activities were as scientist, philosopher, politician, artist, engineer, breadwinner or "head of household"—and then only built on examples of some males, at that! It was a curriculum that took White male examples as examples of human experience and knowledge, as nongendered (nonraced, nonclassed) human experience and knowledge. There was no awareness of a need to prefix that experience and knowledge as "White" or "male." The traditional malestream curriculum simply took whatever characteristics were historically associated with maleness, masculinity, or "man" (such as reason and rationality) and treated them either as defining or exalted characteristics of what it is to be human. To the extent that women failed to exemplify these characteristics, women either were not fully human or were assumed to have characteristics (such as emotionality and irrationality) that were assigned lower status or prestige (Warren, 1988). As the classic Broverman study showed in 1970, when one hundred psychiatrists, psychiatric social workers, and psychologists were asked to describe a normal man, a normal woman, and a normal human, the normal man and the normal human turned out to be the same; the normal woman was different. As philosopher Elizabeth Minnick (1986) puts it, "That means that a woman can be either a 'normal' human and an 'abnormal' woman, or a 'normal' woman and an 'abnormal' human—not both. Man is what human IS; woman is deviant" (p. 5).

The reason, then, that we cannot move simply from the McIntosh Phase 4 ("Woman as _____") to the McIntosh ideal Phase 5 ("_____ to include us all") is that knowing about woman's gendered experience and knowledge is also only part of the story; we need to know about men's gendered experience and knowledge, about "men as _____" (fathers, sons, brothers, husbands, lovers, friends). This is not the same as the old stuff of knowing about males *as* humans. It is knowing about males as "prefixed" or "marked" by gender, as gendered humans in all their gender diversities.

Unfortunately, we currently have very little information about men as men-humans.[2] And before we can have a history, or philosophy, or biology "to include us all"—McIntosh's (1983) "ideal phase"—we need to learn about both women's and men's different gendered (and raced, classed, affectionately oriented, age, abled, religious, ethnic) experiences and knowledge.

This "phase gap" in the McIntosh model must be filled. For at least those subject areas or disciplines whose primary content is sensitive to issues of gender (such as the social sciences and humanities) we will need at least two additional phases, for a total of seven—not five—phases of curricular development. We will need a new, male-gendered Phase 5, "men as _____" and a new female- and male-gendered Phase 6, "gendered_____." This gendered-human Phase 6 will combine what has been learned from a gendered perspective on *both* women and men (from Phases 4 and 5) into an inclusive, rather than exclusive or exclusionary, account of human experience and knowledge. Only then can a final (ideal) Phase 7 follow: "_____ to include us all." These seven phases must make explicit the connections between women, race, and class and provide a blueprint for how related issues of age, affectional preference, religion, and regionalism affect the scholarship on women. And this scholarship on women ultimately will include scholarship of men qua the gendered humans that they are.

This seven-phase model of curricular development assumes that among the goals of feminism are the eradication of all oppressive gender (and related race, class, age, affectional orientation, ability) categories of analysis and the creation of a world in which *difference does not breed domination or subordination*—say, a world in 4001. In 4001, then, a truly inclusive curriculum would be a nonsexist, nonracist, nonclassist, nonheterosexist, nonageist, nonableist, non-anti-Semitic curriculum. But this is not 4001. There currently is no human simpliciter: Every contemporary human is a human of some gender, race/ethnicity, class, affectional orientation, age, and marital status. As long as the current social realities of, for example, sexism, racism, classism, heterosexism, and ageism exist, we cannot leapfrog to some "humanist" place of equality and justice that "includes us all." We must walk through the realities of different genders, races, and classes first if we are ever to arrive at a "_____ which includes us all." That is why the additional Phases 5 and 6 are needed.

For at least primary content subject areas, then, I encourage a seven-phase integrative model of curricular revision (see Figure 4.1).

The second and more significant weakness of the McIntosh model is, paradoxically, a by-product of its main strength: Its focus on the primary content of subject areas—the model's strength—makes the McIntosh model difficult to utilize in courses whose primary content is "gender resistant" (such as math, physics, chemistry). When using only the McIntosh five-phase model of curricular transformation, feminists find themselves in the difficult and unfortunate position of having to think about ways in which $2 + 2 = 4$ or $Na + Cl = NaCl$ are gender biased. By conceiving of feminist curriculum transformation projects in terms of primary content areas, feminists leave largely unaddressed the needs of our colleagues in math and the natural sciences who are struggling to incorporate their feminism into their professionalism and curricula.

What these criticisms of McIntosh's (1983) five-phase model suggest is that any unidimensional approach to feminist curricular transformation in terms of only primary content area, or of only women (i.e., without men), has crucial limitations. This is true even when those limitations are corrected by the inclusion of gender, race, and class issues, such as in my integrative seven-phase approach. This is because there are *other* important contributions that feminism makes to the mainstream curriculum besides the revision of primary content areas. A discussion of these contributions is the focus of the remainder of this chapter.

An important paper by psychologist Kathryn Quina (1986) impressed upon me how a need to rethink "the feminist curriculum" in terms of goals, rather than of content, could make feminist curricular transformation projects genuinely applicable to gender-resistant fields. Quina identifies six "multiple domains" in which feminist curricular change can occur: (1) primary content; (2) secondary or incidental content (e.g., illustrations and examples); (3) methodologies or "modes of analysis"; (4) pedagogy; (5) teachers as professional role models; and (6) worldviews or conceptual frameworks (p. 3). Conceiving of feminist curricular transformation projects as goal focused allows (2)–(6) to be central aspects of any such projects.

Overlaying Quina's (1986) multidimensional curricular domains on my integrative seven-phase model, one could generate a greatly expanded range of goals for feminist challenges to the malestream curriculum. Here I provide such an overlay for only one of Quina's five additional areas, (2) secondary content areas (visual aids, photographs, examples):

Consider Phase 3. In a logic course, if the arguments discussed consistently deal with specifically feminist claims, or with characterizations of women that challenge sex-role stereotypes, one *is* engaged in Phase 3 feminist curricular revision in a secondary content area. Or if in a chemistry course one consistently uses examples of research published by women, regardless of content area,[3] in order to expand students' conceptions of women's contributions, one would be engaged in Phase 3 curricular revision.

Consider now the other three goal areas identified by Quina (1986)— methodologies, pedagogy, teachers as role models, and conceptual frameworks, (3)–(6). Feminist challenges to traditional disciplinary "methodologies" would include examination of gender bias in experimental designs, promotion of a variety of analytic approaches to research problems (such as the use of new statistical techniques to evaluate reported gender differences), and a challenge to gender-biased terminology. A focus on methodology highlights the view, insisted on by feminists, that the methodology one uses, including the questions one asks, affects the answers one gets. For instance, gender bias in traditional primatology and in its assumptions of male dominance hierarchies prevented primatologists from seeing that dominance hierarchies are neither universal nor male.[4] The work of such feminist primatologists as Donna Haraway (1986) and Sarah Hrdy (1986), which challenged traditional androcentric observational and explanatory

Phase	Women/gender	Race/ethnicity	Class
Phase 1	Womanless____	Raceless/ethnicityless____	Classless____
Phase 2	Women in____	Blacks/Native Americans/Hispanic/Asians in ____	Poor people in ____
Phase 3	Women as a problem, anomaly, or absence in ____	Racial/ethnic minorities as a problem, anomaly, or absence in____	Poor people as a problem, anomaly, or absence in ____
Phase 4	Women's ____(includes race/ethnicity, class, age, affectional preference, marital status, nationality, religion)	Afro-American, Native American, Hispanic American, Asian-American ____ (includes racial/ethnic women)	Poor people's (includes women)
Phase 5	Men's ____ (includes White, racial/ethnic minority men, poor men, gay men, older/younger men, religious/nonreligious men, men of different regions/nationalities)		
Phase 6	Gendered (women's and men's) ____ (includes White, racial/ethnic minority, rich, middle-class, poor, lesbian/gay, older/younger, religious/nonreligious, different region/nationality women and men)		
Phase 7	Redefined/reconstructed to include us all		

FIGURE 4.1. Seven-phase integrative model for primary content subject areas.

models for primate social organization, revealed the gender bias of the methodologies and of the underlying assumptions employed in traditional primatology.

In this vein, ponder what non-Western feminist Uma Narayan, in a wonderful paper called "Working Together Across Difference" (1988), says about methodology. Referring to members of an oppressed group as "insiders" and to nonmembers as "outsiders," Narayan argues that in "working together across differences," the outsider must practice "methodological humility" and "methodological caution":

By the requirement of "methodological humility" I mean that the "outsider" must always sincerely conduct herself under the assumption that, as an outsider, she may be missing something, and that what appears to her to be a "mistake" on the part of the insider may make more sense if she had a fuller understanding of the context. By the requirement of "methodological caution," I mean that the outsider should sincerely attempt to carry out her attempted criticism of the insider's perceptions in such a way that it does not amount to, or even seem to amount to, an attempt to denigrate or dismiss entirely the validity of the insider's point of view. (p. 38)

Quina's (1986) fourth domain, pedagogy, is one of the richest areas of feminist scholarship. The research of Roberta M. Hall and Bernice R. Sandler (1982) shows that the college classroom is indeed a "chilly one for women": Men students talk more than women, and what they say often carries more weight. Men interrupt women students far more often than women students interrupt men, and men's interruptions of women more often introduce trivial or inappropriately personal comments that bring the women's discussion to an end or change its focus. Faculty inadvertently reinforce this chilly classroom climate for women in various ways: by calling directly on men students but not on women students; by calling men students by name more often than they do women students; by addressing the class as if no women were present ("Suppose your wife . . ." or "When you were a boy . . ."); by using sexist humor; by referring to males as "men" but to females as "girls" or "gals" rather than as "women"; by asking questions followed by eye contact with men students only—as if only men were expected to respond; by "coaching" men but not women students in working toward a fuller answer ("What did you mean by that?" "Why do you see that as a major turning point?"); by waiting longer for men than for women students to answer a question before going on to another student; by responding more extensively to men's than to women's comments; and by responding to comments or questions perceived as delivered in a "feminine style" as inherently of less value than those stated in a "masculine style."

Feminist pedagogy encourages cooperative learning, classroom interactions that are free of gender biases, critical thinking in the classroom, "problem solving with a quantitative tool kit" rather than merely rote mathematics (Quina, 1986, p. 20), use of examples that grow out of the student's own experiences, recognition of different "learning styles" and "thinking styles" (absolutist and relativist thinking; intuitive, contextual, narrative, "connected forms of thinking"; and" separate," detached, isolated kinds of thinking), appreciation of diversity and life experiences, and legitimate use of human emotion and experience within science (for example, as part of the science problem-solving process). The implementation of feminist pedagogies is central to any feminist curricular transformation project.

In the area of professional role models, Quina's fifth domain, same-gender advisors and mentors have been shown to be important to young women (1988, p. 25). Science teachers need to include our foremothers in the history of science.[5] Merely having women in the classroom in women-underrepresented fields corrects a noticeable absence of women—as teach-

Phase 1	Gender biased	Race/ethnic biased	Class biased
Phase 2	Examples of/from women added in	Examples of/from "racial minorities" added in	Examples of/from "poor people" added in
Phase 3	Examples from women that challenge traditional examples	Examples from racial minorities that challenge traditional examples	Examples from poor people that challenge traditional examples
Phase 4	Examples of/from women predominantly or exclusively	Examples of/from racial minorities predominantly or exclusively	Examples from poor people predominantly or exclusively
Phase 5	Examples of/from men qua men predominantly or exclusively (including Black men, Hispanic men, Native American men, gay men, poor men, fathers, sons, husbands)		
Phase 6	Gendered examples predominantly or exclusively		
Phase 7	Examples that include us all		

FIGURE 4.2. Seven-phase integrative model for secondary content areas.

ers, mentors, colleagues—in ways that are healthy for *all* learners. Simply having more numbers of underrepresented bodies among the faculty and student populations is a necessary (though not sufficient) way to begin remedying the bias created by their absence. This point is made succinctly by sociologist Rosabeth Moss Kanter in her *A Tale of "O"* (1980), with its eye-catching title.

The last area that Quina identifies—worldviews or conceptual frameworks—is of great concern to feminists interested in challenging what I have called oppressive—especially patriarchal—conceptual frameworks. Feminists have convincingly argued that some of the most time-honored and cherished assumptions about scientific practice, such as the idea that it is value neutral, objective, and rational, are incorrect or problematic. Feminists have made similar claims about, for instance, philosophy and psychology—that assumptions of the value neutrality, objectivity, and rationality of "the moral and epistemological points of view" and "theories of human moral development" are incorrect.[6] The feminist critique of conceptual frameworks involves seeing ways in which patriarchal conceptual frameworks have functioned to blind viewers to male gender biases whenever and wherever they occur.

In this chapter I have attempted to say what feminism is, what makes any issue a feminist issue, and how and why the mainstream—malestream—curriculum is a feminist issue. After reviewing the important integrative five-phase model of curriculum revision proposed by Peggy McIntosh (1983), I suggested ways to expand that model to make feminist curricular transformation projects truly inclusive as well as applicable to gender-resistant fields. In particular, I suggested that feminists adopt a seven-phase curriculum model, and, following Kathryn Quina's (1986) lead, conceived of feminist curriculum transformation projects in terms of goals rather than of content. This expanded and reconceived goal model would include primary and secondary content areas, methodological issues, pedagogy, professional role models, and conceptual frameworks as legitimate loci of feminist transformation projects.

The advantages of this sort of multidimensional, expanded, goal-oriented phase model of feminist curricular transformation are many: It takes seriously the conceptual and historical interconnections between sexism and other social *isms*; it clarifies ways in which feminist curricular transformation projects are applicable to gender-resistant subject areas; it gives central importance to "climate issues" in classrooms; it invites faculty members to fit into curricular transformation projects wherever they find themselves or feel able; it provides mechanisms for genuine change that do not require institutional support; it can be accomplished in all disciplines, across all disciplines, and at all levels (elementary, secondary, and postsecondary) of education.

What, then, are the obstacles to these feminist curricular changes? What might prevent feminist curricular transformation projects from succeeding? According to sociologist Victor Rios, there are three circumstances that oppose social change: The change is not understood; the proposed change threatens basic security; and the proposed change is viewed by those it is intended to benefit as imposed on them.[7] Certainly all those obstacles have thwarted feminist curricular transformation projects. My hope is that, by clarifying what feminist curricular changes involve and by suggesting ways in which a genuinely inclusivist curriculum benefits all of us in academia— as teachers, as scholars, as women and men—my remarks will encourage each of us to start, wherever we are, in initiating such changes. If we do so, the feminist challenge to the mainstream curriculum will accomplish a philosophical miracle: It will rewrite the future.

NOTES

1. As Elizabeth Minnick (1986) writes, "We cannot add anything to that which has been defined as the whole. Knowledge that does not fit within that whole cannot be additive—consider the fact that we cannot simply add the idea that the world is round to the conviction that the world is flat" (p. 11).

2. Some of the literature in "men's studies" is an attempt to provide such information. See, for example, Franklin Abbott, ed., *New Men, New Minds: Breaking Male Tradition*, Freedom, CA: Crossing Press, 1987; Eugene R. August, *Men's Studies: A Selected and Annotated Interdisciplinary Bibliography*, Littleton, CO: Libraries Unlimited, 1984; Timothy Benke, *Men on Rape*, New York: St. Martin's, 1982; Harry Brod, ed., *The Making of Masculinities: The New Men's Studies*, Winchester, MA, 1984; *Changing Men: Issues in Gender, Sex, and Politics* (journal); Warren Farrell, *Why Men Are the Way They Are: The Male-Female Dynamic*, New York: McGraw-Hill, 1986; Daniel Garfinkel, *In a Man's World: Father, Son, Brother, Friend and Other Roles Men Play*, New York: New American Library, 1985; Alice Jardine and Paul Smith, eds. *Men in Feminism*, New York: Methuen, 1987; Michael S. Kimmel, ed., *American Behavioral Scientist*, 29(5), special edition on "Researching Men's Roles," 1986, and *Changing Men: New Directions in Research on Men and Masculinity*, Beverly Hills: Sage, 1987; Mirra Komarovsky, *Dilemmas of Masculinity: A Study of College Youth*, New York: Norton, 1976; Robert A. Lewis, *Men in Difficult Times: Masculinity Today and Tomorrow*, Englewood Cliffs, NJ: Prentice-Hall, 1981; Elizabeth H. Pleck and Joseph H. Pleck, eds., *The American Man*, Englewood Cliffs, NJ: Prentice-Hall, 1980; Joseph H. Pleck, *Working Wives, Working Husbands*, Beverly Hills: Sage, 1985, and *The Myth of Masculinity*, Cambridge, MA: MIT Press, 1981; Robert Staples, *Black Masculinity: The Black Male's Role in American Society*, San Francisco: Black Scholar Press, 1982.

3. See, e.g., Patrick Grim, "A Note on the Ethics of Theories of Truth," in Mary Vetterling-Braggin, ed., *Sexist Language: A Modern Philosophical Analysis* (pp. 290–298), Boston: Littlefield, Adams, 1983. For a very interesting set of papers on teaching "feminist logic," see Ruth Ginzberg's "Feminism, Rationality and Logic" and "Teaching Feminist Logic," *American Philosophical Association Newsletter on Feminism and Philosophy*, 88(2) (March 1989), 29–34.

4. For a discussion of this point, see my "Critical Thinking and Feminism," *Informal Logic*, 10(1) (Winter 1988), 31–42.

5. Anne Fausto-Sterling and Lydia English (1985) at Brown University have taught an exciting course titled "Women and Minorities in Science," which was received with enthusiasm by both minority and nonminority students. In my own discipline of philosophy, the absence of women in the history of Western philosophy has led many like myself to despair about attempts to "find" female philosophers. Recently, however, the Project on Women in the History of Philosophy has published two of a four-volume set on the history of women in philosophy. The first volume of *A History of Women Philosophers*, titled *Ancient Women Philosophers, 600 B.C.–500 A.D.* (Boston: Martinus Nijhoff, 1987), ed. Mary Waithe, identifies at least 15 women philosophers in classical Greece. What a thrill it is for me to have access to these materials! There is now no excuse for teachers of the history of philosophy and of classics to offer courses without reference to these materials.

6. See, for example, philosopher Alison M. Jaggar, *Feminist Politics and Human Nature*. Totowa, NJ: Rowman & Allenheld, 1983; Carol Gilligan, *In a Different Voice: Psychological Theories and Women's Development*. Cambridge: Harvard University Press, 1982; and *Mapping the Moral Domain: A Contribution of Women's Thinking to Psychological Theory and Education*, eds. Carol Gilligan, Janie Victoria Ward, and Jill

McLean Taylor, with Betty Bardige, Center for the Study of Gender, Education and Human Development. Cambridge: Harvard University Press, 1988.

7. Victor Rios, my colleague at Macalester College, made these remarks at the Macalester College Faculty Retreat on Cultural Pluralism, Feb. 13, 1988.

REFERENCES

Aiken, Susan H., Anderson, K., Dinnerstein, M., & Temple, J. N. (1988). *Changing our minds: feminist transformations of knowledge*. Albany, N.Y.: State University of New York.

Bleier, Ruth. (1984). *Science and gender: A critique of biology and its theories on women*. New York: Pergamon.

Bleier, Ruth. (Ed.). (1986). *Feminist approaches in science*. New York: Pergamon.

Broverman, Inge K., et al. (1970). Sex-role stereotypes and clinical judgments of mental health. *Journal of Consulting and Clinical Psychology 34*, 1–7.

Bunch, Charlotte, & Sandra Pollack. (Eds.). (1983). *Learning our way: Essays in feminist education*. Trumansburg, N.Y.: Crossing Press.

Culley, Margo, & Catherine Portugues. (Eds.). (1985). *Gendered subjects: The dynamics of feminist teaching*. Boston: Routledge and Kegan Paul.

Daedelus. (1987). Special Issue on "Learning about women: Gender, politics, and power," Fall.

DuBois, Ellen Carol, et al. (1985). *Feminist scholarship: Kindling in the groves of academe*. Chicago: University of Illinois Press.

Fausto-Sterling, Ann, & Lydia L. English. (1985). *Women and minorities in science: An interdisciplinary course* (Working Paper No. 154). Wellesley, MA: Wellesley College Center for Research on Women.

Fisher, Berenice. (1981). "What is feminist pedagogy?" *Radical Teacher 18*, 20–24.

Franzosa, Susan Douglas, & Karen A. Mazza. (1984). *Integrating women's studies into the curriculum: An annotated bibliography*. Westport, Conn.: Greenwood.

Giroux, Henry A. (1977). *Theory and resistance in education: A pedagogy for the opposition*. South Hadley: Bergin and Garve.

Hall, Roberta M., & Bernice R. Sandler. (1982). *The classroom climate: A chilly one for women?* Washington, DC: Project on the Status and Education of Women, Association of American Colleges.

Haraway, Donna. (1986). Primatology is politics by other means. In Ruth Bleier (Ed.), *Feminist approaches to science* (pp. 77–118). New York: Pergamon.

Harding, Sandra. (1986). *The science question in feminism*. Ithaca: Cornell University Press.

Hoffman, Nancy. (1977). White woman, Black woman: Inventing an adequate pedagogy. In *Women's Studies Newsletter*, 1–2, 21–24.

Hrdy, Sarah Blaffer. (1986). Empathy, polyandry, and the myth of the coy female. In Ruth Bleier (Ed.), *Feminist approaches to science* (pp. 119–146). New York: Pergamon.

Journal of Thought. (1985). Special Issue on "Feminist Education." *20*(3) (Fall).

Kanter, Rosabeth Moss. (1980). *A Tale of "O": On being different in an organization.* New York: Harper & Row.

Keller, Evelyn Fox. (1983a). *A feeling for the organism: The life and work of Barbara McClintock.* New York: Freeman.

Keller, Evelyn Fox. (1983b). *Reflections on gender and science.* New Haven: Yale University Press.

Langland, Elizabeth, & Walter Gove, eds. (1983). *A feminist perspective in the academy: The difference it makes.* Chicago: University of Chicago Press.

Maher, Frances A. (1987). Inquiry teaching and feminist pedagogy. *Social Education, 51,* 186–192.

McIntosh, Peggy. (1983). *Interactive phases of curricular revision* (Working Paper No. 124). Wellesley, MA: Wellesley College Center for Research on Women.

Minnick, Elizabeth. (1986). *Conceptual errors across the curriculum: Towards a transformation of the curriculum,* Memphis, TN: The Research Clearinghouse and Curriculum Integration Project, at the Center for Research on Women, Memphis State University.

Narayan, Uma. (1988, Summer). Working together across difference: Some considerations on emotions and political practice, *Hypatia, 3,* 31–48.

Nelson, Cary. (Ed.). (1986). *Theory in the classroom.* Urbana: University of Illinois Press.

Porter, Nancy. (1982). Liberating teaching, *Women's Studies Quarterly,* X, 19–24.

Quina, Kathryn. (1986). *Teaching research methods: A multidimensional feminist curricular transformation plan* (Working Paper No. 164). Wellesley, MA: Wellesley College Center for Research on Women.

Schuster, Marilyn, & Susan Van Dyne. (1985). *Women's place in the academy: Transforming the liberal arts curriculum.* Totowa, N.J.: Rowman and Allenheld.

Signs: A Journal of Women in Culture and Society. (1987). Special issue on "Reconstructing the Academy." *12*(2) (Winter).

Spender, Dale, ed. (1981). *Men's studies modified: The impact of feminism on the academic disciplines.* New York: Pergamon.

Vetterling-Braggin, Mary, ed. (1983). *Sexist language: A modern philosophical analysis.* Boston: Littlefield, Adams.

Waithe, Mary Ellen, ed. (1987). *A history of women philosophers, Vol. 1: Ancient women philosophers, 600 B.C.–500 A.D.* Boston: Martinus Nijhoff.

Warren, Karen J. (1986, Spring). Feminism and ecology: Making connections. *Environmental Ethics, 8,* 3–20.

Warren, Karen J. (1988). Critical thinking and feminism. *Informal Logic, 10*(1), 31–42.

Warren, Karen J. (1989). Male gender bias and western conceptions of reason and rationality. *American Philosophical Association Newsletter on Feminism and Philosophy,* (88), (March), 48–52.

Wolff, Mary Ann. (1986). According to whom? Helping students analyze contrasting views of reality. *Educational Leadership* (October), 36–41.

Women's Studies Quarterly. 1987. XV, nos. 34: Special Feature on Feminist Pedagogy (Fall/Winter), 6–124.

ABOUT THE AUTHOR

Karen J. Warren is an Associate Professor and Chair of Philosophy at Macalester College in St. Paul, Minnesota. She received the 1996 Macalester College Excellence in Teaching Award. She has published more than 40 articles, mostly in the area of environmental philosophy, and has produced two videos, one of which ("Thinking Out Loud: Teaching Critical Thinking Skills," from Alliance Productions) won First Place at the Chicago International Video and Film Festival, Education Division, 1994. She currently is completing a book titled *Ecofeminism: A Philosophical Perspective on What It Is and Why It Matters.*

CHAPTER 5

Resistance to Generalizations
in the Classroom

Susanne Bohmer

From my own teaching experiences over the past few years, both in women's studies and in sociology, as well as from conversations with colleagues, it seems that the resistance to generalizations on the part of students about which I wrote in 1989 is not something of the distant past, but very much a part of life in the current classroom. Although I have not encountered a class quite as "resistant" as the one I described in the article, I still regularly have to convince my students of the value of generalizing about groups in society.

What I do differently in my teaching today from at the time when I wrote the article is that I do not wait until the students object to generalizations based on research, but now make a discussion of the issue part of my courses within the first two class sessions. I summarize for students many of the points from the article that underscore the benefits and need for making (what I now call) "empirical generalizations." Since one of the motivations for objecting to general statements about entire groups is based on fear that this involves stereotyping, I have found it useful to follow this discussion with group work that asks *students* to distinguish between empirical generalizations and stereotypes. I then put their answers on the board, and we discuss them as a whole class.

Typical answers involve differences in the process of arriving at these two types of generalizations. The empirical kind requires extensive and systematic study, whereas stereotypes are often based on hearsay or involve an overgeneralization derived from personal experience.

Another difference typically listed by students is that stereotypes tend to be emotionally loaded and judgmental whereas empirical generalizations are more neutral, aimed at describing the world around us. This leads us to a discussion of the motivation for using these two types of generalizations. At least in the ideal, we make empirical generalizations to better understand our society and the people within it by providing both description and explanation. In contrast, when we stereotype, we are not interested in understanding or explaining the traits of the target group, but simply want to judge and maintain our distance. Students also recognize on their own that stereotypes tend to be rigidly applied to all members of the group, whereas empirical generalizations give us averages or typical characteristics and thereby leave room for exceptions. Finally, we discuss that empirical generalizations are always open to reexamination and that their content changes to accommodate new evidence. Stereotypes, in contrast, often are resistant to evidence.

I have found that the process of having *students* come up with differences between these two types of generalizations raises their level of acceptance for the empirical kind. In addition, of course, it allows us to refer back to this class session whenever objections to general statements about social groups come up later in the term.

Teacher: To this day, women spend more time on housework and child care than do men, in spite of the fact that many women are full-time members of the labor force.

Student: But my mother worked outside the home and never did any housework. It was my father who took care of the household chores and children.

This was my second term coteaching an introductory women's studies course.[1] The class met twice a week for lectures, panels, or films and was accompanied by weekly small group discussions. During class sessions we typically provided students with background information on a given topic, followed by discussion, a film, or both. Part of this information consisted of a summary of current research describing the conditions and experiences of members of different groups in society and was often comparative. This descriptive information, of course, involved generalizations about groups, such as women of color, lesbians, White women, or White men. Examples included women's and men's average yearly earnings, gender differences in the number of interruptions in conversations, and the relatively high number of sterilizations of women of color.

When we taught this course the first time during the fall, students were eager for the type of information that documents inequalities in our society. Although they occasionally asked how we came to know about such differences between groups on a given topic, they accepted the legitimacy of these generalizations and saw them as useful and meaningful. We were surprised to find a very different response when we taught the introduction the following term. This time, a considerable number of students objected to such generalizations, either by saying that we needed to consider each individual in their own right or, as illustrated by the exchange above, by giving us exceptions to the general trend we had just discussed. We were particularly surprised about this response because we had begun the course with a discussion of the different types of oppression (such as racism, classism, and sexism) and had stressed the importance of considering how our personal experiences are shaped by our membership in particular groups.

Within three class sessions (each taught by a different person), a pattern of interaction had been established that seemed disruptive, at times even hostile, and in which the speaker spent considerable time defending the information she had presented. This pattern did not allow us to go beyond description to more interesting questions, such as the reasons for existing differences or how we can effect change. My coteacher and I decided to address the issue directly by telling students about our concerns. I prepared a talk about generalizations and their relationship to exceptions. I want to share some of these points here since I found in conversations with other instructors that resistance to generalizations about members of different groups in society is fairly common, particularly in courses that deal with politically charged topics, such as gender, race, or class oppression. Below, I will first summarize my presentation to our class and then explore some of the reasons that I believe underlie students' objections to generalizations.

NEED FOR GENERALIZATIONS

The first point I wish to make is that generalizations can indeed be problematic and objectionable. We are all familiar with the ways in which stereotypes generalize about members of different groups. Most of us would rightfully object to this type of generalization, not only because stereotypes often involve a flawed representation of the group in question, but also because they are evaluative, "insensitive to evidence, and . . . applied indifferently to members of the target group" (Philips, 1988, p. 55). Stereotypes ignore or deny differences between group members. In contrast, the types of generalizations about which I want to talk here are primarily descriptive. They are based on empirical evidence and are thereby open to revision, and they involve a consideration of the frequency with which an event, activity, or characteristic occurs.[2]

When we say, for example, that we have more rainfall in the winter than in the summer, we are making a generalization about the weather. This statement gives us a description of our weather pattern and is based on records of rainfall during the two seasons. Furthermore, this generalization is still valid even though we have some rainy summer days and some dry winter days. Similarly, when we state that women do more child care and household work than do men, we are describing differences in the activities of these two groups based on research findings. We are not saying that *all* women do more of this unpaid labor than do *all* men. Rather, we are talking about the relative amount of time that women and men spend on the average on these tasks. Generalizations do not mean that something always happens in a set way, but that it occurs with greater frequency. These types of generalizations, unlike stereotypes, allow for variations within groups.

Generalizations are an important and necessary part of our everyday lives. As we move through our daily activities, we are continually informed by our knowledge of what happens typically or generally under given circumstances. When we plan how much time we need between rising in the morning and arriving at work, we usually do not just consider this particular morning but generalize from our previous experiences. We know how much time it takes us on average, on most mornings, to get ready for work. Of course, if we have to run an errand on a particular day, we will allot extra time for this activity. But we do not consider anew each time how long it takes us to shower, get dressed, have breakfast, or travel to work. These types of generalizations, then, allow us to accomplish our activities more efficiently. They put order into the world around us and help us orient ourselves within it.

Generalizations about members of different groups in society are not all that different from those used in everyday life. They are actually often better documented, since most are based on research that is typically more comprehensive than what we surmise when we generalize from our personal experiences. Generalizations are necessary if we want to analyze our society and the positions of women within it. If we considered every individual separately, we would be overwhelmed by the wealth of information and unable to comprehend how we organize our lives in a community.

Furthermore, generalizations allow one to look beyond one's personal experiences by placing one's own life in relation to those of others and by their leading to an understanding of how one's behaviors and thoughts are influenced by the society in which one lives. Our lives are not only regulated by our own values and desires but also by the people with whom we interact and by the structures of the community around us. Generalizations about the experiences and conditions of members of different race, age, class, or gender groups provide us with insights into our own personal experiences as well as those of others, and they help us comprehend how we organize our society.

Since many of the generalizations we make are based on research findings involving averages, I find it useful to explain briefly how these averages are calculated statistically. This explanation allows students to understand that many generalizations already take account of exceptions. When we take a random sample of women in the workforce, for example, and ask them about their yearly earnings, we find that a few of these women are likely to have very high earnings. When we average the incomes of *all* women in our sample, however—that is, when we add them up and divide by the number of cases—we find a lower average than when we do the same procedure for men.[3] This occurs even though we have included women with exceptionally high earnings in our calculations, because *most* women earn less money than *most* men. Averages, while they include the experiences of exceptional cases, reflect the characteristics that are most frequent for a particular group.

Another way of explaining the usefulness of generalizations based on averages is through the use of the normal curve.[4] This shows students that averages are indeed good representations of characteristics of members of different groups since, under the bell-shaped curve, the vast majority of cases fall closely around the mean and very few are out under the tails.

I also argue that responding to a generalization by listing all the cases that are exceptional prohibits us from learning more about the topic at hand. It means that we close our eyes to the experiences of most people in our society while considering an exceptional few. That the majority of women have relatively low incomes is significant because it affects their lives in all areas, and it tells us that women and men are treated differently in our society. If we accept such generalizations as valid and meaningful, we can move on to examine the reasons for the gender gap in wages, the consequences of low earnings, and possible solutions to these inequities.

Finally, I point out to students that we are most likely to ignore or challenge generalizations when they do not fit our personal experiences. It is useful, however, to be aware of how one's life differs from those of most others around one. To know that one is different in some regard helps one to better understand one's own experiences and might lead to further questions, such as, Why am I different? or How has this difference affected my life? "Exceptional" experiences can be useful learning devices if we consider them in relation to those of others in society.

The response of students to these explanations was positive, overall, and clearly improved classroom interactions. The question that remains for me, however, and that was not answered by our students, is why we find such resistance to these types of generalizations in the classroom. Under what conditions do students suspend their everyday belief that generalizations remain valid in spite of exceptions? In what follows, I want to explore some of the reasons that I believe underlie objections to generalizations about members of different groups in society.

Some students, being aware of the political nature of women's studies courses, believe that any information given in these classes is necessarily biased and should therefore be challenged or debated. At the beginning of this term, several students asked us how we would be able to grade assignments and tests in a course that was highly political, and whether or not we would grade them down for disagreements. I think these are valid concerns. I was surprised, however, that I had not been asked these questions when teaching and assisting in sociology classes, an area that is no less political and in which some of the topics are closely related to those covered in women's studies. I suspect that differences in students' approaches to class materials in the two fields are due to the different manner in which we teach women's studies and sociology courses. In women's studies we are explicit about the political nature of our field and present ourselves as feminists, that is, as members of a political movement. In sociology we tend to be less overtly political. Although we might briefly discuss our "leanings," we typically do not present ourselves as unequivocally as feminists as we do in women's studies courses. How students respond to generalizations might thus be related to the degree to which we highlight our political stance. Information in courses that are presented in an overtly political manner seems to be perceived by students as biased, leading them to reject generalizations more readily.

Students who challenge information due to the political nature of women's studies courses, then, do not necessarily object to the use of generalizations per se, but they doubt the validity and objectivity of the research on which they are based. During the term, we were asked several times who conducted a particular study and how it was executed. Again, I consider these to be valid and important questions, yet I was surprised by this concern with methodological issues since it was very unlike students' behavior in the statistics course in sociology that I had taught the previous year. There, I continually had to encourage awareness of biases in empirical studies because students tended to accept findings uncritically, especially when more sophisticated statistical models were used for analysis. Statistics courses, they seemed to believe, dealt with nonpolitical and therefore objective or "scientific" materials. Whether students readily accept generalizations based on empirical research thus also depends on the topic at hand and on their belief that certain courses are more scientific than others.

Most objections to generalizations are clearly a way of denying differences and inequalities in our society based on group membership. As Philips (1988) states, "The refusal to generalize is not a sign of moral purity but of willful blindness" (p. 60). In this case, even students who accept the validity of research findings object to the use of generalizations, arguing that we need to consider individuals in their own right rather than as members of groups. This is not an uncommon line of thinking given the strong emphasis placed on values such as individualism and personal achievement in the United States. Insisting on the uniqueness of every individual and the belief that success or failure is based solely on our actions as individuals is a way of ignoring or denying structural inequalities.

Most of the material covered in women's studies courses deals directly or indirectly with oppression. This is an unfamiliar and uncomfortable topic for most students, particularly for those who are members of privileged groups. Men do not think much about their privileges in a sexist society, Whites do not often consider the benefits associated with belonging to this racial group, and middle- and upper-class people often remain ignorant of the economic struggles of members of the working class. It is not surprising, then, that most of the objections to generalizations were made by our male students as well as by White, middle-class women. Students of color and White working-class students more readily accept information that documents oppression because they can integrate it into their own lives and because they do not struggle with feelings of guilt or defensiveness.

When I gave a lecture on oppression at the beginning of the term, I stressed that oppression always involves two groups—the oppressed and the privileged—and therefore affects all of us, and not just those who are the target. What I believe we failed to do, however, in subsequent class sessions was to examine truly the dynamic relationship between the two groups. Although we often gave comparative information on oppressed and privileged groups, our focus remained on the former. Of course, in a women's studies class our emphasis will be on the experiences of women, but when we make comparisons between the sexes, it is useful not only to point to the barriers that women face but also to how these perpetuate male privilege. The same needs to be done for comparisons between people of color and Whites, lesbians and heterosexual women, or working- and middle-class people. As Paula Rothenberg (1989) points out, "Instead of focusing exclusively on the pathology of racism and sexism, white students can be asked to analyze the implicit privileges they enjoyed growing up white" (p. 40).[5]

Such an analysis does not mean that we neglect the experiences of members of oppressed groups but that we show how oppression and privilege are related to one another, since one group cannot exist without the other. Margaret Andersen (1987) calls this the "fourth phase" in transforming the curriculum, where members of oppressed groups "become seen as society, not *in* society" (p. 19). This approach goes beyond seeing women, people of color, or lesbians as victims and will further our understanding of the relationship between oppression and privilege. In classrooms where many students are from privileged backgrounds, such an investigation would also help them relate the materials more directly to their own lives and thereby, as Rothenberg (1989) puts it, undercut "resistance to acknowledging the force and nature of both racism and sexism" (p. 40).

Furthermore, awareness of privilege helps us discover the intersections between different types of oppression. Again, although I talked about the experience of multiple group membership in my initial lecture, stressing that any one individual might be a member of both oppressed and privileged groups, we did not fully integrate this information into our following presentations. In many instances, what seems to be an exception actually indicates membership in a privileged group. When students respond to information about the gender gap in wages, for example, by saying that they know women who are in professional and well-paying jobs, we should point out that these women are members of a privileged group with regard to class standing. This allows us to make the link between gender and class.

In addition, an awareness of multiple group membership guards against a tendency toward making universal statements about women. Much of our research to date is based on the more privileged groups of women, and we often generalize from these to all women. Although this issue did not seem to be at the root of the concerns of our students this term, I believe that it is important to let students know the limitations of our information. I am thus not advocating here the blind acceptance of all types of generalizations. I consider objections valid and necessary when the generalization in question homogenizes women and ignores the diversity in the life experiences and conditions of women of different backgrounds.

NOTES

1. I want to thank my coteacher, Joyce Briggs. This paper has benefited greatly from our many discussions.
2. This is of course a simplistic way of describing the type of generalization I am discussing. No piece of information is ever purely descriptive, since it is al-

ways embedded in a particular social, economic, and political context. The concept of empirical evidence is similarly problematic since evidence is at least in part socially constructed rather than merely "discovered." I believe, however, that this representation of generalizations is useful given the overall point I wish to make to my students. For the remainder of this paper, the term *generalization* is used in this narrow and somewhat "unproblematic" sense.

3. Mean, rather than median, income is used here because most averages are based on the mean and to emphasize the consideration of outlying cases.

4. I am grateful to Lisa Leimar for bringing this point to my attention.

5. [Paula Rothenberg's essay is reprinted in the present book. Ed.]

REFERENCES

Andersen, Margaret L. (1987). *Denying difference: The continuing basis for exclusion in the classroom.* Memphis, TN: Center for Research on Women, Memphis State University, 1987.

Philips, Michael. (1988). Racist stereotypes. *Sweet Reason, 7*(3), 54–62.

Rothenberg, Paula. (1989). Integrating the study of race, gender, and class: Some preliminary observations. *Feminist Teacher, 3*(3), 37–42.

ABOUT THE AUTHOR

Susanne Bohmer is a full-time instructor of sociology at Edmonds Community College in Seattle. She teaches, in addition to introductory sociology, courses in sex and gender, race and ethnic relations, and social inequality. She also teaches Introduction to Women's Studies for the women's studies program. She received her PhD in sociology in 1992 from the University of Oregon.

CHAPTER 6

The Power of No

Martha E. Thompson

When *Feminist Teacher* first published "The Power of No" in 1990, I had successfully used the technique described in what follows several times. Seven years later, I still find a "NO circle" an effective technique to use in conjunction with discussions of violence against women. Students indicate that they suppress their feelings when discussing violence in classroom settings and that a NO Circle gives them an opportunity to release the physical and emotional tensions that arise. This brief and focused exercise is one way to acknowledge students' feelings and memories without requiring them to reveal their personal experiences or emotions. In my experience as a teacher, I have found that acknowledging the emotional and physical consequences of violence facilitates students' willingness to grapple intellectually with scholarly work on violence against women.

"Let's gather into a circle. Breathe deeply. Ground your feet firmly. Make yourselves as tall as you can. If you feel comfortable doing so, hold hands or put your arms around the women next to you.[1] Let's each call out something we would like to say no to, something we want to stop happening."

"Rape! beatings! harassment! racism! discrimination! poverty! unemployment! fear! homophobia! women as sex objects! child abuse!"

"Look around the circle. See what beautiful and powerful women we are. We have a right to our own bodies and our own

---

space. Whatever you are feeling right now—pain, fear, anger, sadness, whatever—channel it into your voice. On the count of three, let's say NO together. Let's say NO to all that which limits us. One . . . two . . . three."

"NO!"

It had been one of those days: A woman in my class brought up the incident of a brutal rape that had recently been in the news, and one student after another described a woman's murder, rape, beating, or assault, and the indifferent reactions of others to the event. The women in the class needed to tell these stories and to share with supportive women our collective anger, fear, and disgust.

As women in the class talked, I felt my own anxiety and anger increasing. My stomach was in knots; my neck and back muscles were tense. I wanted to quit listening. I can't stand the pain and terror each woman who is brutalized must experience, the fear and anger I feel when hearing these stories, the wrenching pain I experience when others ignore or trivialize a woman's degradation.

I was angry that we would leave the room in a few moments carrying the weight of the stories we had just heard and knowing that in order to merge again with the world outside the classroom, we would shove these stories into our subconscious. What could I do to channel the emotions stirred by these horror stories into constructive energy?[2]

Drawing on my experience as an IMPACT self-defense instructor, I asked the class to do a NO circle, described at the beginning of this chapter, before we left the classroom.[3] The NO circle transformed the energy in the room. Before forming the circle, tension, anxiety, and fear had permeated the room. Our voices and bodies had seemed to become smaller and smaller as we talked. After the NO circle, we had high energy and we were large and powerful. We were still angry and fearful, but we had focused our feelings on despicable acts against women. These feelings were no longer gnawing at our self-esteem, nor were vague or free-floating. When we saw a slide show on pornography later in the term, students commented on how crucial the NO circle had been earlier in the course for helping them transform their feelings of powerlessness and victimization. We did a NO circle that day, too.

THE NO CIRCLE

What is it about the NO circle that enabled us to turn our feelings of victimization and powerlessness into powerful energy focused on stopping violence against women? On the surface, a NO circle is a simple exercise. The underlying principles, however, are complex and instructive for those of us who teach about violence against women.

Directly or indirectly experiencing violence affects the total person. A key assumption underlying the NO circle is that we carry violence in our bodies, minds, and spirits. When we are powerless, we develop strategies to "get us through" the violence; for example, we may leave our bodies, shut down emotionally, block memories of violence, or deny that people have violated us. These tools may help us survive when we perceive no other options, but they perpetuate our individual isolation. Instead of focusing our anger and fear on the agents and acts of violence, we may turn our emotions inward and experience depression and powerlessness. Or we may carry an unfocused anger with us, randomly and inappropriately discharging it.

From my experience as a teacher, I have come to believe that women use distancing strategies in classrooms to enable them to hear and read about violence against women. As a consequence, they may experience paralyzing depression or unfocused anger. Even when the classroom materials portray women as survivors and not as victims, women are often unable to transfer this idea to their own lives: "That woman is a survivor, but I'm not." "I would be ruined for life if something like that ever happened to me."

I analyzed the instructions I gave in the NO circle described above because of the success of this technique in encouraging women to convert feelings of powerlessness into power. In my analysis of the NO circle instructions, I found four themes that represent principles of empowerment. By empowerment I mean a process of transforming feelings of victimization and powerlessness into feelings of power and confidence with which to act purposefully and justly on our own and others' behalf. I identify below these four principles of empowerment and how they are represented in the NO circle.

PRINCIPLES OF EMPOWERMENT

1. For empowerment to occur, we must make emotional and physical connections with other women. For instance, "Get in a circle." "Hold hands or put your arms around the women next to you." "Look around the circle. See what beautiful and powerful women we are." "Let's say NO together."

2. For empowerment to occur, we must assert our right to establish our own boundaries, to exercise autonomy and self-determination, and to do what we need to do to protect ourselves from victimization. Therefore,

I always add, "If you feel comfortable doing so." and "We have a right to our own bodies and our own space."

Asserting our rights does not simply mean that we talk about our rights; it also means that we act on them. Acting on our own behalf may make others uncomfortable and may publicly disrupt ongoing activities. In the NO circle, when we take steps to protect ourselves from victimization, we make a loud noise when we yell "NO!" Yelling no gives women a chance to practice acting on our right to say no even when it may disturb others. For instance, the first time I set up the NO circle in my class, one woman expressed her concern about the noise we would make when we yelled no together.

"We're going to make a lot of noise. Won't people wonder what we are doing? Won't we bother other people?"

"*We* need to do this to be able to step out of this room and move confidently in the world. If people come looking, let's ask them to join us in saying NO to violence against women."

3. For empowerment to occur, we must engage our whole selves in the process. We must unite our minds, bodies, and spirits. The instructions given in the NO circle direct participants to come into our bodies: "Let's gather into a circle. Breathe deeply. Ground your feet firmly. Make yourself as tall as you can." The facilitator in the NO circle encourages women to acknowledge our myriad emotions about violence and bring them into the circle: "Whatever you are feeling right now—pain, fear, anger, sadness, whatever—channel it into your voice." The facilitator urges women to think about and name the violence. "Let's each call out something we would like to say no to, something we want to stop happening."

4. For empowerment to occur, we must act collectively to challenge violence against women. The NO circle gives women an opportunity to experience the power of a collective voice. "On the count of three, let's say no together. Let's say no to all that which limits us. One . . . two . . . three. NO!"

In sum, course material on violence against women may stir women's memories and fears of violence. To protect ourselves from these memories and fears, we may leave our bodies, disregard our feelings, or deny the extent of violence that exists. Because they maintain our isolation and victimization, these are not effective strategies when we try collectively to understand and challenge violence against women.

To facilitate women's empowerment, teachers need to devise techniques that give students opportunities to develop relationships with others in the classroom, to exercise their right to say no to victimization, to integrate their bodies, minds, and spirits, and to collectively challenge violence against women.

Acknowledgments. I would like to thank Susan Stall, Demetria Lazzetto, Jim Lucas, Shelley Bannister, and Vicki Byard for their comments on an earlier version of this essay. Thanks also to Dianne Costanzo, Theo Pintzuk, Judith Roth, and Mary Tesoro for their encouragement, and to the students in American Women for inspiring this article.

NOTES

1. If men are present in the classroom, it is important to include them in the circle and to acknowledge them as allies. Wherever appropriate, use language that is inclusive.
2. For other ideas, see Elizabeth Adler's "It Happened to Me: How Faculty Handle Student Reactions to Class Material," in *Feminist Teacher*, 3(1), pp. 22–26; and the responses by Joanne Belknap and Nancy Brooks in the same issue.
3. I teach IMPACT self-defense, which is a highly specialized self-defense program. Women learn a knockout defense against an assailant of any size. The course is taught by a female and male instructor team with the female instructor serving as the team leader and the male instructor playing a dual role of instructor and mock assailant. With the support of other students, class assistants, and the female instructor, students learn to use full-force defenses against the padded mock assailants in simulated rape scenarios. IMPACT organizations are located in Chicago, Indianapolis, Los Angeles, Minneapolis, San Francisco, and Washington, D.C.

ABOUT THE AUTHOR

Martha E. Thompson is a professor of sociology and women's studies at Northeastern Illinois University in Chicago. She also teaches IMPACT self-defense in Chicago and in other locations in the Midwest.

CHAPTER 7

Reflections on Teaching: "Gender, Race, and Class"

Joy James

It's been several years since I have taught in women's studies, although I continue to focus on issues of gender, race, and justice. The varied research and teaching environments in which I have found myself have altered my approach, or approaches, to pedagogy. For instance, I no longer consider academe to be singularly depoliticizing or deradicalizing as an environment. So the doubts expressed toward the conclusion of "Gender, Race and Radicalism: Teaching the Autobiographies of Native and African American Women Activists" (Chapter 19 in this volume) have been alleviated somewhat. Specifically, can one maintain one's integrity as a dissenting voice, as a progressive voice, in a corporate structure? My response today is yes, as long as you are more than a professional thinker, as long as you have a political life outside of academe that seeps across academic borders. And an ethical drive that calls you to want more than competency or excellence in the classroom. So, I have been criticized for wanting too much from academe, too much from students, and too much from myself. In the essay "Reflections on Teaching: 'Gender, Race, & Class'" my "exacting" demands are apparent and have been dismissed by some academics as being too political/polemical and unrealistic.

Perhaps I trust myself and my students more. Perhaps I have become more detached. But the urgency that shapes these two essays no longer always appears as a feature in my classes—unless perhaps my students bring this with them.

This chapter originally appeared in *Feminist Teacher*, 1991, 5(3), 9–15.

The Feminist Teacher *Anthology: Pedagogies and Classroom Strategies.* Copyright © 1998 by Teachers College, Columbia University. All rights reserved. ISBN 0-8077-3741-0 (paper), ISBN 0-8077-3742-9 (cloth). Prior to photocopying items for classroom use, please contact the Copyright Clearance Center, Customer Service, 222 Rosewood Drive, Danvers, MA 01923, USA, telephone (508) 750-8400.

The phrase *gender, race, and class* has become a litany in the attempt to transform Eurocentric patriarchal studies into multicultural, nonracist, nonsexist, nonelitist education. A few years ago, as a visiting scholar at a White, midwestern, "public Ivy League" university, I became part of a team-teaching core for a first-year required class, Gender, Race, and Class: Perspectives on Oppression, Power, and Liberation. The course was taught by three African American women and one European American man, with degrees, collectively, in social geography, psychology, political philosophy, and art and architecture. The objective of our course was to teach 100 first-year students to recognize and analyze racism, sexism, heterosexism, and classism both in themselves and in society, in other words, to question the foundations of their thought and culture.

As an African American womanist educator from New York City, my previous academic experience consisted of teaching ethics at a New York City seminary to African and Latin American working-class, middle-aged church activists. I had taught about structural oppression before but never to a population—European American, upper middle-class—so invested in privilege stemming from others' oppressions. My apprehension about teaching this course to such students also led me to be cautious (if not pessimistic) about my own expectations of the students' receptivity to the material and their willingness and ability to engage in critical analysis. I did not want to participate in the ridicule and contempt directed at White students that I had witnessed months earlier at a women's studies conference panel.[1] Nor did I want to become so alienated by and disgusted with students' racism and sexism that my teaching "shut down."

TEAM-TEACHING

In liberal programs that grapple, theoretically, with the issues of domination and distortion in education, there is little active support from faculty or administration for maintaining racial, sexual, and class biases. Yet the passive reinforcement of race, class, and gender biases is often pervasive. Such passive support is evident in the syllabi of Eurocentric male faculty in which womanist/feminist critiques and analyses are absent or marginalized; it is also evident in Eurocentric feminist faculty syllabi that use the works of women of color as addenda and fail to analyze the racialization of gender and the racial identity in all women.

Traditionalist colleagues ignore the validity of "different ways of knowing" altogether.[2] Even among the faculty teaching our course on Gender, Race, and Class, acceptance of nonhegemonic approaches to knowledge, including the interrelatedness of doing and knowing, was not uniformly shared. The most reluctant member of the team felt that students should not be required to participate in antiracist/antisexist research activities, because such action might contradict their political beliefs (i.e., their racism and sexism).[3] Faculty unquestioningly accepted the beneficial role of activity outside the classroom in chemistry, physics, or architecture (half of this class majored in architecture), where students are expected to act in ways that deepen their understanding of theoretical models, but were resistant to applying the same standard within this course. (In private interviews, my students informed me that what they resented was not the request to act outside the classroom [which they did in other classes], but the request to engage in antiracist or antisexist action.) This double standard indicates the racial and sexual politics of the professorial worldview and places action confronting bigotry as outside of the learning process. Patricia Hill Collins (1989) describes the ideology of this worldview:

> Several requirements typify positivist methodological approaches. First, research methods generally require a distancing of the researcher as a "subject" with full human subjectivity and objectifying the "object" of study. A second requirement is the absence of emotions from the research process. Third, ethics and values are deemed inappropriate in the research process, either as the reason for scientific inquiry or as part of the research process itself. Finally, adversarial debates, whether written or oral, become the preferred method of ascertaining truth—the arguments that can withstand the greatest assault and survive intact become the strongest truths. (p. 754)

EPISTEMOLOGY AND ETHICS

Rejecting the claim of education as value neutral, we employed a theory of knowing and "extracurricular" activities to promote interdisciplinary study; critical thinking that challenges racist, sexist, classist, and nationalist biases; and students' active rather than passive role in what we hoped would be a humanistic learning process. In this learning process, in which class, race, and gender biases were stumbling blocks, ethical action—activity in which the objectives are moral and egalitarian consequences—became indispensable. Our course epistemology rejected the dichotomy between knowing and doing. Students were asked to approach learning with a critical mind and an activist outlook, with the epistemological assumption that only when we act upon the material studied can we say that we know it, and so become an integrated person. To help them understand this theory of knowledge, students were asked to apply to themselves Paulo Freire's concept of "integrative" versus "adaptive." Freire defines the adaptive person as the conformist determined by socialization, with limited choices and capacity for critical thought; the integrative person transcends imposed limitations and acts in the world in such a way that deterministic socialization is negated.

We used Bernard Lonergan's (1970) concept of human knowing as a four-part process—experience, reflection, judgment, and action.[4] This is the process by which people (knowingly or unknowingly) learn. Action is indispensable to the learning process: One knows how to ride a bicycle or drive a car not from merely reading books about bicycles or cars, but from riding or driving one as well (more in-depth knowledge is derived from constructing or building one). One knows how to live, learn, and teach without patriarchal, White supremacist, or class elitist assumptions by doing activities that confront and diminish racism, sexism, and classism.[5]

This four-part process organized the course. We chose readings to stimulate and challenge students to expand their experiences in race, class, and gender relations. Their reflections in weekly journal entries facilitated expanding their worldviews. Through judging and participating in "active engagements" by means of implementing projects they designed, hoping to demystify and challenge oppressive relationships, they inserted themselves physically into the subject. The course created a holistic approach to learning, where experience, reflection, judgment of personal and cultural values, and collective and individual action became central to the course's progression.

In their active engagement assignments, students designed their own "direct actions." These included a video asking students whether they thought racism existed on campus; a poster board critiquing sexist advertising of women; a letter petition for the university to change the name of its athletics teams from "Redskins"; and organizing around the impending Ku Klux Klan and neo-Nazi skinhead rally to be staged in the local town.

LANGUAGE AND POLITICAL THINKING

Early in the semester the difficulties in critiquing pervasive and denied practices of institutionalized oppression without a shared, supportive language became apparent. We then introduced the class to the concepts of social philosophers, using them as models for a political language and thinking that demystifies dominant norms. We began searching for a common political language by examining definitions of political terms central in discussions of oppression and liberation (students had already acknowledged the need for a common political language in their group work). The class was given handouts with definitions of *paradigm, power, hegemony,* and *ideology.* Since these terms were explained through simplified or working, rather than comprehensive or complete, definitions, students were encouraged to eventually read works in which these terms are extensively discussed. I found that the following working definitions enhanced students' political vocabulary and ability to debate, critique, and reconstruct political concepts.

We began with Thomas Kuhn's (1962) use of the term paradigm in order to talk about personal and cultural mind-sets. Paradigms, according to Kuhn, are worldviews, self-contained systems of social meanings that explain and provide guidelines for thinking and acting. Judged by its ability to explain reality and allow integrated action, a paradigm or worldview "fails" when it can no longer offer adequate explanations or when its problem-solving abilities prove inadequate. When the faltering paradigm or worldview is replaced by another more capable explanatory view—a "scientific" (conceptual or intellectual) revolution—a "paradigm shift" occurs. This move from one set of beliefs to another occurs when experiences problematic to the current worldview can no longer be ignored or assimilated. This definition is also consistent with Freire's notion of epochs of change or epochal crises based on social upheavals; the need for new social meanings and worldviews is revealed through crises that engender critical and creative thought.

We linked the concept of a paradigm as a worldview and as social construction (Berger & Luckman, 1984) to Antonio Gramsci's (1971) notion of hegemony. Hegemony was defined as domination through institutions and therefore control over social meanings in the state and society. Since it is institutional and systemic, hegemonic control is pervasive and usually not attributed to a controlling group but to the "nature" of society. Eurocentric male-centered control over the construction and dissemination of information (education) means that whoever controls text, media, and language has hegemony. Hegemonies shape the collective worldview and perceptions of freedom and thus legitimize or delegitimize hierarchies, systems, and relationships of domination. Hegemonies are vehicles through which domination is made to appear "normal" and valued. They are buttressed by compatible ideologies, which we defined as systems of beliefs. These definitions can function in the liberating role of theory. Theory promotes questioning, exploration, and problem solving, in other words, the creation of radically expanding worldviews. Ideology can also function as dogma, a closed, reified set of beliefs. We eventually labeled ideologies that legitimate oppression as closed (rather than open), static (rather than dynamic), and authoritarian (rather than egalitarian).

In constructing a common political language, students disagreed most on the meaning of *power*. Assigned writers did not clearly distinguish between two contradictory notions of power: power as control or domination (the most common understanding); and power as democratic, noncoercive action. We advocated a definition of power as collective or communal action dedicated to achieving a common good, for example, democracy. Power here becomes "power to," or empowerment, rather than "power over," or domination. Power over, coercion or domination, is a corruption of democratic power as an ideology and practice; power as domination leads to violence, which in its ultimate form is fascism (Arendt, 1958). With their deeper understanding of political language, students familiarized themselves with the implicit and explicit use of these terms or concepts by womanist or feminist writers. We began the course by studying womanist/feminist writers such as Audre Lorde, Peggy McIntosh, Angela Davis, Maria Mies, and bell hooks in order to analyze ideas for human liberation as well as critiques of oppression.

bell hooks's (1981) definition of feminism, which implicitly critiques self-centered individualism, an ideological pillar in U.S. society, served as a model for a theory of liberation:

> Feminism is a commitment to eradicating the ideology of domination that permeates western culture on various levels—sex, race, and class . . . and a commitment to reorganizing society so that the self-development of people can take precedence over imperialism, economic expansion, and material desires. (pp. 194–195)

Native and African American worldviews, as well as feminist/womanist thought, entail theories of liberation. Students were asked to consider the political and ethical implications of worldviews in which they are accountable to their community, their ancestors, and future generations. Examples given for them to reflect on included African philosopher John Mbiti's *African Religions and Philosophies* (1969), which outlines a worldview according to which the individual, although sacred, cannot exist outside or alienated from the development of the whole community. We also referred to Paula Gunn Allen's *The Sacred Hoop: Recovering the Feminine in American Indian Traditions* (1988), which describes the North American Indigenous concepts of "seven generations" and "sacred hoop" as guides for ethical action and right relationships with oneself, society, and nature.

IMAGES, COMMUNITY AND PLAY

Before midterm, the uniqueness of the course, its threatening content, and the complexities of theory were met by student resistance. To break the intellectual impasse in students' encounters with womanist/feminist theory, we brought sugar cubes to class and asked students to build cube models of their theories of oppression and liberation. Working in small groups or collectives, students played and created nonlinear, multilayered depictions of the intersections of gender, race, and class in society. ("Play," or creative interaction, had already been set to end the course in that students created a wall mural incorporating the themes that had been studied, as part of their final grade.) This play allowed the class to veer off from lectures and question-answer or discussion format. Tactile work with peers diffused tension while still providing a focus for theoretical concerns in oppression and liberation struggles.

First, before constructing their models, students were asked to restudy assigned readings, filling in a grid that listed authors' names under the headings *Gender, Race, Class, Power* (G, R, C, P). Using the grid as a data sheet to aid memory, students summarized the writers' stances on these four categories. This became a learning tool for students overwhelmed not only by content and critique but also volume (weekly readings consisted of 100 pages and as many as four authors). Power was identified as the dynamic, or energy, that flowed through the model and as the necessary requisite for change. We asked that students use political terms defined earlier whenever possible in synthesizing feminist/womanist theories of gender, race, and class. They did not need to agree with all positions taken by the writers, but students had to identify, document and synthesize these positions.

The second part of this process entailed students' constructing models by color coding the sugar cubes: blue=gender; black=power; red=class; green=race. Black arrows were drawn to denote the flow of power from different cubes. Once G, R, and C cubes were identified, they were related to each other by P cubes. Some students chose to mark cubes with several variables, for example, a cube half-red and half-green represented sexual racism. Identifying relations of power in the model changed with evolving definitions of power. Students in one section chose to represent two types of power and relationships, a negative power for relationships of domination and a positive power for democratic relationships.

Finally, students sketched their models (on their study sheets containing the grid identifying feminist/womanist theorists) and translated the images into language or theory retaining the various dimensions present in their cube models. Asked to examine existing relations of dominance and oppression as well as emerging relations of liberation, students created both actuality and potentiality in the model (as in the Aristotelian concept that embedded in an acorn is simultaneously actuality [seed] and potentiality [oak tree]). Most students were able to construct physical models and to translate their construction into theoretical (explanatory) language.[6] The request, however, that students place themselves in their work and identify the ways in which their actions supported or challenged the model was addressed by only a few of them. This absence of the *I* in most group reports was conspicuous, and pointed to a reluctance to engage in self-critique and to identify personally with the issues.

At the end of the semester, more students placed themselves more fully in the project in which each seminar group of 20 students created a wall mural reflecting the themes explored. The course culminated in this group activity, wherein students drew and painted images and, following a reception for their artwork open to the public, displayed their murals on the ground floor of their residential and classroom buildings. During the semester, students had written reflective and analytical papers on and sketched, drawn, or constructed images of the social and political relationships they were studying, thus expressing themselves and their worldviews in several media—verbal, written, and visual.

RESISTANCE, AMBIVALENT
ACCEPTANCE, TRANSFORMATION

Student responses to the course Gender, Race, and Class: Perspectives on Oppression, Power, and Liberation went from resistance to ambivalent acceptance to transformation to resistance, and so forth. *Transformation* does not imply that students accepted the social critiques presented; rather, many became less dependent on their previous socialization into class, race, and gender bias and more willing to think critically. The most difficult critique for them was that on racism. Students resisted critiques and calls for action concerning racism at a much higher level than they resisted calls to critique or demystify sexism or classism.[7] In seminar, students agreed that there was a dominant gender in the United States (male) and a dominant class (wealthy), but rejected the notion that a dominant or colonizing race (white/European) existed. A small core of students consistently resisted any action to demystify and confront classism, racism, or heterosexism.

Rutledge M. Dennis (1981) states that for the White population, racism breeds irrationality, inhibits intellectual growth, and negates democracy. We hoped that Gender, Race and Class would nurture in our students rational and critical thought, analytical skills, and communal or democratic values. Their resistance came from the emerging contradictions in their socialization. Resistance was a response to stress, in a learning process largely shaped by African American women faculty, with readings and assignments that established ethical antiracist/antisexist action as normative. Anxiety and fear were identified as part of that resistance. Other students found the call to action challenging.

Student emotional response to the readings and the film and video viewings (particularly the video *Ethnic Notions,* which critiques racist images of African Americans in U.S. culture) exhibited anxiety, denial, and hostility. Hostility (reserved for the African American women faculty) ensued in proportion to the severity of the critique. White students, primarily female, also retreated into a form of passivity and silence followed by complaints of being asked to "save the world" or "shoulder the weight of oppression." (This last complaint reminded me of my own first year in college, where I first read Ayn Rand's *Atlas Shrugged* and its glorification of unhindered, expanding, self-centered egoism.) A significant number of students poorly grasped the assigned readings, misrepresenting authors' positions or reducing them to superficialities. Students had difficulty reading and retaining information that was critical of rather than repetitive of previous schooling. Enrollment in a "special program," a liberal college within a conservative university, added to an additional pressure on those who sought to fit, or conform to, their image of the enlightened, young adult.

As faculty, we pointedly encouraged the students to struggle with their unfamiliarity and dissonance. In the opening lecture, we pointed out that few, if any, had ever been taught by one (let alone three) African American women. Although cautioned not to let their feelings become a retreat from a critique, students were repeatedly asked to explore their feelings and anger against the writers and African American women professors, which they did through discussions, drawings, and writing. To read works by people of color and women analyzing racism, classism, heterosexism, and the roles of government in maintaining oppressive structures was understandably extremely disorienting for students schooled in an hegemonic absence of African women's voices and critical thought. Recognizing that relationships are instrumental in the learning process, we began meeting with students individually for private discussions about their attitudes towards the class and their first year at college. Personal interactions with faculty, play, and creative space in constructing the wall mural helped students (and faculty) to put aside their defenses. In end-of-term course evaluations, most students gave Gender, Race, and Class high ratings. Student acceptance of multicultural, antiracist/antisexist education, although ambivalent, still established the ground for future development.

CONCLUSION

Gender, Race, and Class courses are a tool in constructing enlightened and democratic education. An inherent limitation in such courses is that they themselves are susceptible to becoming a "litany," a catchall for all oppressions. When these courses are so ambitious, so encompassing that they lose focus, they become "crash courses in humanity" and sensitivity training to unlearn racism and sexism. When forced to function as correctives for entire programs, they remain isolated, with little reinforcement in or support from upper-division courses. The ghettoization of these courses places a stressful burden on the faculty teaching them to provide a permanent intellectual and ethical base for students compelled to take one critical/antiracist course that is an aberration in their schooling. (The disparate interests and commitments of faculty when these causes are team taught further compounds the problem.) However imperfect, these courses, or variations of them, remain an important part of the critical pedagogy that dismantles the parochialism and chauvinism of university education.

The historic role of schools in "severing consciousness from education, and education from political movements" is continuously challenged by such courses.[8] Clarity about the political nature of teaching means more than changes in style or "inclusivity" or "minority representation" in syllabi. A superficial litany is easy. It is more easily accommodated by and assimilated into the dominant pedagogy than is an integrated analysis. Critical thought (particularly that of womanist theorists) and critical teaching do not append to Eurocentric patriarchal "education." They dismantle it. Teaching critical theory that analyzes the interrelatedness of oppression and liberation is a political and subversive act. Integrating critical theory into one's worldview is likewise political and helps to transform the irrationality and antidemocratic bias that shapes, if not dominates, our encounters with each other.

NOTES

1. At that conference, two White women panelists ridiculed their students for their racism and sexism and for their misreading of Toni Morrison's *The Bluest Eye*. An African American woman in the audience pointed out that students, like faculty, reflect their socialization and education in a patriarchal, White supremacist culture. With generally poor analytical skills and little accurate historical, sociological, or political information on African people, students have no adequate context or consciousness within which to "experience" Black or feminist fiction or narratives. If these students had been prepared, by examining the social dynamics of race, sex, and class oppression in the United States prior to reading the novel, they would have had a greater opportunity to understand and appreciate the work. Generally most students' analytical skills are underdeveloped. Unskilled in what Freire calls "critical consciousness," they reflect their years of education by rote learning and indoctrination in cultural biases.

2. For further discussions of womanist/feminist epistemology and pedagogy, see Belenky et al., *Women's Ways of Knowing: The Development of Self, Voice, and Mind*; Myers, *Understanding and Afrocentric World View*; and Collins, "The Social Construction of Black Feminist Thought." Current texts by White feminist educators,

for example, the work of Michelle Fine, Mary Belenky, and Carol Gilligan, critique the patriarchal assumptions, but not the racial (White supremacist) assumptions, in education. The research on the effects of White supremacy on Whites is relatively undocumented.

3. The classes in which students felt they had the most leeway to rebel were the seminar sections taught by the European male professor. Students in his class, when asked to engage in an activity in response to readings and videos, made statements that they would not have expressed to the other faculty and that were based on real or imagined support for their hostility. For example, when asked what community action they would engage in to reflect course content, one responded, "Does this mean that we can join the KKK?"

4. Theologian Bernard Lonergan's epistemology is similar to the African (Afrocentric) ethical paradigm in which knowledge exists for the sake of communal good and human liberation, ends that are not oppositional.

5. The claim that social sciences are above politics, in other words, nonpolitical or value neutral, has already been extensively critiqued (e.g., see Ira Shor and Paulo Freire, *A Pedagogy for Liberation,* South Hadley, MA: Bergin and Garvey, 1987).

6. Out of a class of 100, only 5 failed to do so. One group of students resistant to the course placed their cubes in a shot glass, added water and stirred. After dissolving or destroying their model, they sketched a dot with arrows pointing out towards the periphery of a swirl (spiral) under which they wrote their explanatory theory on oppression and liberation. "Power [arrow] expands, and as it does it widens, the gap increases the void between class, gender, and race. ... [B]y combining our cubes we demonstrate our belief that all forces are interlocking and intertwined." A retreat into superficial generalizations is one response on the part of students required to depict and critique social/political relationships of oppression and liberation when their identities are intermeshed with these relations.

7. One student described her group's initial response: They labeled the construction of a model as "dumb" and complained of being tired of feminist/womanist theory because "Okay, so Black women are oppressed, so what?"

8. This point was made by Michelle Fine in a presentation titled "Ventriloquy and Voices," in which she defined ventriloquy as the "white out" of authorship and as intellectually dishonest calls for research that is value neutral and that has no politics. She also posited that never using the word *I* in the text is a trick of ventriloquy. "Voices," for Fine, represented the lack of interior analysis and the use of narratives or other voices to take positions the author holds but refuses to state personally.

REFERENCES

Arendt, Hannah. (1958). *The human condition.* Chicago: University of Chicago Press.
Allen, Paula Gunn. (1988). *The sacred hoop: Recovering the feminine in American Indian traditions.* Boston: Beacon Press.

Belenky, Mary F., Clinchy, Blythe, Goldberger, Nancy, & Tarule, Jill. M. (1986). *Women's ways of knowing: The development of self, voice, and mind.* New York: Basic Books.

Berger, P. L., & Luckman, T. (1984). *Social construction of everyday reality.* Harmondsworth, England: Penguin.

Collins, P. H. (1989). The social construction of black feminist thought. *Signs, 14,* 745–773.

Dennis, R. M. (1981). Socialization and racism: The White experience. In B. P. Bowser & R. G. Hunt (Eds.), *Impacts of racism on White Americans* (pp. 71–85). Beverly Hills: Sage.

Fine, Michelle. (1990). *Ventriloquy and voices.* Paper presented at Miami University, Oxford, OH.

Freire, Paulo. (1970). *Pedagogy of the oppressed* (M. Bergman Ramos, Trans.). New York: Herder and Herder.

Gilligan, Carol. (1982). *In a different voice: Psychological theory and women's development.* Cambridge: Harvard University Press.

Gilligan, Carol, Lyons, Nona, & Hanmer, Trudy. (1990). *Making connections: The relational world of adolescent girls at Emma Willart School.* Cambridge: Harvard University Press.

Gramsci, Antonio. (1971). *The prison notebooks.* Q. Hoare and G. Nowell Smith (Trans. and Ed.). New York: International Publishers.

hooks, bell. (1981). *Ain't I a woman: Black women and feminism.* Boston: South End Press.

Kuhn, Thomas. (1962). *The structures of scientific revolutions.* Chicago: University of Chicago Press.

Lonergan, Bernard. (1970). *Insight: An understanding of human knowing.* New York: Philosophical Library.

Mbiti, J. (1969). *African religions and philosophies.* London: Heinemann.

Myers, L. J. (1988). *Understanding the Afrocentric world view.* Dubuque, IA: Kendall-Hunt.

Shor, Ira, & Freire, Paulo. (1987). *A pedagogy for liberation.* South Hadley, MA: Bergin and Garvey.

ABOUT THE AUTHOR

Joy James teaches feminist and political theory in the Department of Ethnic Studies at the University of Colorado at Boulder. She coedited *Spirit, Space and Survival: African-American Women in (White) Academe* (Routledge, 1993), which won the Gustavus Myers Human Rights Award, and is the author of *Resisting State Violence: Radicalism, Gender and Race in U.S. Culture* (University of Minnesota Press, 1996). James's most recent work is *The Angela Y. Davis Reader* (Blackwell). She is currently working on issues of prisoners' rights.

CHAPTER 8

Reshaping the Introductory Women's Studies Course

DEALING UP FFRONT WITH ANGER, RESISTANCE, AND REALITY

Ardeth Deay and Judith Stitzel

When we were given the opportunity to review and update our 1991 article on teaching Introduction to Women's Studies, we hesitated. Of course, we were pleased to be asked, but the article was based on our teaching a course during the 1980s that neither of us was teaching any longer, and we were apprehensive that our approaches and analyses might no longer be relevant. We decided to invite responses form three graduate assistants currently teaching the course. Despite their heavy teaching and personal responsibilities, our colleagues, Dee Quaranto, Cindy Snow, and Carrie Stone, accepted our invitation eagerly and met with us for 3 hours on a sunny Saturday morning in June.

The teachers found the specific exercises valuable, as confirmations of approaches that they were already taking; as new approaches; and as starting points for their own adaptations. They remarked that it was helpful to be reminded that there are patterns of student response/resistance that can be anticipated. In particular, they were relieved to know that others besides themselves and their students could be angry and defensive, and they saw how anticipating that anger could help shape approaches to construction. They agreed that getting students involved in collecting the information that they later analyzed—whether from the media, the classroom, or campus graffiti—was an excellent

This chapter originally appeared in *Feminist Teacher*, 1991, 6(1), 29–33.

The Feminist Teacher *Anthology: Pedagogies and Classroom Strategies.* Copyright © 1998 by Teachers College, Columbia University. All rights reserved. ISBN 0-8077-3741-0 (paper), ISBN 0-8077-3742-9 (cloth). Prior to photocopying items for classroom use, please contact the Copyright Clearance Center, Customer Service, 222 Rosewood Drive, Danvers, MA 01923, USA, telephone (508) 750-8400.

means of encouraging students to attend to their own experiences within a feminist context. Likewise, they thought that the exercises helped to ground teachers in student realities that they did not necessarily share. The teachers suggested the need for additional exercises that document positive social change. As Cindy said, "I don't want my students to only gather stuff that bothers them or that would bother them once we analyze it . . . I want some empowerment."

Obviously, we were pleased to learn that our article was relevant to current teaching needs and classroom situations. But something more significant happened that warm June morning. We took extraordinary pleasure in each others' company and came away refreshed and renewed. Dee, Cindy, and Carrie were grateful for the opportunity that our article gave them to think about their own teaching. They pointed out that while they had met regularly during the year to plan, discuss, and share, the logistics of running the course had consumed their sessions. For us, listening to this new generation of gifted feminist teachers was an equally appreciated boost. Their 3 hours of energetic, committed, inventive conversation about pedagogy energized us and revalidated our commitment to feminist teaching and scholarship. Furthermore, the experience of working together confirmed yet another important discovery of our original article: Collaborative learning and teaching is the very heart of women's studies.

Teaching women's studies in the 1990s and beyond will make different demands on each of us, depending on whom we teach, how long we've been teaching and where we are in our own lives. Our work in redesigning our Introduction to Women's Studies course was a struggle for authenticity and sanity. First, we had to acknowledge what was happening to us— and what was happening, we discovered, was that the class was making us angry. We had been teaching the introductory course together for over 5 years in a state university. No longer an elective chosen by a self-selected group of feminist students hungry for self-assertion, self-reflection, and theory, our introductory course had become one of several courses available to students to fulfill a general education requirement in women's, minority, or international studies. Many of these students came to the course with little preparation, either intellectual or emotional. And more and more, we found ourselves seeking refuge in a few students who, for whatever reason, were more "right-thinking" (i.e., thinking as we did), and we were becoming impatient with the others.

In addition to having more students in the introductory course who resisted rather than embraced feminism, we found ourselves coping with the more general swing toward conservatism in the university, as elsewhere. The lack of responsiveness in our classes made us tired and cranky. Yet like K. Edgington, who writes honestly and articulately about her fiasco (her word) in an American literature course in which she fails to engage the class,[1] we also had to confront the fact that we could not simply blame our unhappiness with our students on an increasingly conservative environment. We had to take some responsibility.

When we allowed ourselves to think about what was happening rather than justifying it, we discovered that we could make some changes in our course that would simultaneously help us and our students. It is these changes that we would like to discuss.[2]

The first thing we noticed when we discussed our unhappiness was that there were a number of student responses that we were beginning to anticipate and dread. We also realized that, instead of passively waiting for them to occur, we could bring them to the fore, and be prepared for them as useful stages in a process. Among these responses were (a) the tendency of students to focus on exceptions, for example, "My mother is a doctor," "I know a woman conductor," "My sister played football in high school"; (b) their tendency to insist that discrimination was a thing of the past and that their instructors—we—were man-haters who denied the hope and opportunity that they saw for their own lives; and (c)—growing directly out of (a) and (b), in other words, out of a focus on the individual and an ahistorical consciousness—the alarming tendency to deny the existence of oppression and the interrelationships of institutional structures and the fabric of their own lives and the lives of others.

Whereas we had been feeling that these tendencies were getting in the way of our teaching—if only they weren't there, we could get on with it—we began to see that they were the *it* we must get on with. We felt that we had to deal much more directly with the fact that the students were not making the connections that we wanted them to make, that the connections did not come automatically, and that it was our responsibility to challenge the students' ideology of individual success and to establish as an underlying theme of the course the interrelationships of one's own experiences, the experiences of others of different races and classes, and the patriarchal institutions that shape all experience. At the same time, paradoxically, we had to do this in an atmosphere in which our challenges to the students would not be felt as threats, and in which their experiences would be valued and attended to in ways not usually found in the traditional classrooms in which some of the students felt more at home.

In short, the change in the atmosphere had to begin with a change in us. We needed to change the tone of the class. But how do you "operationalize" tone? To some extent, the changed tone came from rethinking our objectives for the course, writing them out in greater detail, and linking assignments to them. Putting them in writing was important—identifying and acknowledging what bothered us and getting it out there for both of us to look at. The objectives gave us a reality check several times a semester. They relaxed us. And because we were less tense, we were more responsive.

We cannot stress how important that *us* is in this discussion. Although it is certainly possible for an individual teacher to identify and change problem areas in her or his teaching, coteaching contains a built-in hormone, which makes growth happen faster and less painfully. Working collaboratively, we helped each other keep her balance. Additionally, as coteachers who respected each other's learning styles and needs, we were eventually able to appreciate that student growth also involves internal conflicts and ambivalence; this led us to reshape the course to take account of the pace and the stages of the students' development.

In addition to the clarification that came from focusing and writing out the objectives and the mutual support that came from the coteaching, the most important change in our teaching was our supplementing course readings, writing assignments, and class discussions with a set of field exercises. These exercises were designed to ground our students in the present tense of their own lives, to encourage them to be responsible investigators, and to inspire them to use their experiences and evidence as one context for responding to class readings, lectures, and discussions.[3] They would not have to passively accept the instructors' expertise. They would not have to take what we said on faith.

We had always asked students to *pay attention* to what was happening in their environment, but the field exercises provided an opportunity and obligation for them to *keep track* of their experiences as well. The specific information and, when appropriate, numbers that they brought in for class discussion made it harder for them to use the exceptional case to avoid acknowledging sexism, racism, and other forms of oppression. Furthermore, denial was more difficult when they had themselves provided the data for the discussion.

The exercises were also a way for us to learn about students' lives outside the classroom. We were often disappointed at their naïveté and their romanticization of experience. But we were grateful to know what they were thinking and feeling, since this was where we needed to begin in order to meet our responsibility as feminist teachers, remaining respectful of our students' needs while challenging their assumptions.

A brief description of the 10 exercises that we developed for the course follows:

Exercise 1: Media Awareness—Advertising. The first exercise is designed to help students develop their awareness of the pervasiveness of sexism and racism in advertising. We ask them to identify 6 to 10 advertisements that illustrate stereotypes *or* promote positive images for women or men. They are encouraged to draw their examples from magazines, newspapers, advertising circulars, television, radio, and so on.

Students are given this assignment the first day of class, during which they view the film *Still Killing Us Softly*, with Jean Kilbourne. In the past, we had viewed this film and informally suggested that students notice advertising during the week that followed to see examples in their daily lives of the points that Kilbourne makes. Many would come back to class with examples. But many also came back expressing concern that "bias was in the eyes of the beholder." They saw the sexual innuendoes and put-downs of women as something that feminists read into ads, rather than as genuinely oppressive acts by advertisers.

This field exercise changed that experience. Having the students actually collect examples, so that at class time we have 180–300 examples, which are reviewed in small groups, focuses the class discussion on the students' observations. These observations, which also document that women of color are both ignored and exploited, allow for discussion of the intersection of racism and sexism in advertising.

It is also helpful to ask for examples that promote *positive* images of women and men and people of color. Students do find some, and these examples are acknowledged and celebrated. Nonetheless, there are so few of them that the overriding tenor of advertising cannot be dismissed or written off as the result of a man-hating perspective. Likewise, we can acknowledge exceptions without allowing them to be used to discount the pervasiveness and power of oppressive institutions.

Exercise 2: Television Messages. This assignment requires students to examine gender messages communicated by television programming. Students are asked to watch 4 hours of tv and to keep track of the number of major roles, supporting roles, and speaking parts by gender, race, and economic class. They are directed to look at the roles played by women and men of different races and classes, examine them in terms of stereotypes, and pay particular attention to variations on the stereotypes to see if there are any *fundamental* challenges, rather than cosmetic changes, to them.

When students tally the numbers of female and male actors of different races present on their favorite television programs, they are astonished by the imbalance; and their own accounting reinforces research that documents an imbalance in media representation of women and minorities. Even more revealing to them are the tallies for speaking parts, major roles, and supporting roles. The evidence is overwhelming. As they discuss their findings in small groups and then report to the whole class for a group compilation, the manipulation of our perceptions through television becomes undeniable.

Exercise 3: Textbook Messages. Students are asked to look at how basic information about women and gender is conveyed to them through the textbooks required for their university courses. Students are assisted in their analysis by Myra and David Sadker's (1982) definitions of the kinds of bias found in curricular materials (invisibility, stereotyping, imbalance/selectivity, unreality, fragmentation/isolation, linguistic bias, and photographs).[4]

In preparation for the textbook analysis, students are asked to read some short excerpts to determine if sex bias is present and to revise the excerpts to eliminate bias. The following preliminary exercise is helpful in identifying the levels of student awareness of linguistic bias and in reinforcing acceptance of a variety of perspectives:

DIRECTIONS: Read each excerpt and determine if sex bias is present. If you find bias, indicate which form is present. By the way, as in the case in so many of our textbooks, you may come across more than just one form of bias in each excerpt. Finally, assume the role of author and rewrite the excerpt so that bias is no longer reflected.

Sam led, and Helen went after him. Helen held his hand in a hard grip. She was timid in the darkness. . . . Helen fell and Sam helped her get up.

Is sex bias present? _____
What form of sex bias is present? _____
Suggested Revision: _____[5]

Some Sample Student Responses:

Helen led and Sam went after her. Helen held Sam's hand tightly. He was timid in the darkness. Sam fell and Helen helped him up.

Together, Helen and Sam walked along the path. The two clutched each other's hands. Because of the darkness a timid feeling soon engulfed them. . . . They kept each other from failing.

Sam and Helen went together. They held hands firmly. When one fell down in the dark, the other helped.

The first of these responses revealed, and therefore allowed us to discuss, the common misconception that feminists want a role reversal rather than a restructuring of power relationships, whereas the other two responses allowed students and instructors to appreciate that removing bias is not just a linguistic trick but provides access to a richer description of experience.

Exercise 4: Classroom Messages. Students are asked to pay attention to what is happening in their university classes. Readings in Roberta Hall and Bernice Sandler's *The Classroom Climate: A Chilly One For Women* (1984),[6] provide the background for their own data collection of the numbers of men and women in their classes, the numbers of students of different races, and the sex, race, and rank of their instructors. In addition, they are requested to discuss for each course whether the instructor uses nonsexist language (using the National Council of Teachers of English Guidelines[7] and Hall & Sandler as guides).

When students document what goes on in their own classrooms, they find an overwhelming White male representation among their professors, whereas their student colleagues are somewhat more diverse. Again, this documentation, when compiled by the class, reveals for them an environment far more skewed in favor of the patriarchy than they have realized. At the same time, by paying attention to specifics, we are able to acknowledge and find satisfaction in those situations that were demonstrative of an academic world that, under pressure, is slowly changing and becoming more inclusive. Students seem to appreciate the occasions that we provide in which to see where and when progress is made and what makes it possible.

Exercise 5: Campus Messages. This week students are asked to tune into campus life beyond the classroom, to look and listen for incidents of prejudice that devalue persons who are perceived in our culture and society as deviating from the White/heterosexual "norm." They are asked to focus on sexism, racism, homo/lesbophobia, anti-Semitism, anti-ethnic behaviors or remarks, and to their intersections.

When students record examples of prejudice that they see and hear around them in the student union, in their residence halls, and in their fraternities and sororities, they are shocked and astounded, and their preconceived ideas about equality and openness in our society have to be reexamined in the face of their own experiences. As a result of their own personal observations, some students acknowledge that, in the future, they will be more likely to speak up and object to disparaging remarks and "jokes" made by friends, relatives, dorm mates, and boyfriends; they realize that they are not so funny after all. The ability of our students to have ignored the oppression around them for so long does, of course, distress us; but that distress does not by itself provide the strategy to move them beyond their narrowness. This exercise begins to do so.

Exercise 6: Who Whistles? Who Sings? Both male and female students are asked what messages they received about appropriate behavior for females from their environments, for example, family, school, church. They are required to write down at least five specific messages that they remember or still observe in their lives. They are encouraged to reconstruct these messages from play, work, or school situations. Sharing them with their peers helps our students acknowledge that they have received very clear messages about "woman's place." Some examples from our students' own experiences are

"My brother received a car on his 16th birthday, despite the fact that two females turned 16 without receiving a car before him."

"My aunt Edie once told me that little girls should not turn cartwheels because it was unladylike and could cause female problems later. I was 5 years old at the time."

"Nice girls do not curse."

Although none of these discrepancies seems in itself appalling, they are discrepancies that the students have experienced and about which they have strong feelings. This provides an excellent place from which to begin to discuss the effect on their own lives of what might otherwise be seen only as theoretical issues.

Exercise 7: Religion and Spirituality. For this assignment, students are asked to take at least 5 minutes to free-associate with each of the terms *spirituality* and *religion*. When they share their lists in class, we end up with two composites. The composite on spirituality includes words such as *soul, community,* and *personal,* whereas the stimulus of *religion* elicits words such as *god, commandments,* and *church.* This exercise illustrates differences between internal personal experience and external societal structures and makes it easier for students to affirm the values of both and, where appropriate, reject the restrictions of the latter.

This is particularly valuable with students who might worry that feminism necessitates a rejection of all values that they hold dear, including religious traditions within which they may, in fact, have found strength. In many communities in the United States, urban as well as rural, we lose opportunities to reach our students if we do not understand the central role that traditional religions have played and currently play in their lives.

Exercise 8: The Marriage Contract. Students are asked to read the marriage contract that first appeared in *Ms.* magazine (June 1973, pp. 62–64, 102–103) and answer the following questions:

1. What items in the contract do you find most likely to lead to a satisfying marriage? Why?
2. What items in the contract do you find most likely to interfere with achieving a satisfying marriage? Why?
3. Is the institution of marriage necessary to achieve a satisfying permanent relationship? Why or why not?
4. The authors of this contract are a male/female couple. How would/could/should the contract be altered for use by two women or two men?

In the past, although we did use the marriage contract, we did not require an itemized response in preparation for our discussion. Students found it cold and objectionable, asserting that any written description of such a highly personal and intimate relationship was dysfunctional. Completing the exercise helped students be clearer, more articulate in their objections and more open in acknowledging some of the advantages of the contract, or, at least, in talking about the issues raised in it.

In addition, for a group of students, most of whom are looking forward uncritically to a traditional marriage, a discussion of marriage is a good way to focus their attention both on the assumptions behind and constraints implicit in the institution, assumptions which include heterosexism and class bias.

Exercise 9: Men's Lives. We had used the film *Men's Lives* successfully when we first taught this course. In recent years, students' reactions had seemed to focus on aspects of the film that seemed dated to them rather than on the still prevalent messages in men's lives that are the point of the film. Answering the following questions—which they take home, write out, and bring to the next class for discussion—helps students to structure and focus their thoughts, relate the film to their lives, and develop their responses in more depth:

1. What attitudes and values do the men in the film express?
a) about themselves
b) about women
2. What are the dangers associated with these attitudes and values?
a) for men
b) for women
3. How does the film cause you to rethink your own relationship to work/career?
a) why you chose your career
b) how your work constrains/expands you
c) what control you might have over your work/career

Exercise 10: Portraits of Courage is the final field exercise and is completed at home for discussion on the last day of class. This exercise allows us to end the semester on a simultaneously affirmative and realistic note and acknowledges the pain and courage, the tenacity and beauty, of the women in our lives. Students are asked to describe an act of female courage, be it physical courage or an example of the courage that novelist Gloria Naylor describes, "a certain tenacity, a willingness to do in the face of everything." They often report stories of their mothers, grandmothers, sisters, and themselves. We see genuine pride and joy from students as they envision themselves and other women as able to stand up, be counted, and survive with dignity.

When we began teaching women's studies, our students were likely to be our peers, close to us not only in age but also in their feminist consciousness. Many of our current students are neither, and we have a different responsibility to them. We do have an obligation to lead them beyond the narrow individualism that angers and frustrates us, but because we no longer share as many assumptions or experiences, we need a strategy that simultaneously allows us to learn who our students are while providing avenues to where we would like them to be. We believe that by developing these simple straightforward exercises to connect course materials to students' lives, we have helped our students and ourselves in ways that are both respectful and pedagogically sound.

NOTES

1. K. Edgington, "Stumbling Through the Minefield," *On Our Minds,* 3(1) (Spring, 1989), 4. *On Our Minds* is a newsletter of the Women's Studies Program, Towson State University, Baltimore, Maryland.

2. We first presented this material at the 1989 National Women's Studies Association conference, where it was clear that others shared our concerns, were grateful for our airing of the problems, and appreciative of some of our solutions. Since that time, we have received additional responses, all of them helpful and some justifiably critical of the insufficient attention to issues of racial diversity and sexual orientation/preference in our exercises.

We have taken these comments very seriously, have changed the introductory course in response to them (in cooperation with our colleagues at West Virginia University, Marian Jensen and Marianne Ebend), and have incorporated these changes in this paper. Some narrowness may remain, in part because the origin of this article is the experience of teaching the class we reported on initially. But we hope that most of the ideas are usable and that all are provocative. We look forward to continued dialogue and critique.

3. Our colleague Lillian Waugh at West Virginia University contributed significantly to the design of these exercises.

4. Myra Sadker and David Sadker, *Sex Equity Handbook for Schools*, New York: Longman, 1982.

5. Ibid., p. 74.

6. Available from the Project on the Status and Education of Women, Association of American Colleges, 1818 R St. N.W., Washington, DC 20009.

7. Guidelines for Nonsexist Use of Language in NCTE Publication (Rev. 1985). Urbana, IL. NCTE.

ABOUT THE AUTHORS

Judith Stitzel is a professor of English and women's studies at West Virginia University. She was the founding director of the WVU Center for Women's Studies and, in the late 1970s, developed the first introduction to women's studies course at WVU, which she cotaught for many years with several colleagues, including her friend and coauthor Ardeth Deay. Judith is currently teaching feminist theory, methods, and perspectives in women's studies, and creative writing. She is a member of the Publications and Policies Committee of the Feminist Press and has published short fiction and articles in *Colorado Quarterly; College English; Women's Studies Quarterly; Frontiers: A Journal of Women's Studies; Feminist Teacher;* and *Women's Studies International Forum.*

Ardeth Deay is an associate professor of curriculum and instruction at West Virginia University. Her current work with educators focuses on developing awareness, knowledge, and skills to increase their effectiveness in their work with various ethnic, gender, and SES (socio-economic status) groups. Her responsibilities in this area include teaching a graduate course, Education for Cultural Diversity, chairing the Diversity Task Force for the College of Human Resources and Education, and providing liaison and consulting services to professional development schools in West Virginia.

CHAPTER 9

Enhancing Feminist Pedagogy

Berenice Fisher

This article represents a midway point in a process of thinking about
feminist pedagogy that began for me in the mid-1970s and continues
today. When I wrote my first piece on the subject at the beginning of
the 1980s, I wanted to identify the features of a liberatory, feminist
pedagogy, in contrast with the prevailing liberal feminist image of
teaching for higher education. My idea of pedagogy drew on Dewey's
progressive education, Freire's image of student-teacher dialogue, and the
community organizing tradition developed so dramatically in the civil
rights movement. But my notion of feminist pedagogy also drew—and
continues to draw—on the insights of radical feminist consciousness-raising
of the late 1960s and early 1970s, in particular the insight that women
coming together to explore the connections between the personal and
the political could lead to new understandings of women's oppression
and new ways of resisting it. My vision of feminist pedagogy has nur-
tured me. It has helped to keep alive in me a commitment to social
justice, a faith in the human capacity to learn and grow, a hope for
community, a belief that our bodies and feelings play a crucial role in
our struggle to understand the world, and my own deep desire to live
as a freer woman. I have kept this faith alive in part through interactions with students in my women's studies classes and in part by

This chapter originally appeared in *Feminist Teacher*, 1992, 6(3), 9–15.

practicing feminist pedagogy outside the classroom. In retrospect, I can see that the extracurricular feminist workshops that I discuss in my article had even greater limitations than I had noted at the time. If I had incorporated the concerns of the participants more fully, I might have expanded the options for women who had difficulty relating to parts of the workshops. I might have built in more support for facilitating actions that could have flowed from the workshops. I might have tried them in a variety of locations to see how different groups of women responded to them. But these limits for me do not negate the value of such efforts. In politically hard times, I believe it is especially important for progressive teachers to continue creating new forms. Moreover, doing feminist educational work outside higher education helps those of us who labor in the academic vineyards keep ourselves grounded in the multiple realities of daily life—keep us from getting too drunk on the excitement of our own ideas.

For feminist teachers, women's studies offers an exciting, demanding, and frustrating context for educational work. Excitement stems from the great potential for exploring the connections between women's personal experience and our political realities. Demand arises from the difficulty of teaching students who may resent, resist, and ultimately reject that vision. Frustration grows out of both student resistance and the institutional constraints under which we operate. Like all teachers, we work under limiting conditions and must conform to a variety of institutional and professional regulations.

Given the ways in which these demands and frustrations curb our excitement about teaching, it is little wonder that some of us dream of teaching women's studies without such limitations. For me, the dream was realized in part by my creating and offering the multimedia workshops that I describe in this essay.[1] The workshops had two purposes. The first was to explore two topics of importance to women: our relation to the newspaper and our notion of home. The second was to enhance the theory and practice of feminist pedagogy by integrating into it alternative media for consciousness-raising—drama, movement, and visual art.[2]

My interest in women's experience of reading the newspaper and of coming to grips with the meaning of home arose out of my own struggles in these areas. I developed the newspaper workshop after a close friend, named Miriam, announced to me that she had canceled her longstanding subscription to the *New York Times*. She said that newspaper reading had become an addiction; it filled her with rage and despair and drained energy away from things she wanted to do with her life. At first, I was horrified at what seemed to be my friend's withdrawal into a more "privatized" way of living. But the more I thought about her decision, the more I had to acknowledge that, in the spring of 1985, I found it harder and harder to read the paper myself. In the face of rampaging Reaganism, even the alternative press was giving me little comfort. Miriam's prosaic act touched on painful feelings about my current relation to public life. Thinking that other women might have such feelings, I imagined an event in which we explored the meaning of reading the newspaper. I called that workshop Miriam Cancels the *Times*.

The topic of the second multimedia workshop occurred to me about a year later, when I was struggling with the issue of living together with my lover. For me, home always had two contradictory associations: that of a refuge and that of a trap. The refuge association grew out of my mother's almost exclusive involvement with "private" life, the trap association grew out of my father's focus on travel and "public" activities. Mulling over this contradiction, I realized that many women found making a home problematic. The meaning of home also was gaining tremendous public attention because of the growing homelessness in New York City and elsewhere. I was not sure about the relationship between these issues, but I thought some sense of connection might emerge in the workshop titled Home is Where the Heart Lies.

My interest in exploring the power of alternative media for feminist pedagogy grew out of problems I had encountered in the classroom. Although feminist pedagogy emphasizes the sharing of experiences and feelings, I found that students often had difficulty describing their experiences and expressing their feelings. Psychotherapy had taught me how deeply rooted such constraints might be. Explorations with Gestalt therapy, psychodrama, and movement and dramatic improvisation showed me the power of symbolic and nonverbal communication. I sensed the need to integrate these forms of communication into the feminist teaching process.

Both my interest in the newspaper and home and my experiences with alternative media suggested to me the importance of going beyond our usual concept of the classroom. Most higher education rigidly distinguishes between theory and practice and between what is serious and what is fun. Yet the more I allowed myself to let my varied learning experiences inform my teaching, the richer it became: the more fun the students could have with serious matters, and the more I encouraged the interaction of feeling, doing, and thinking. Breaking down received distinctions about what is "educational" seemed to me a crucial element of feminist pedagogy.

In discussing these workshops and the feminist pedagogy implicit in them, I want to focus on three interweaving processes: my own process of developing the workshops, the workshop process itself, and the process engaged in by the workshop participants. My hope here is to offer an example, rather than a static "model" of feminist pedagogy. As any teacher who uses participatory methods knows, the conditions under which we work demand tremendous flexibility, involving continuous reassessment of our own responses to students, sensitivity to their changing responses to us and to each other, and an awareness of how shifting social conditions impact on the classroom. Flexibility is both a necessity and a source of power for feminist pedagogy. It is necessary because we cannot anticipate all the complex relationships we will discover between personal experience and political life. It is powerful because it supports our effort to learn from each other rather than from a fixed tradition that negates so many of our realities.

BACKGROUND OF THE WORKSHOPS

My own educational experience has involved a long love affair with participatory learning. The affair began when I attended an experimental school founded by John Dewey. It continued at a college famous for its small-group discussions. It waxed as I began to teach college and gravitated toward the "discussion method." It culminated in my involvement with women's studies, where I realized the need to expand my notion of participation.

I was not alone in discovering that the feminist vision of participation required a new sort of educational process. From the early years of women's studies, feminist teachers began to incorporate journal writing, role-playing, photographs, autobiography, drama, and a widening range of techniques to bridge the gap between "extracurricular" life and the classroom experience.[3] For me, Gestalt therapy and psychodrama were especially important in expanding my notion of participation in the classroom context. Through these techniques, I learned how feelings and experiences could be expressed with relative "safety" when they were projected into symbols or roles. (In Gestalt therapy, for example, speaking in the voice of a tense stomach can lead to understanding the meaning of that tension.) Similarly, work in movement improvisation taught me to speak through my body, to "say" what I wanted, to listen to others, and to respond to their movements in order to improvise with them.[4]

In some ways, my experiences with expressive media culminated in my encounter with Brazilian director Augusto Boal's Theater of the Oppressed.[5] Two techniques seemed particularly relevant to enhancing feminist pedagogy. In the first, "statue" or "image theater," participants use their own bodies and the bodies of other participants to "sculpt" feelings about themselves and the world. Such sculptures might involve movement, sound, or both, but they are not explained or discussed. The second technique, "forum theater," involves a group-improvised or scripted play in which a protagonist struggles to solve a problem familiar to the audience. After the play is performed, members of the audience replace the protagonist and attempt to solve the given problem in a more satisfactory way.

In my women's studies classes, I used various adaptations for forum theater to help students explore feminist texts and the relation of feminist thought to women's experiences.[6] But space limitations, as well as my own hesitation to go beyond verbal communication, kept me from incorporating movement and other media into classroom teaching. Longing to experiment in what felt like "free space," I found the opportunity with a New York feminist organization called the Crystal Quilt.[7] Through this community educational organization, I was able to reach a somewhat heterogeneous (although mostly urban and middle-class) audience of women who were friendly or at least not hostile to feminism. Miriam Cancels the *Times* and Home Is Where the Heart Lies were each presented through the Crystal Quilt at least three times over 5 years. During that time, I continually changed the workshops to respond to my own concerns and to criticisms made by participants. In the following account, I generalize from a number of workshops and indicate some ways in which they evolved.

THE MULTIMEDIA WORKSHOPS

My experience studying and watching Boal's forum theater convinced me that the language of drama could be a powerful force in consciousness-raising. Yet I had certain reservations. It seemed difficult to create an effective forum script, and I was not prepared to become a playwright. I was impressed by how women's groups could improvise forum plays, but I knew from experience that when women simply talk about their own oppression their words have a highly dramatic quality. I wanted to capture this sense of drama in the workshops.

My experiences in feminist journalism and research interviewing provided the clue. For each workshop I created a dramatic reading based on interviews with nine women. I chose nine voices so that the reading could reflect a wide range of experiences without overwhelming the listeners. Through my friendship and political networks, I located women of various ages, races, ethnicities, sexual orientations, and physical ability. I did not attempt to represent all possible experiences in the scripts. My purpose in creating a given reading was to establish a context in which participants could feel safe in sharing their own particular experiences. I hoped that the dramatic readings would foster trust among women who, as strangers, were about to spend 3 (later expanded to 4) hours together working on a topic they might never before have discussed with others.

The interview material turned out to be extraordinarily complex and dramatic. For the newspaper script, women talked about how the daily paper frightened and angered them. Some admitted their shame at not being able to respond to all the oppression and wrongdoing in the world. Others described how avidly they read the paper, how they saved articles and virtually created archives. Women talked about how newspapers could foster a sense of connection with others—with neighbors, with members of the same racial or ethnic group, with people who held similar political values. Some women talked about their anger at women's invisibility, how "the news" meant men and male activities. They grieved, celebrated, and raged at the events that were reported.

For the Home script, one woman described the tremendous sacrifice and joy involved in building her home. Others talked about their fears of homelessness. One woman described the difficulty of being home alone after the death of a partner; others talked about their home as a refuge or a nest. Still others talked about home as a setting for violence or the exploitation of domestic workers. One woman described how she had been able to reclaim her home after having been raped there.

In shaping the scripts, I relied a great deal on intuition. I imagined these women talking with each other, responding to specific themes or feelings that emerged as others talked, bringing up their own experiences to echo or contrast with what had been said. To heighten their dramatic impact, I tried to alternate voices so that "speeches" varied in length, intensity and tone. At first, I treated the interviews as though they were newspaperquotes or research material, carefully preserving each word. But as I shaped the material, I gradually allowed myself to edit interview excerpts to sharpen their impact. When the scripts were completed, I found three women who wanted to read the parts and join me in presenting the workshop.

Both workshops had the following format: I would begin by explaining the purpose and character of the workshop, sometimes using a brief warm-up to help the participants feel comfortable with each other and the setting. (In one warm-up for Home, I invited each woman to explore the space we were using, to get to know her surroundings and to greet others with whom she would share this temporary "home.") In introducing the three women who would present the dramatic reading, I explained that each would read three voices: Participants should imagine that they were hearing the voices of women speaking in an adjoining room—voices they might not always be able to identify. The performers sat facing the audience as they read from the scripts, and participants sat nearby on chairs and pillows.

At the conclusion of the reading, I asked participants to divide into groups of four or five (between 10 and 20 women attended each workshop) for a half-hour discussion. The groups were asked to make sure that each woman had a chance to share her response to the reading and her own experiences and feelings about the topic. The performers joined the various groups, and I watched and listened from close by. I could see how intensely the women discussed the topic. Often they shared their own experiences. Sometimes they focused on certain "voices" that had resonated within or disturbed them. Many times they wanted to continue their discussions rather than move on to the next part of the workshop.

This second segment focused on exploration and communication of feelings through the body. Here, I used a variety of warm-ups to help participants relax and become attuned to their bodies. Sometimes I adapted traditional games to the theme of the workshop (for example, using a children's "telephone" game in which a whispered message is passed around the circle as one way of exploring how the news becomes distorted). Sometimes I used visualization (for example, asking participants to visualize a past or current home, to imagine themselves moving around that home, and to notice the responses they felt in different parts of their bodies). For the newspaper workshop, I asked participants to select actual articles from pages of various newspapers lying around the room and bring their attention to the ways in which their chosen article affected their bodies. For the Home workshop, I asked participants to select a key word connected to the theme of the workshop, and, by reciting it silently or quietly, begin to explore their body response.

The hands-on-the-newspaper strategy and the keyword technique provided especially good warm-ups for Boal's self-sculpture method. As participants focused on their physical responses, I asked them to allow their bodies to take a shape that in some way expressed these responses. They could add movement, sound, or both to this self-sculpture. At first, I followed Boal's lead by having each individual show her self-sculpture to the group. But gradually I realized that many women found this demand for individual exposure too frightening. Instead, therefore, after the self-explorations, I asked the participants to form new small groups to make group sculptures. Here, each individual used the bodies of the others in her group to shape a sculpture that captured the spirit of her self-sculpture.

I introduced this task by demonstrating (with the aid of my performer-assistants) how to respect the body integrity of others in the group (through words or gestures discovering whether and how people wanted to be touched, what positions or movements were physically possible and physically or psychologically comfortable for them). Although participants could reveal the word or image that informed their sculpture, I asked them not to explain or discuss what they were doing.

After the groups had created their sculptures, they showed them to the other participants without comment or discussion. This nonverbal work was dramatic and often deeply moving to both performers and audience. Sometimes the point of the sculpture was obvious: the horror of violence, the desire for security, the impulse to resist domination, the need for rest. Sometimes the meaning was more elusive: the sculptures displayed confusion, strength, direction, stasis. Even where the "point" was not clear, participants could grasp the feeling/tone of the piece.

After a 10-minute break (essential for both physical and psychological reasons), I introduced the third and final part of the workshop: visualizing the future. Developing this segment proved especially difficult. In creating the workshops, I had seen the beginning segment as an introductory exploration of feelings and experiences. I intended the second segment to move participants to a level of deeper self-understanding and trust. The body work and movement often brought out feelings of pain, anger, and despair—a recognition of external and internalized oppression that (although not the same for each woman) could be shared and understood. I thought that the third segment should facilitate both a sense of vision and consciousness empowerment through cooperation.

I introduced this segment of the workshop in a variety of ways. In the most successful version of Home, I asked everyone to sit in a circle. Then, we went around the circle a number of times, with each woman giving one- or two-word associations to the notion of home. (Participants could repeat their own or others' words as often as they wished.) I listed the words and, when the group felt satisfied that they had expressed enough associations, slowly read the list. Then I asked participants to group the words into large categories. In doing so, they came up with themes such as "solitude," "comfort," "intimacy," "precariousness," and "safety." At this point, I asked participants to divide again into small groups according to the theme with which they wanted to work. I gave out supplies (each group had a thick bulletin-board-like base about three by four feet in size, construction paper, colored markers, and glue) and asked the groups to discuss and construct a vision of home that related to the theme they had chosen. They were reminded that they came to this project with different experiences and feelings and that in order to collaborate on a construction they might have to negotiate to find a commonly accepted vision.

Both the Home and Newspaper constructions were exciting and evocative. In the Newspaper workshop, where small groups were asked to construct a page from an ideal newspaper, one such page included a lead article on the arrival of Halley's comet that asked readers to reflect on the human attempt to dominate nature. This ideal newspaper also stressed reader participation and response to much of its content. A piece on apartheid in South Africa invited readers to write about apartheid in relation to racism in our country. The article ended with a space for the reader to write her own comments. The column on books included readers' recommendations and discussions of their reading. The list of upcoming events stressed reader involvement in community affairs. An article on lesbian retirement communities included reports from the women themselves.

In Home, on construction on the theme of solitude included a large central cone with the wide end attached to the base. The cone was surrounded by symbols of comfort and communication—music, a telephone, a bathtub. The construction included the face of a woman crying. Around the edge of the construction, participants had placed signs and symbols of their political concerns: AIDS, apartheid, homelessness. After the constructions were completed, when each group displayed and talked about what they had created, the women who made this cone construction talked about the need for solitude, to be at home with the self. Home, in their vision, would allow each person, including the smallest child, his/her own "home." The group members saw this as a prerequisite for being conscious of and acting in response to suffering and injustice.

After each group had given the others a "tour" of its construction, we gathered together to discuss the implications of our work. It is impossible to summarize the discussions that took place in the various workshops, but I was particularly struck by several recurring themes. In the Newspaper workshop, participants suggested that their feelings of powerlessness and alienation from mainstream papers arose out of the sense of their own invisibility and irrelevance in what was defined as news. Although a few women (like myself) read alternative (including women's) newspapers, these were not perceived as an adequate counterbalance to the publicly legitimated news media. Participants wanted not only women's news or feminist news but a sense that they themselves made the news. They talked about the need to read mainstream papers (or watch television newscasts) critically so as to reject false pictures of themselves and to draw out those aspects of the news that helped them empower themselves in relation to ongoing events.

In Home, I was interested and surprised to find that burnout was one of the leading themes discussed. Many of the Home constructions suggested the tremendous strain that women experience in meeting their own needs and fulfilling their sense of obligation to others—in their families and intimate relationships and in their work and political worlds. Through discussion, women identified many conditions that contributed to this burnout. They also offered each other support and hope.

EVALUATION AND IMPLICATIONS

It is difficult to assess the impact of educational and political work, and these workshops were no exception. After each event, I invited participants to fill out a simple evaluation form, adding fuller comments if they wished. Following some workshops, I talked extensively with participants as well as with the performers. I thought a lot about the workshops and their impact on me.

The first few times I offered the workshops, I felt tense about combining so many ways of working, and I was unsure about possible reactions to such loaded subjects. Over the 5 years in which the workshops were offered, I grew increasingly comfortable with the material, methods, and format. My confidence increased because of the support of the performers, the responses of the participants, and my own growing sense of the organic character of the work.

The women who attended the workshops expressed a wide range of responses. Most were favorable; many were highly enthusiastic. Their positive responses emphasized how the workshop heightened awareness about or encouraged reflections on the given topic. They described the readings, discussions, and various exercises as "clarifying" the meaning of newspapers or home in their lives, as promoting "understanding," "relearning," or "enlightenment" on these issues. They often commented on how important it was to connect to and work with other women. A number talked about rediscovering their bodies, becoming aware of feelings, enjoying the opportunity for creativity or play. Although I was gratified by these positive responses, I sensed that participants themselves could not always find words to describe the deeper impact of the workshops.

In a way, I learned more from the negative responses—painful as they may have been on some occasions. Most negative responses came when I first offered the workshops and my own grasp of the process was weakest. Some women saw the workshops as politically incorrect: They thought that the news was not "a woman's issue." They felt that I had sentimentalized Home, or downplayed or ignored home as the setting for incest or battering. They disliked the viewpoints of other participants and, in effect, wanted me to structure the workshop to emphasize what they considered good politics. Some participants thought that the workshops were not "professional," that I should not include the movement or art, or that the whole project smacked of dilettantism ("parlor therapy," one critic suggested). Several women were very unhappy because they felt that their unique experiences were not addressed. Although the workshop had been described as involving movement and art, a few women felt uncomfortable being asked to move or do visual work or indicated that they found such techniques childish or demeaning.

The most searching criticism I received concerned the group process involved in constructing a vision of newspaper or home. A woman making one such criticism pointed out that there was a difference between an ideal newspaper and the ideal news. The first time the newspaper workshop was offered, several pages included fanciful items that ridiculed or distorted the news (e.g., "Nancy [Reagan] Comes Out!"). In later workshops, I emphasized that the purpose of this exercise was to try to imagine how newspapers might serve women as a means of communication. But, given this guideline, the newspaper constructions continued to include a lot of ideal news. The home constructions also contained a mixture of ideal and reality. In the end, I saw this tension between ideal and reality as intrinsic to developing a vision and, therefore, a valuable part of the workshop process.

The other main criticism of this segment concerned the group process. My original plan for the workshops was to move from individual expression to increasingly collaborative work. But difference sometimes became a stumbling block in collaboration. In early presentations of the Newspaper workshop, some women became angry with each other for wanting to include articles with which they did not agree. Rather than talking through their disagreements, they censured each other or withdrew in silence. During one of the home workshops, one group had constructed an enclosed community to respond to the theme of safety. One group member told me afterward that she had not expressed her concern that the community's locked gate would be used to exclude people on the basis of race or class: She hesitated to say this because she and her husband owned a small summer home. She was afraid that if she raised the issue of elitism, she would be accused of it herself.

My response to these conflicts was twofold: to stress to the participants the importance of working through differences and to try to deepen the level of work before presenting the final, collaborative tasks. The more effectively the first two segments enabled women to share their experiences and feelings, the less likely they were to dismiss each other's ideas or fear expressing their own.

IMPLICATIONS FOR FEMINIST PEDAGOGY

I created the Home and Newspaper workshops in the spirit of feminist consciousness-raising, which I see as the core of feminist pedagogy.[8] Consciousness-raising has four components: Participants relate experiences and listen nonjudgmentally to each other; they express feelings about these experiences; they analyze their feelings and experiences to develop a theory of women's oppression; and they act to challenge and end that oppression. Each of these four components was reflected in the workshops. The dramatic readings encouraged participants to share experiences. The nonverbal activities tapped strong feelings. The discussions supported theorizing. The constructions called for collaborative, albeit symbolic, action.

Yet, these components also posed knotty problems. One concerned the risks involved in participation—the psychological risks involved in sharing pain, fear, or anger, the physical risks involved in doing various activities, the cultural risks involved in behaving in ways that some of us had been taught were shameful or demeaning. Through interacting with participants, I learned a lot about the kind of support needed in response to each kind of risk. I watched members of a sculpture group put their arms around another member when a painful memory caused her to burst into tears. I talked with physically disabled women about accessibility and learned not to prejudge what they could do (a mobility-impaired woman could participate in group sculpture while seated; a blind woman could help construct a newspaper page by discussing it with her group). I discovered that some women found movement or art activities anxiety provoking because they had been introduced to them by rigid or judgmental teachers. When a woman pulled away from the activities, I tried to find some adaptation that would enable her to participate comfortably or to remain connected to the event even if she did not directly participate.

The problems connected with theory development were knottier still. Early in this feminist wave, activists sought theory in order to guide ongoing actions. Twenty years later, feminist theorizing has become strongly identified with academic scholarship, with students and other scholars as its consumers.[9] In the Newspaper and Home workshops, I tried to reclaim the role of theory maker for nonspecialist women. By naming the themes that underlay their experiences, workshop participants produced the central categories of an analysis—much as feminist researchers extract themes or categories from the words of the women they study.[10] These themes were explored through activities that connected experience and feelings to ideas. Thus, (in line with the arguments of many feminist academics), the workshop structure challenged the dichotomy between reason and emotion: Discussion remained firmly rooted in the experiential material out of which it was generated.[11]

Finally, the relation of these workshops to action remained an even more difficult problem.[12] Since the early years of this feminist wave, feminists have argued about the meaning of *action*. Whereas some activists criticized consciousness-raising as a diversion, others saw it as the heart of feminist activism. I did not develop the Newspaper or Home workshops to promote specific actions, although I can easily imagine adopting the format to such an end (e.g., a union trying to formulate its policy on child care; a women's center trying to help women respond to sexual harassment). Rather, I developed them at a time of waning feminist energy in the hope of reinvigorating the personal–political connection, of helping women to explore the subtle ways in which gender oppression permeates our lives.

In fact, I believe that the workshops did have an impact on action. Like many women who attended the Newspaper workshop, I found myself reading the paper differently. In any case, I became more willing to engage with the "bad news" (e.g., the Israeli-Palestinian conflict) and to ally myself with feminist activists working on such issues (e.g., the Jewish feminist peace movement). One woman told me how the Home workshop helped her to complete her grieving for her husband, because she was able to reinterpret the meaning of home without him. Another woman talked about the relevance of the Home event for her work as an organizer in community planning. The workshop suggested to her how expressive media might be used to help people understand their community needs. Still another participant in the Home workshop overcame some of her skepticism about political "rhetoric" to grasp the connections between political activism and the problems of the homeless population.

The workshops left questions unanswered: about how risks shape the feminist educational process, about the role of theory in consciousness-raising, about the links between feminist pedagogy and political action. Yet the small changes that these workshops inspired represent a distinct contribution to the possibility of women's liberation. The workshops also contributed to the possibility of women's liberation in another way: by validating women's emotional, social, and intellectual needs. For if we hope to encourage women to become more active as feminists, we must recognize what it takes to sustain activism: daily material survival, supportive relationships, recuperation, and moral validation.[13] Without some balance in meeting these needs, women (and men) rarely remain politically active. In this respect, consciousness-raising and feminist pedagogy (which may be the only form in which most women in this era will experience consciousness-raising) serve as more than an introduction to the meaning of women's oppression and liberation. These forms of feminist learning serve as a constant source of renewal. They offer an opportunity to rethink and refeel the meaning of gender in our lives, to connect and reconnect with others through our experience, to explore the meaning of injustice and to ask ourselves how we can struggle against it.

NOTES

1. I am deeply grateful to Linda Nathan Marks, director of the Crystal Quilt Consulting Service for Women, who encouraged my creation of the multimedia workshops, and to Suzanne Carothers, Yvonne Fisher, and Barbara Witenko, who performed the readings and helped bring the workshops to life. I also want to thank Sherry Gorelick and Lorraine Cohen for their perceptive criticisms of this paper and the following teachers, who work with movement, dramatic improvisation, or both and whose work has directly or indirectly contributed to the workshops: Augusto Boal (and the members of the Center for Theater of the Oppressed in Paris), Robert Dunn, Martha Eddy, Simone Forti, Stephanie Glickman (and members of the Paris Project in New York City), Anna Halprin, Paulette Sears, and Ruth Zaporah.

This reprinting and its new introduction are dedicated to the memory of Barbara Witenko, who died in 1993 at the age of 49.

2. See my "What Is Feminist Pedagogy?" *Radical Teacher, 18* (1981) (pp. 24–29). The long list of resources on feminist pedagogy includes Charlotte Bunch and Sandra Pollack (Eds.), *Learning Our Way: Essays in Feminist Education*, Trumansburg, NY: Crossing Press, 1983; Margo Culley and Catherine Portuges (Eds.), *Gendered Subjects: The Dynamics of Feminist Education*, Boston: Routledge, 1985; *Women's Studies Quarterly*, especially the special issue on feminist pedagogy (see note 6); *Radical Teacher, Feminist Teacher*, and the publications of the National Women's Studies Association.

3. See, for instance, Charlotte Bunch, "Not by Degrees" (originally published in 1979), in her *Passionate Politics: Feminist Theory in Action* (pp. 240–253), New York: St. Martin's Press, 1987; Helen Keyssar, "Staging the Feminist Classroom: A Theatrical Model," in Culley and Portuges (pp. 108–124) (see note 2); Sue V. Rosser, "Warming Up the Classroom Climate for Women," *Feminist Teacher*, 4(1) (Spring 1989), 8–13. [This essay is republished in this collection. Ed.]

4. See, for example, Frederick S. Peris, *Gestalt Therapy Verbatim* and *In and Out of the Garbage Pail*, Lafayette, CA: Real People Press, 1969. The method of psychodrama developed by J. L. Moreno is reviewed by Lewis Yablonski in *Psychodrama: Resolving Emotional Problems Through Role Playing*, New York: Gardner Press, 1981; on art as a medium for consciousness-raising, see my essay "Exorcising 'Failure': Joan Arbeiter's 'C.A.A. Job Search,'" *Frontiers: A Journal of Women Studies, 9* (1987), 1–77. One experience with movement improvisation is described in my "Master Teacher Robert Ellis Dunn: Cultivating Creative Impulse," pp. 84–87, *Dancemagazine, 57* (January 1984), 84–87. Also see the many discussions in *Contact Quarterly*.

5. Augusto Boal's ideas are available in English in *Theater of the Oppressed*, New York: Urizen Books, 1979. I have described my experience with this method in "Learning to Act: Women's Experience with 'Theater of the Oppressed,'" *off our backs, 16,* (October 1986), 14–15.

6. See my discussion, "The Heart Has Its Reasons: Feeling, Thinking and Community Building in Feminist Education" pp. 47–58 in Frinde Maher and

Nancy Schniedewind (Eds.), "Feminist Pedagogy," [Special issue], *Women's Studies Quarterly*, 15 (Fall/Winter 1989), 47–58.

7. The Crystal Quilt Consulting Service for Women was founded by Linda Nathan Marks in 1981 to offer workshops, support groups, and cultural and educational events to women. In 1990 it became a nonprofit corporation, the Crystal Quilt, Inc.

8. Some important early arguments on the nature of consciousness-raising can be found in Pamela Allen, *Free Space: A Perspective on the Small Group in Women's Liberation*, New York: Changing Times Press, 1970; and Kathie Sarachild (Amatneik), "Consciousness-Raising: A Radical Weapon," in Redstockings (ed.), *Feminist Revolution*, (pp. 144–150), rev. ed., New York: Random House, 1978.

9. For some sense of that context, see Jo Freeman, *The Politics of Women's Liberation*, New York: David McKay, 1975; Sara Evans, *Personal Politics: The Roots of Women's Liberation in the Civil Rights Movement and the New Left*, New York: Knopf, 1979; Alice Echols, *Daring to Be Bad: Radical Feminism in America: 1967–1975*, Minneapolis: University of Minnesota, 1989; and Carol Anne Douglas, *Love and Politics: Radical Feminist and Lesbian Theories*, San Francisco: Ism Press, 1990.

10. I am referring to naturalistic or ethnographic research methods in which analytical categories and "grounded theories" are developed from accounts and observations of lived experience. See, for example, discussions in Gloria Bowles and Renate Duelli Klein (Eds.), *Theories of Women's Studies*, London: Routledge, 1983.

11. See, for example, the chapter on "Integrating Reasoning and Emotions," in Sara Lucia Hoagland, *Lesbian Ethics: Toward New Value*. Palo Alto: Institute of Lesbian Studies, 1988.

12. See Allen and others cited in note 8. Action projects can be required for women's studies classes, although such assignments may raise ethical questions. See, for example, Suzanne Rose, "The Protest as a Technique for Promoting a Feminist Activism," *NWSA Journal*, 1(3) (Spring 1989), 486–490.

13. Linda Marks has argued the need for structures such as the Crystal Quilt to bring feminists together to renew themselves: "So many feminists were feeling fragmented, burnt out, and highly stressed. To be effective 'out there' we needed to feel more balanced, grounded, and clear about our energies and priorities. It was important to create an atmosphere where women could make connection with each other, where there could be serious discussion about the *work* we do, and where there would be a sense of intellectual, emotional and spiritual excitement and vitality" (talk presented at the New York State Women's Studies Association conference, 1984). Also see my "Over the Long Haul: Burnout and Hope in the Conservative Era," *Frontiers: A Journal of Women Studies*, 7(3) (1986), 1–7.

ABOUT THE AUTHOR

Berenice Fisher is professor of educational philosophy and cofounder of the Women's Studies Commission at New York University's School of

Education. Her feminist essays cover a wide range of subjects, including guilt and shame in the women's movement, the meaning of role models for women, the impact of disability on friendship between women, and a feminist theory of caring. She has been writing on the topic of feminist pedagogy since the late 1970s and her book on the subject will be published by Rowman and Littleford.

CHAPTER 10

This Class Meets in Cyberspace

WOMEN'S STUDIES VIA DISTANCE EDUCATION

Ellen Cronan Rose

Unfortunately, there are many places at which to cross any frontier, and what you learn to get past one checkpoint successfully may not be remotely pertinent at the others. I had a second chance to teach a women's studies course via distance education in the spring of 1997 and discovered to my chagrin that what I learned from teaching feminist theory to students at the University of Nevada-Las Vegas (UNLV) and the University of Nevada-Reno (UNR), using compressed video and a class E-mail account, was almost totally inapplicable in this instance. As I said in "This Class Meets in Cyberspace,"[1] I learned four things from teaching feminist theory via distance education: (1) that it is vital to bridge the actual and psychological distance between students at the primary and remote sites; (2) that E-mail can be an effective means of building that bridge if students are given adequate instruction in using the technology; (3) that it is important to establish equivalent requirements and prerequisites for enrollment in the course by students at both primary and remote sites; and (4) that I must never allow technology to dictate my pedagogical practice. Lesson 3 took care of itself. The course I taught this time—WOM 101, Gender, Race, and Class—is an introductory course that satisfies a general education requirement, so the students were all novices, those at UNLV as well as those at remote sites. And I steadfastly refused to alter my pedagogy to accommodate distance ed technology (Lesson 4). That proved to be a problem.

When I taught my first distance ed women's studies course, there were five students in Las Vegas and four in Reno, and we could sit opposite each other, as it were, trading comments back and forth from one TV monitor to another. This time, I had 19 students in Las Vegas, seated in the usual women's studies circle of chairs. The particular distance ed technology we use at UNLV allows for only two microphones, which I placed in the middle of the circle, as I had placed them on the table around which the five UNLV students sat in WOM 301, another course that I taught. But a circle whose radius is 15 feet is a lot bigger than a five-foot long table: Students at the remote sites could not hear, much less participate in, the lively, knowledge-constructing discussion taking place in the UNLV classroom. Nor did the remote sites have access to the Internet (Lesson 2), which would have allowed students there to engage in virtual, if not actual, discussion with their UNLV classmates via a class E-mail account. Hence, there was no way to implement the most important lesson of all: to bridge the gap between students at primary and remote sites.

Two thirds of the students who enrolled in WOM 101 from remote sites withdrew before completing the course; the others scraped by with Cs and Ds, on the basis of what they could learn on their own from reading the text, augmented by my written comments on their journals, which I reviewed at 3-week intervals.

In short, nothing I learned from my two experiences teaching women's studies courses via distance education persuades me that—however appealing it may be to cost-cutting administrators intent on achieving economies of scale—distance education can accommodate, much less facilitate, the goals of feminist educators.

Educational theorists and policy makers alike are currently fascinated with a range of technologies called distance education, because they see in these technologies possibilities for addressing a number of problems—from meeting the instructional needs of a demographically diverse student population (including many who work full-time or who live at inconvenient distances from institutions of higher education) to pooling scarce resources in an increasingly stringent economy.[2] Women's studies administrators, faculty, and students are all eager to avail themselves of the benefits of distance education and wary of its possible pedagogical limitations. On the plus side, women's studies practitioners see in distance education a means of reaching out to homebound or rural women who would otherwise be unable to take courses. It also offers small programs with limited resources an opportunity to share faculty and courses with other similarly small programs with equally limited but different resources. But how congenial are these technologies to the kind of participatory, collaborative learning that is the hallmark of the feminist classroom? It was, in part, to answer that question that I agreed to offer my Feminist Theories course via distance education to students at the University of Nevada, Reno (UNR) as well as at my own institution, the University of Nevada, Las Vegas (UNLV). Although my reflections on the experience of trying to teach a women's studies course in a distance learning environment can make no more than a qualitative, experiential, and anecdotal contribution to the small but growing literature on women's studies and distance education, I believe that they raise questions we need to ponder before unconditionally embracing these technologies.[3]

THE INSTITUTIONAL CONTEXT

Shortly after I arrived in Las Vegas in July 1993 as UNLV's first full-time director of women's studies, I learned about distance education and began to wonder whether it might help solve some of the problems facing UNLV's and UNR's women's studies programs, both young, small, and strapped for resources. Since 1992, UNLV has offered both an undergraduate major and minor in women's studies; UNR offers only an undergraduate minor. At both universities, most women's studies courses are departmental cross listings. Developing a coherent interdisciplinary women's studies curriculum is difficult when so much depends on the willingness of faculty members from a range of disciplines to develop courses that meet criteria for cross listing with women's studies and the cooperation of department chairs in scheduling these courses regularly. Consequently, there are gaps in both programs. It seemed evident to a number of us at both universities that we would all benefit from sharing our resources, perhaps making courses from each program available to students at both, through distance education. In the fall of 1994, the acting director of women's studies at UNR told me that Reno would not be offering their feminist theory course in the 1994–95 academic year and asked if I would be willing to allow UNR students to enroll, via distance education, in the feminist theory course I planned to teach spring semester. In her request, I recognized an opportunity to see how accommodating to feminist education distance education might prove to be.

FEMINIST EDUCATION

The proliferation of curriculum transformation projects across the country, designed to integrate the experience of women and other marginalized groups into the standard postsecondary curriculum, might suggest that feminist education happens when professors revise their syllabi in the light of feminist multicultural scholarship. Most women's studies practitioners, however, believe that how we teach is as important as what we teach. For many people, the word *pedagogy* signifies classroom techniques designed to transmit knowledge from teacher (and text) to students. Traditional pedagogies employ what Brazilian educator Paulo Freire (1968/1983) calls "the 'banking' concept of education," in which "knowledge is a gift bestowed by those who consider themselves knowledgeable upon those whom they consider to know nothing."[4] In this model, students are "containers" or "receptacles," to be "filled" by the teacher: "The more completely he fills the receptacles, the better a teacher he is. The more meekly the receptacles permit themselves to be filled, the better students they are" (p. 58).

By contrast, Freire developed what he called "problem-posing education," which "consists in acts of cognition, not transferals of information":

> Through dialogue, the teacher-of-the-students and the students-of-the-teacher cease to exist and a new term emerges: teacher-student with student-teachers. The teacher is no longer merely the one who teaches, but one who is himself taught in dialogue with the students, who in turn while being taught also teach. They become jointly responsible for a process in which all grow. (1968/1983, p. 67)

Despite Freire's (or his translator's) unredeemed use of the generic *he*, many principles of feminist pedagogy are derived from his model of problem-posing education.[5] Each member of the feminist classroom is a learner and a potential teacher. Each brings something to contribute to the collaborative construction of knowledge, which, collectively produced exceeds, ideally, what any member—including the teacher—knew when she entered the class. Members of a feminist classroom respect each other and share responsibility for constructing knowledge. But the egalitarianism of the women's studies classroom does not mean that all statements made therein are equally validated. Rather, students and teacher develop what Nancy Schniedewind (1993) identifies as "skills for sharing feelings about difference and constructively confronting conflicts" (p. 27) as they acknowledge that they are "situated knowers," simultaneously privileged and handicapped by their class, race, gender, sexuality, age, and ability.[6] The feminist classroom is a learning community in which epistemological—and other—differences are acknowledged, respected, and used to transform social relations, in the classroom to begin with, but ultimately in the world outside the academy.

REFLECTIONS OF A PIONEER
PREPARING FOR THE TRIP

Would it be possible to create any community, much less a genuinely feminist learning community, within the technological parameters of distance
education? My initial anxieties occurred months before registration for
spring semester and were all related to an unknown, mysterious, and rather
frightening technology. At a workshop in October, sponsored by UNR's
Instructional Media Services, I was exposed for the first time to the mission of the University and Community College System of Nevada's distance education project ("to provide quality education outside the geo-
graphical area of the university" [Distance Education Workshop, 1994,
p. 2]) and the array of technologies available to realize it. I was also given
a thick handbook to guide me in preparing my course for "delivery" to Reno
via compressed video. As the words *provide* and *delivery* should suggest,
the educational philosophy animating distance education assumed a banking model pedagogy. The diagrams of classrooms specially equipped to
"deliver" or "receive" distance education classes show an instructor's po-
dium at the front of the room, facing rows of tables or individual desks for
students. Students at both home and remote sites are provided with push-
button microphones so that they can "ask questions or participate in discussion," but both the layout of the room and the technology assume a
lecture format for the class (*Distance education faculty handbook*, 1993, p. 18).

The notion that knowledge is a commodity that can be packaged and
delivered is implicit in the handbook's injunction that the distance education instructor prepare an "extended syllabus" that contains—in addition
to the usual information (course objectives, required texts, topics to be
covered, grading policy)—"for each class meeting: lesson objectives, lesson key ideas, lesson study activities, [and] lesson visual materials." The
idea is to provide students with "a highly organized study guide" (*Creating materials for distance education courses*, 1993, p. 2) that will allow them—
should they choose—to work on their own, at their own pace.

As it turned out, I was able fairly easily to subvert the technological
imperative to lecture. Enrollment in the course was small enough that students at each site could cluster around a small table and thus be visible on
the TV monitors as a group to students at the other site.[7] It was, I thought, a
reasonable facsimile of the circular arrangement of chairs characteristic of
many women's studies classrooms. (As it turned out, I was mistaken: What
we had was less a circle than two rows of students, confronting each other
over a 450-mile expanse.) I left the first class meeting hopeful that we could
overcome technological barriers to effective communication and succeed in
transforming the distance education classroom into a feminist classroom. I

had not reckoned on the lack of parity between UNR's and UNLV's women's studies programs, the material significance of the 450 miles that physically separated the two groups of students, and the impact on class dynamics of ancillary technologies such as the E-mail accounts that I had set up for all class members. Above all, I had not anticipated the lingering and wide-ranging effects of that extended syllabus, a 14-page document detailing course objectives and requirements, stipulated texts, grade distribution per-centages, and a detailed calendar, not only designating readings for each class period but providing three or four study questions for each reading.

SEPARATE AND UNEQUAL

When the acting director of women's studies at UNR asked if her students could enroll in my course, I did not make sufficiently clear to her that WOM 301, Feminist Theories, was designated as the second in a three-course interdisciplinary sequence required of all women's studies majors and minors at UNLV, with WOM 101, Introduction to Women's Studies, or con-sent of the instructor, as its prerequisite. UNLV students who registered for WOM 301 had to demonstrate either that they had previously taken WOM 101 or that they had had a sufficient number of cross-listed courses to persuade me that they had a firm grasp of core women's studies concepts and some experience of feminist pedagogy. The analogous course at UNR—WS 450, Feminist Theory and Methods—is required of minors, but WS 101, Intro-duction to Women's Studies, is not required of students wishing to enroll in the theory course. UNR students registered for the course in Reno, with-out needing to seek my permission to do so. Only one had taken a women's studies course, an Introduction to Women's Studies offered at one of the community colleges, and none identified herself as a women's studies minor. Beginning with registration, therefore, there was a lack of parity between students in Reno and Las Vegas.

   This was further exacerbated because four of the five UNLV students who stayed the course were women's studies majors. They knew each other well. Not only had they taken one or more courses with each other, but, more importantly—at a university where women's studies is a small, relatively new, not widely understood or supported program—they formed with the other 10 majors a tightly-knit support group. They knew me, too. Two of the UNLV students had taken Introduction to Women's Studies with me, and as the director of women's studies, I am academic advisor to all majors. By contrast, none of the UNR students had known each other prior to enrolling in this course, and I was an utter unknown to them all, as—of course—were the UNLV students.

The students were, from the beginning, keenly aware of these differences. On the first day of class, as I went over the syllabus with the students, I emphasized that this was not an introductory class. "You will have great difficulty in this course," I said, "if you have not had at least one women's studies class prior to this one." The UNLV majors chimed in, expressing their desire for at least one course where they would not be (as they are in most cross-listed courses) the "experts" in a room of novices. One of them, Pam, came right out and said, "I'm looking forward to a class where we don't have to define epistemology, pedagogy, hegemony, and paradigm—where we all know what those words mean and can move on to how particular thinkers understand them." When class ended, we in Las Vegas turned off our mike, but the Reno folks didn't, so we were inadvertent eavesdroppers on their postmortem. What we heard revealed that the UNR students were both envious of and daunted by what they read as a spirit of camaraderie and community among the UNLV students and between them and me, and they were intimidated by Pam's four words.

I now bitterly regret that I did not begin the second class by revealing to the Reno students that we in Las Vegas had overheard their comments after the first class had formally ended. Not only would such a confession have been ethically preferable to suppressing the truth (as I did, though not by conscious intention), but it might have proved pedagogically useful as well, since it would undoubtedly have put the subject of perceived differences between the two groups of students on the immediate conversational agenda.

As it was, however, by the sixth class (we met twice a week, for 75 minutes at a time), a severe case of us versus them had set in. Not very subtly, the UNLV students were signaling their impatience with the UNR students, who seemed—to them—ignorant of what the UNLV students regarded as "fundamental" terms and concepts, such as essentialism, social constructionism, patriarchy, and sex-gender system. Understandably, the UNR students—including a very bright graduate student in English, who was concurrently taking a course in critical theory in which she was reading, among others, Foucault and Bakhtin—bridled at what they perceived as "the majors'" arrogance and condescension. It didn't help that the monitor in the Reno classroom was mounted high on the wall above the students. Literally, as well as figuratively, they had a good reason to feel "talked down to."

It took only a few more weeks for an eruption to occur. Perhaps because the extended syllabus suggested to at least some of the students that I had privileged access to a body of "knowledge" that I could introduce them to, perhaps because some of the students had been convinced by the majors that they needed instruction, but more probably because I believed that my particular contribution to the collaborative construction of knowledge was my insistence that we begin discussion of any theorist or theoretical school by explicating the assigned text, I found myself "lecturing" (or at least *talking*) more than I had in 10 years of teaching women's studies. And in class on Thursday, March 9, one of the UNLV majors called me on it. "I've taken a lot of feminist classes," Gayle said; "and this isn't one of them. In a feminist class everyone shares information with and learns from each other. But Ellen is using the 'banking model of education' and lecturing—conveying information to empty vessels called students." Ashley, in Reno, said this didn't bother her, because I was the teacher; I had constructed the syllabus, posed the study questions, and administered the midterm and she, for one, wanted to do well on the midterm.

Laura, in Reno, said that she had been bothered long before Gayle had at having knowledge "extended" to her, though it quickly became clear that she didn't think of me as the principal extender. Pam said, "The problem is that we don't all start from the same place." She used the analogy of a footrace, where those who were further ahead than others were waiting for them to catch up. For Laura, the problem was "that those who are 'ahead' are pushing those who are 'behind' to catch up. I don't mind Ellen being coach and saying, 'Hey, Laura, straighten out your legs or you'll never make it over the hurdle,' but I mind other students telling me what I 'should' know." "So what can we do," Pam asked, "to be less intimidating?" Laura, the graduate student in English, suggested starting with language. "In my research, I've learned about a 'feminine' speech pattern, marked by 'well, I don't know, but I just thought,' or 'it's just my opinion, but.' You guys [in Las Vegas] have done a fabulous job of overcoming this socialized speech pattern, but maybe in this class, you might adopt it again." By now, we were out of time (the compressed video turned off, relentlessly, at the end of the allotted class time, leaving us frozen on TV), and there was a general agreement that students should continue this discussion on E-mail during spring break.

If we had had more time, or if this had not been the last class before spring break, so that we could have resumed this discussion in 2 days rather than 2 weeks, I hope that we would have been able to analyze this exchange and detect what is now, in retrospect, glaringly apparent to me. Pam's disclaimer notwithstanding, the problem with this class *was* pedagogical. The three majors who had taken the greatest number of women's studies courses prior to enrolling in WOM 301—Gayle, Pam, and Joan Eve—viewed their comments in class as contributions to the collective construction of knowledge. The UNR students (and at least one UNLV student, as I later learned) heard the majors' remarks not as contributions to discussion among equals but as lectures to (perceived) inferiors. Some students felt intimidated by the majors; others felt, resentfully, that they were not being taken seriously as intellectual peers. Earlier in the semester, I had flown to Reno to conduct a class from there, hoping thus to convey to UNR students that they were as much my students as the majors—and I their teacher. We went out for dinner afterwards, and by the end of the evening had at least begun to attach personalities as well as bodies to what had hitherto been small faces on a TV monitor. But the students at both sites were strangers, despite the sophisticated technologies that ostensibly enhanced communication between them. During spring break, the inadequacy of technology to substitute for face-to-face conversation became painfully evident.

THE E-MAIL WAR

At the beginning of the semester, I made arrangements with System Computing Services to open E-mail accounts for all students enrolled in WOM 301. Students had the option of communicating individually with me or with another member in the class or of posting a message to us all, using the class "address book." I hoped that this would provide an additional forum for discussion and, in the early weeks of the course, several students did in fact use E-mail to continue discussing a topic raised in class. For Jaime, a UNLV student who rarely spoke up in class, E-mail offered an opportunity to express her ideas and engage in discussion with the one or two students willing to join in.

Yet, on balance, computer-mediated communication in this course did not result in the "enhanced discussion" that Sharon O'Hare and Arnie Kahn (1994) describe in their account of using a computer bulletin board in their introductory women's studies course. Of the eight students in WOM 301, only three regularly posted messages. Most did not have modems at home and hence could gain access to E-mail only in campus computer labs, a problem for students who work from 20 to 40 hours a week in the paid labor force, as do most UNLV and UNR students. And at least three were just plain terrified of the technology. So nothing like a "full discussion" of various issues occurred.

Furthermore, the very format of E-mail encourages altercation. Pine, the mail server we use, allows you to respond to a posting by repeating it and then interjecting comments. This encourages "you said/I say" discourse—the rhetoric of debate, not dialogue.

This was particularly apparent during the semester break, when more messages were posted to the class address book than at any other point during the semester. This subject thread was initiated by Laura, responding to a suggestion made during the last class before break that students use E-mail to continue the discussion of class dynamics that had been abruptly terminated when we went "off air." Following up on her remark in class that the UNLV students were "extending knowledge" to the UNR students, Laura wrote, "I feel that my opinions do not carry the same weight in class as that given to the opinions of others." Jaime replied that she didn't think that the Renoites' "perceptions/insights/questions [are] being devalued nearly as much as you seem to feel they are, but I will not discredit your feelings. . . . We all need to be more sensitive to how what we say makes others feel." Then Gayle weighed in, expressing "total disagreement" with Laura's suggestion in class "that we start to talk in a more feminine tone of voice with phrases such as *in my opinion, could it be,* etc. To suggest that I take a step backward and start to speak in 'feminine' terms is to deny me the personal growth I have strived for during the past 4 years." Gayle went on: "Don't ask me to be different than what I am, for I have struggled long and hard to become what I am." Laura responded by repeating Gayle's message, intervening frequently to disagree or remonstrate. Gayle responded by repeating Laura's response, which—of course—itself contained Gayle's first posting. The length—and acrimony—of the postings expanded exponentially, as Laura responded to Gayle responding to Laura responding to Gayle, until finally Gayle gave up: "There is no way that I can now clarify what I was trying so hard to get across in my message. It is best that I drop it altogether." At this point, as spring break drew to a close, Jaime proposed a truce:

> I would like to "agree to disagree" with regard to communication styles. Some of us are more direct, others of us are not. This should not constitute a hindrance to class discussion. . . . We have a common goal, by virtue of having signed up for this class, of learning more about feminist theories. I suggest we study and discuss feminist theories. If anyone has a problem with something said in class, point it out, discuss it, and move on. Let's be Nike and "just do it."[8]

Because so few students participated in this discussion (although, as I later learned, a number of them had observed the escalating conflict between Laura and Gayle without intervening), it quickly "degenerated" into what looked, to Jaime at any rate, like "a very personal battle of wills." Personality conflicts arise in many classes, of course, including women's studies classes. But in my experience, when they are quite consciously addressed in the context of a general discussion of classroom politics, they provide an opportunity for students to learn valuable "feminist process skills," such as participatory decision making, problem solving, and conflict resolution (Schniedewind, 1993, p. 21). Perhaps if we hadn't gone on spring break, the students in WOM 301 could have continued that Thursday night discussion in the next class, to good effect. One thing is certain. Voluntary participation in an E-mail discussion group proved to be an inadequate substitute for face-to-face interaction. And, unfortunately, I will never know whether or not the E-mail conflict between Laura and Gayle would have been resolved once classes resumed after the break or whether it would have poisoned the rest of the semester for all of us, because Gayle came down with a severe case of pneumonia that confined her to bed for the last 6 weeks of the semester.

LET'S BE NIKE AND "JUST DO IT."

Spring break lasted for 2 weeks, because the two universities' calendars are out of sync. During the first week, while UNLV was on break, the UNR students met with Susan, their site facilitator, a graduate student in psychology who works part-time at UNR's Women's Resource Center; the next week, when the UNR students went on break, I met with the UNLV students. The assigned reading was bell hooks's *Feminist Theory: From Margin to Center* (1984), and one chapter in particular seemed to students at both sights to speak to the current crisis in WOM 301. In chapter 4, "Sisterhood: Political Solidarity Between Women," hooks rejects the romantic (and specifically White, bourgeois) idea that sisterhood "is the natural consequence of women's common oppression ('a false and corrupt platform disguising and mystifying the true nature of women's varied and complex social reality' [p. 44])." Rather, sisterhood is a sense of solidarity to be achieved through hard work. "Women need to come together in situations where there will be ideological disagreement," hooks insists, "and work to change that interaction so communication occurs":

> This means that when women come together, rather than pretend union, we would acknowledge that we are divided and must develop strategies to overcome fears, prejudices, resentments, competitiveness, etc. . . . Expression of hostility as an end in itself is a useless activity, but when it is the catalyst pushing us on to greater clarity and understanding, it serves a meaningful function. (p. 63)

Susan reported that the UNR students found hooks "very relevant to what is going on in the class." One of them, in her reflection paper on the hooks reading, said that it "explained much of the frustration our class has been experiencing. [hooks's] definition of Sisterhood could be taken to heart in our class with much benefit to all. Ellen, I do not think you could have planned a more appropriate 'lesson' for us to ponder for our spring break." And Jaime's motion to "move on" was based on her feeling that, in the spirit of hooks's injunction to "actively struggle in a truly supportive way to understand our differences" (hooks, 1984, p. 64), "we have actively struggled to determine what is 'wrong' with this class, we now understand our differences, and (hopefully) have taken steps toward changing 'misguided, distorted perspectives' that everyone has had regarding people's meaning, intentions, and styles of communication."[9]

Something else happened during spring break that had far-reaching pedagogical consequences in the second half of the semester. One of the Reno students, named Memory, remarked that if some students didn't like it that I was directing discussion, maybe the students were themselves partly to blame, because they had failed to assume responsibility for initiating and directing discussion. When Susan reported this comment to me, I finally knew how I wanted to begin our first post–spring break class meeting. Combining the wisdom of Jaime and Memory, I would say that extensive conversations over the break had established that there were a variety of conversational styles in this class and perhaps some personality clashes, but that everyone seemed to agree that common ground existed in everyone's desire to study and discuss feminist theories. So let's get on with it, resolving to handle conflicts, as they might arise, on the spot, not on the Net. And I would ask for a volunteer to initiate discussion of the assigned texts for each reading, relieving me of the obligation (and the temptation) to "lecture."

SO WHAT'S THEORY GOT TO DO WITH IT?

Class meetings in the second half of WOM 301 were remarkable for their cordiality and genuinely collaborative efforts to construct knowledge. The debacle of the last class before our consecutive spring breaks alerted everyone to the fact that *something* was going wrong. The sometimes acrimonious exchange on E-mail subsequent to that class, coupled with bell hooks's reflections on the necessity of working through conflict in order to achieve feminist solidarity, led the students' expressed desire to make the class work. And when members of the class, rather than I, assumed responsibility for summarizing the assigned text and initiating discussion, the tyranny of the extended syllabus—with its preconstructed "study questions"—was overthrown. The last vestiges of "banking" education crumbled as the class moved—hesitantly at first, but with increasing confidence—towards dialogic, "problem-posing" knowledge construction.

I think it is also noteworthy that in the second half of the semester, we focused on postmodernist feminist theory and Black feminist thought. bell hooks was the pivot, in more ways than one, between the first and second halves of the course. Earlier, in the context of discussing social feminism, students had read Nancy Hartsock's essay, "The Feminist Standpoint: Developing the Ground for a Specifically Feminist Historical Materialism" (1987). To my surprise, almost none of the students understood the essay. Their reflection papers, as well as their comments in class, suggested that they found Hartsock's language impenetrable. When, however, they heard virtually the same ideas expressed in bell hooks's more accessible prose, it was as if they had for the first time encountered standpoint theory, and they found it very appealing.

Of course, as the students quickly realized, the prose of the postmodernist feminists they read after hooks was, if anything, more impenetrable and jargon laden than Nancy Hartsock's.[10] And yet, some more willingly than others, they struggled through it, perhaps because the postmodernists' emphasis on pluralism, difference, and diversity, on partial vision and particular location, struck a resonant chord among students who had, so recently, experienced divisiveness and discord. I am only guessing here, since no one made a connection in class between what we were reading and the turbulence the class had encountered midway through the semester.

In many women's studies classrooms, as Frances A. Maher and Mary Kay Thompson Tetreault (1994) document in their ethnographic study of feminist classrooms in six colleges and universities across the nation, students learn about difference as they come to acknowledge their "situatedness" in particular social class formations, ethnicities, racial and sexual identities. Our tiny class did not yield much diversity along those lines, so our discussion of white privilege, for instance, remained fairly abstract and academic. But, as was painfully evident by midsemester, the class was teeming with differences—of temperament, intellectual style, prior experience in women's studies, exposure to theory in general and specific theories (e.g., psychoanalysis, Marxism) in particular. In the second half of the course, students began to use their diverse positions self-consciously and creatively to bridge the gaps that had divided them and to construct knowledge. A great deal of self-disclosure took place. One student confessed that she "just didn't understand a word of tonight's assignment [Donna Haraway's "A Manifesto for Cyborgs" (1989)] because that kind of language is really hard for me." Another student reported that the same text had taken over her dream life: "I dreamed of Haraway's cyborg last night, and guess who it was? Michael Jackson!" Alliances were formed across sites—between Laura and Joan Eve, for example, who discovered in postmodern feminism a description of reality they recognized, as self-avowed members of Generation X (or the *13th Gen*, as in the title of a book that Laura introduced Joan Eve to [Howe & Strauss, 1993]). Ashley in Reno and Pam in Las Vegas, on the other hand, were extremely skeptical about postmodernism, because they couldn't see that it led to any coherent political agenda.

Knowing "where they (each) were coming from," to reduce postmodernist positionality to colloquial cliche, the students could—and did—modulate the way they articulated their understandings of specific texts to speak to their classmates' anxieties. Postmodernists Laura and Joan Eve, for example, pointed out to Pam and Ashley the frequent advocacy by both postmodern feminists and feminists of color of a politics of "overlapping alliances" (Fraser & Nicholson, 1989, p. 35), "conscious coalition" (Haraway, 1989, p. 198), and shared "partial perspectives" (Collins, 1990, p. 236). By the time we reached the last assigned reading, Maria Lugones's "Playfulness, 'World'-Traveling, and Loving Perception" (1990), even the skeptics had come to recognize the epistemological, ethical, and political value of the kind of speculative playfulness that so delighted Laura and Joan Eve.

By the end of the semester, the students had succeeded, albeit more by accident than by design, in creating a feminist classroom, a learning community in which the acknowledgment and discussion of epistemological differences among its members resulted in transformed social relations. By highlighting differences between students in Las Vegas and Reno, distance education created problems for this class. It also—paradoxically— may have provided them pedagogical opportunities that would not have arisen had they been, as I know they would have preferred to be, in the same room.

(IN)CONCLUSIONS

At the end of the semester, the acting director of women's studies at UNR called me. "Well, how did it go?" she asked; "Would you do it again? Can and should we expand the number of women's studies courses we offer via distance education?" I said I'd let her know, and set about finding the answers by writing this essay.

Yes, I would do it again—but differently; I learned much from the mistakes made this semester. And yes, I believe that distance education is one way in which those offering women's studies programs can collaborate to pool resources and serve our students better. The technologies involved need not raise insuperable barriers to feminist pedagogy. But they may, unless certain precautions are taken and certain conditions met.

Here is what I learned. First, it is vital to bridge the (actual and psychological) distance between students at the primary and remote sites. I believe that one reason the UNR students did not blame me for the breakdown in communications that happened midsemester was that I had visited Reno and spent an evening working and socializing with them. Had the students had an opportunity to meet each other in the same fashion, I suspect that the distrust and hostility that nearly destroyed the class would never have developed. As Jaime said, in an E-mail to the class towards the end of spring break:

> One last thing. Anyone who knows me will tell you I never pass up a chance to hang out and talk over some beers. If we were in the same city, this would have occurred, and I really think much of this [conflict] could have been worked out by simply getting to know each other better.

If possible, a meeting between students at both sites should be planned for the beginning of the semester. If travel money cannot be administratively budgeted (as my plane fare to Reno was), then students could be assessed a "lab fee." That's how important I think it is to establish real, face-to-face contact between class participants.

Second, if I decide to set up a class E-mail account the next time I teach a distance education course, I will do more than I did this time to make it an integral element of the course. The opportunity to extend discussion beyond the allotted 150 minutes a week is appealing and, as the example of Jaime testifies, some students feel more comfortable expressing themselves in writing, having had time to reflect, than they do in class. Many students will also feel comfortable using this means of continuing discussion after class because they are accustomed to surfing the Net. But for others, the prospect of traveling on the information superhighway is as scary as flying to the moon. I did invite the manager of System Computing Center's user liaison office to class early in the semester to explain verifying, logging into, and using the class E-mail account, but I did not make special arrangements for hands-on workshops in both Reno and Las Vegas. Next time, I'll know better.

Third, if distance education is one component of a collaborative effort between two programs, such as the women's studies programs at UNLV and UNR, a set of equivalent requirements and prerequisites for enrollment needs to be established. Although I believe that some of the tension that marred the first half of our semester was the result of distance and the limitations of technology ("Not being able to see the body language of the other group is a big problem," more than one student complained), it is at least equally true that the UNLV majors *were* frustrated to discover that their counterparts in Reno did not have the same grounding as they in core women's studies concepts, even if they later came to realize that that didn't mean that the UNR students weren't as "smart" as they were, or as capable of sustaining lively, provocative discussion.

Finally, and most important of all, never again will I let awe of technology dictate my pedagogical practice. I was so terrified of this unknown technology that I slavishly followed the advice of "the experts," in this case, the professional staff of UNR's Instructional Media Services. "The 'extended syllabus' is integral to the Distance Education course," they said (*Distance education faculty handbook*, 1993, p. 7), so I dutifully created one, not stopping to reflect that its mere existence contradicted everything I believed— and would tell the students—about the social and incremental construction of knowledge. To identify the objectives and key ideas for each class period over a 15-week semester and prepare study questions for the last assigned text before I'd even met the students obliged me to "construct knowledge" and made a mockery of my remarks to the students on the first day of class, my avowal that the course would be conducted according to the principles of feminist pedagogy, in which knowledge is socially constructed in the classroom. Of course, as Maralee Mayberry and Margaret Rees (1995) remind us, any course syllabus sends a message to students that knowledge can be "organized, prearranged, and transmitted from the professor to the student" (pp. 8–9). But syllabi can be altered and, in fact, rewritten in consultation with the students once the semester gets underway, as has repeatedly happened in courses I have taught. Some syllabi, however, may look less alterable, more cast in stone, than others.

In short, as I look back over the semester, I believe that the impediments to feminist pedagogy we stumbled up against in WOM 301 could have been removed, had we anticipated them. What I have attempted to provide, with the aid of students' retrospective reflections, is a map of one cyber classroom so that others can see the hazards before crossing the electronic frontier.

NOTES

1. For the title, and much else in this paper, I am indebted to Jaime Phillips. She, Laura Akers, and Susan Trentham generously shared with me their written reflections on this cyberclass.

2. *The Electronic University* (1993) lists 90 colleges and universities in 48 states and 5 in Canada that offer courses, degrees, or both via distance education.

3. For discussion of other experiments in teaching women's studies via distance education, see Burge and Lenskyj; Carl et al.; Lenskyj; Moran; and Rutherford and Grana.

4. In what follows, I borrow freely from Kaplan and Rose, as shared with and modified by Mayberry and Rees.

5. There is by now an extensive literature in feminist pedagogy. See Shrewsbury's 1993 bibliography. For a feminist critique of Freire, see Weiler.

6. "Situated knowers" is an allusion to Donna Haraway's influential essay, "Situated knowledges: The science question in feminism and the privilege of partial perspective." The theoretical basis of feminist pedagogy is, I believe, feminist standpoint theory.

7. Eight students enrolled from UNR, seven from UNLV. By the end of the semester, there remained three students in Reno and five in Las Vegas.

8. Reflecting on the class afterwards, Jaime felt "a little ashamed of my impatience with the 'disruption' in the class." She came to realize that, in a class "embracing feminist pedagogy, it was *very* important that some students felt unheard."

9. Thanks to Maralee Mayberry for pointing out to me that the students' ruminations on bell hooks illustrate the pedagogically contradictory nature of distance education. The anger and divisiveness that erupted midway through the semester was certainly exacerbated, if not solely caused, by the students' physical separation from each other—an inherent characteristic of distance education. But without having experienced this episode of confusion, frustration, and pain, the students might not so readily have understood the significance and relevance of hooks's insights about the necessity to work through conflict, rather than deny it, in order to achieve feminist solidarity.

10. In Linda Nicholson's (1989) anthology, *Feminism/Postmodernism*, they read essays by Nicholson and Nancy Fraser, Jane Flax, and Donna Haraway.

REFERENCES

Burge, Elizabeth, & Lenskyj, Helen. (1990). Women studying in distance education: Issues and principles. *Journal of Distance Education, 5*(1), 20–37.

Carl, Diana R., Keough, Erin M., & Bourque, Lorraine Y. (1988). Atlantic Canada perspectives. In Karlene Faith (Ed.), *Toward new horizons for women in distance education: Internal perspectives* (pp. 107–120). London and New York: Routledge.

Collins, Patricia Hill. (1990). *Black feminist thought*. New York: Routledge.

Creating materials for distance education courses: Extended syllabus format guide. (1993). Reno: Instructional Media Services, University of Nevada-Reno.

Distance education faculty handbook. (1993). Reno: Instructional Media Services, University of Nevada-Reno.

Distance Education Workshop. (1994). Reno: Instructional Media Services, University of Nevada-Reno.

The electronic university: A guide to distance learning. (1993). Princeton, NJ: Peterson's Guides.

Flax, Jane. Postmodernism and gender relations in feminist theory. In Linda Nicholson (Ed.), *Feminism/postmodernism* (pp. 39–62). New York: Routledge.

Fraser, Nancy, & Nicholson, Linda J. (1989). Social criticism without philosophy: An encounter between feminism and postmodernism. In Linda Nicholson (Ed.), *Feminism/postmodernism* (pp. 19–38). New York: Routledge.

Freire, Paulo. (1983). *Pedagogy of the oppressed.* Trans. Myra Bergman Ramos. New York: Continuum. (Original work published in 1968)

Haraway, Donna. (1988). Situated knowledges: The science question in feminism and the privilege of partial perspective. *Feminist Studies, 14*(3), 575–599.

Haraway, Donna. (1989). A manifesto of cyborgs. In Linda Nicholson (Ed.), *Feminism/postmodernism* (pp. 190–233). New York: Routledge.

Hartsock, Nancy. (1987). The feminist standpoint: Developing the ground for a specifically feminist historical materialism. In Sandra Harding (Ed.), *Feminism and methodology* (pp. 157–180). Bloomington: Indiana University Press.

hooks, bell. (1984). *Feminist theory: From margin to center.* Boston: South End Press.

Howe, Neil, & Strauss, Bill. (1993). *13th gen: Abort, retry, ignore, fail?* New York: Vintage.

Kaplan, Carey, & Rose, Ellen Cronan. (1990). *The canon and the common reader.* Knoxville: University of Kentucky Press.

Lenskyj, Helen. (1991). Tele-communication: Women's studies through distance education. *Resources for feminist research, 20*(1/2), 11–12.

Lugones, Maria. (1990). Playfulness, 'world'-traveling, and loving perception. *Lesbian philosophies and cultures.* Jeffner Allen (Ed.). Albany, NY: State University of New York Press.

Maher, Frances A., & Tetreault, Mary Kay Thompson. (1994). *The feminist classroom.* New York: Basic Books.

Mayberry, Maralee, & Rees, Margaret. (1995). Feminist pedagogy, interdisciplinary praxis, and science education. Unpublished essay.

Moran, Louise. (1990). Inter-institutional collaboration: The case of the Australian inter-university women's studies major. *Journal of Distance Education, 5*(2), 32–48.

Nicholson, Linda J., ed. (1989). *Feminism/postmodernism.* New York: Routledge.

O'Hare, Sharon L., & Kahn, Arnie S. (1994). A computer bulletin board in women's studies courses. *Transformations: The New Jersey Project Journal, 5,* 64–73.

Rutherford, Leane, & Grana, Sheryl. (1994, October). Fully activating interactive TV: Creating a blended family. *T.H.E. (Technological Horizons in Education) journal, 22,* 86–90.

Schniedewind, Nancy. (1993). Teaching feminist process in the 1990s. *Women's Studies Quarterly, 21*(3/4), 17–30.

Shrewsbury, Carolyn M. (1993). Feminist pedagogy: An updated bibliography. *Women's Studies Quarterly, 21*(3/4), 148–60.

Weiler, Kathleen. (1991). Freire and a feminist pedagogy of difference. *Harvard Educational Review, 61*(4), 449–474.

ABOUT THE AUTHOR

Ellen Cronan Rose is director of women's studies at the University of Nevada-Las Vegas. In a former incarnation, she published books and articles on contemporary women writers—principally Doris Lessing and Margaret Drabble. Now she practices feminist pedagogy in subject areas ranging from Introduction to Women's Studies to gay and lesbian history and knows more about academic administration than in her former professorial years she had ever hoped to know.

Part II

Bringing the World into the Feminist Classroom

CHAPTER 11

Integrating the Study of Race, Gender, and Class

SOME PRELIMINARY OBSERVATIONS

Paula Rothenberg

I don't know whether to be pleased or distressed that so many of the issues and strategies covered in this article still seem relevant today. Its deficiencies, to my mind, have more to do with what's left out. For example, "race" is implicitly constructed as a dualism (as Black and White) and issues of sexuality receive no attention. Certainly were I writing it today I would feel compelled to talk about issues of heterosexism, heterosexuality, and homophobia and to broaden the discussion of race to encompass issues of race and ethnicity in much more inclusive terms.

I would probably begin with a brief discussion of the difference between teaching "multiculturalism" and teaching from an "antiracism" perspective and would emphasize the need to do both simultaneously. Today's students continue to need to be taught both to understand and value cultural differences and to understand the history of racism, sexism, class privilege, and heterosexism, which provide both the antecedents and the continuing context for everything that happens in U.S. society today.

Ten years ago it seemed as if we were on the verge of integrating the study of race, class, and gender into our scholarship and our teaching. But reality has fallen short of those expectations. Whereas

This chapter originally appeared in *Feminist Teacher*, 1988, *3*(3), 37–42.

The Feminist Teacher *Anthology: Pedagogies and Classroom Strategies.* Copyright © 1998 by Teachers College, Columbia University. All rights reserved. ISBN 0-8077-3741-0 (paper), ISBN 0-8077-3742-9 (cloth). Prior to photocopying items for classroom use, please contact the Copyright Clearance Center, Customer Service, 222 Rosewood Drive, Danvers, MA 01923, USA, telephone (508) 750-8400.

135

women of color have taken a leadership role within women's studies
and multicultural studies in carrying out this project, many White
feminists still do not "do" race and many still think that talking about
race is for and about "them" and not "us." Although it is true that the
conversations about race/ethnicity, gender, class, culture, and sexuality
will vary enormously depending on who's in the classroom, the commitment to examining the intersections and disjunctions should not be a
function of how many "representatives" of each category are present at
any given time. Yet this is all too often the case.

Finally, I continue to believe that our ability to engage students with
these critical issues is enhanced by helping them recognize that most of
us are victims of a system that uses racism, sexism, and heterosexism to
protect and extend class privilege. Seen in this way, the racist and sexist
speech and behavior that many of us perpetuate unthinkingly can be
interrogated, not as indications of some corrupt personal nature, but as
testimony to the system's success in persuading us to internalize a
misguided sense of self-interest and to misdirect blame for the system's
inequities and our own sense of dissatisfaction and injustice.

The value of examining the ways in which race, class, and gender intersect in the construction of reality has not always been obvious. For some,
the fear was that comparisons would be used to invalidate or subordinate
the oppression of one or more groups to some single and absolute paradigm
of oppression or exploitation. For others, there was the well-intentioned
insistence that they were leaving out race or class or gender in their study
of one of the other two, not because it wasn't important but simply because
it wasn't "relevant" at that moment.

It has taken us a long time, but we find ourselves in a period when
people are open to integrating the study of race, class, and gender. This is
no accident. Where the 1970s were characterized by separation and suspicion and spawned autonomous movements for racial and gender liberation, the 1980s appear to be a period for collaborations and connections.[1]
At one time it seemed as if our ability to obtain resources for our particular struggle had an inverse ratio to the same ability on the part of others.
There was a lot to go around, but each group wanted exclusive rights to
the pie. Now, in a period of relative scarcity, many of us involved in progressive struggles have come to believe that our survival may well depend
on a combined struggle to oppose cuts and cutbacks. And our approach to
theory now reflects the connections we have begun to forge in practice.
Many of us have come to understand that talking about gender without
talking about race and class or talking about race without bringing in class
and gender is simply another way of obscuring reality instead of coming

to terms with it. Many of us have come to believe that using race, class, and gender simultaneously as categories for analyzing reality provides us, at least at this historical moment, with the most adequate and comprehensive understanding of why things occur and whose interests they serve.

During the past 6 years I have been engaged in several teaching projects designed to integrate this perspective into the curriculum. Drawing on the insights gained from each of them and focusing on my experience teaching a required introductory course called Racism and Sexism in a Changing America, I will examine some of the problems that arise from teaching about the intersection of race, class, and gender.[2] In particular, I will talk about why it is often so difficult to persuade students that racism and sexism continue to be fundamental forces in our society—forces that, along with class, play a primary role in shaping the kinds of lives people live.

I speak from the perspective of a middle-class, White woman who tries to guard against the danger of equating her reality with *the* reality but who nevertheless will more than likely do just that at least several times in the course of the discussion that follows. For that reason, it is probably best to set aside the persona of universal theoretician and begin speaking in my own voice (see also Lugones & Spelman, 1983). Adopting this voice is essential for talking with students and others about racism and sexism. They are legitimately hostile when confronted with abstract lecture-sermons from remote authorities who claim some special ability to recognize and then criticize racist or sexist behavior. If we expect others to talk openly about deeply felt beliefs and experiences, we must make clear our own willingness to do the same.

I grew up in a White, upper-middle-class, urban, Orthodox Jewish family. From the start, I knew I was a girl. The distinction between males and females in Orthodox Judaism is clear and inescapable. Fortunately for me, I was an only child for the first 6 years of my life, and my place as first-born and only child compensated somewhat for the limitations on opportunity that would otherwise have been imposed unrelentingly by my gender.

The first people of color I ever knew were large, loving Black women who came to take care of me, or clean our apartment, or wash our clothes. Later, as our family became more successful, they were replaced by slender young women from the West Indies and later still by young White "girls" from Ireland, France, and Canada. Each of them treated my mother with varying degrees of respect or tolerance, but all of them treated my father with absolute regard. My parents were liberal Republicans with Democratic tendencies. They taught my brother and me the standard liberal rhetoric about equality and justice at the same time that their conversation reflected stereotypical views of people of color and working people.

They called Black people *Chvartsas* and meant no disrespect. Towards the end of her life my mother still spoke on the phone regularly with V., a middle-class Black woman who came to work for us part-time after my father's business began to fail and we could no longer afford the young White "girls" from Europe. By then my mother said *Negroes* instead of *Chvartsas,* and she and V., who preferred to speak of "colored people," spent long hours on the phone with each other, irate over the "black power movement" and the linguistic alterations it recommended.

BEING WHITE

Like most of the White students I now teach, I was not particularly aware of being White during most of my early life. My Black students tell me that they either realized or were taught that they were Black very early on and often have very specific memories of how and from whom they learned their racial identity. In this respect one's awareness or lack of awareness of racial identity can be compared to the difference in the way men and women experience their gender identity. Simone de Beauvior (1952) expressed it this way: "If I wish to define myself, I must first of all say: 'I am a woman'; on this truth must be based all further discussion. A man never begins by presenting himself as an individual of a certain sex; it goes without saying that he is a man" (p. xv). It went without saying that I was White, so of course, I never said it. I was, however, aware of my class. I recognized that my family was a lot better off than most people, and I felt sorry for other people. But simultaneous with an awareness that there was poverty in the world came the belief I held, with absolute certainty, that people who were poor deserved to be so, because they did not work hard enough, or study hard enough, or save carefully enough. So in my world, race was invisible, and class was regrettable but deserved.

Many of the students I teach still believe this to be true. They are victims of the American Dream/Myth of Success. They believe that ability, hard work, and good intentions will be rewarded, that anything is possible. They tell me that they think of themselves as persons or human beings, not women or men, Blacks or Whites. And they are often puzzled and angered by my insistence on noticing race, class, and gender differences. They are embarrassed by my inability to look beyond these identifications and even tell me that noticing that someone is Black is itself racist. In the course of casual conversations that require pointing out a person across the room, they will spend endless time describing the individual in order to scrupulously avoid indicating the person's race or color even when that is the most obvious and easiest way to refer to them. Perfectly comfortable with pointing out "the redhead sitting at the table," they would never be so gauche as to say "the Black man at the front of the line." Of course this is perfectly understandable. Contemporary conservatism extols the virtues of a color-blind public policy, pursuing "equal treatment" with a vengeance, and thereby perpetuating gender, race, and class oppression. Like Ronald Reagan and countless other public officials, today's students confuse failing to notice race and gender with the absence of racism and sexism. No wonder they are so uncomfortable with our insistence on noticing them and insisting that they do the same. And there are other reasons as well.

Race, class, and gender are not abstract categories; they are the prisms through which people see themselves and others; they are the chasms that separate us; they are the "realities" that engulf us. For this reason, many people have trouble acknowledging their existence. They are too much a part of us to permit us the perspective we need to specify them unless we have had the kind of education, formal or informal, that exposed us to this way of thinking. The initial challenge in teaching about race, class, and gender is to persuade students that these are meaningful, indeed crucial, categories for analyzing experience and simultaneously to persuade them that these are not merely abstract categories that we as academics seek to impose, but that they are the lived reality of their lives that has gone unnamed and unnoticed.

DEFINITIONS

The problems involved in trying to get students to deal with racism and sexism directly emerge at the start of any discussion about definitions. Whereas in an ordinary course in epistemology or logic, students willingly copy definitions of terms off the board, classes in race and gender studies erupt over the question of definition. Here the fundamentally political nature of the project of definition, denied or ignored in other contexts, becomes inescapably clear. As with discussions of topics such as abortion or human nature, the nature of the debate, indeed its very outcome, will be shaped by the definition we choose. Adequate definitions of race, class, and gender oppression describe a particular sociopolitical phenomenon, but in the course of doing so, they also point a finger at those whose interests are served by them. Students sense this at once. Their resultant resistance is good evidence for the pragmatists' claim that *ought* can be derived from *is*.

Students are somewhat comfortable defining racism and sexism in terms of "prejudice" as long as the definition allows them to talk about some women being sexist (those who dislike and actively discriminate against men) and some people of color being racist (those who dislike and actively discriminate against White people). Comforted by the apparent reality that "everyone is oppressed," students often move on to discuss instances of discrimination based on ethnic background or religion. They share experiences involving ethnic slurs against Italians or the Irish and talk about experiences their friends and family members have had. This is often followed by some mention of anti-Semitism that usually prompts some of the Christians in the class to talk about prejudiced treatment from Jews. The class is rapidly moving toward the comfortable but untenable conclusion that racism and sexism are just like discrimination based on ethnic or religious background. "Prejudice is everywhere," they agree. All of them have experienced it at one time or another, so why are women and people of color demanding special attention? After all, the Irish and Italians and Jews were able to work hard and succeed, so others should be able to do so as well. If they can't, that simply proves that their subordination reflects some failing in those groups. In this way, they attempt to dismiss the uniquely virulent nature of racism and sexism.

Definitions of racism and sexism that move beyond prejudice to power are experienced as very threatening. One such definition was offered in a report issued by the United States Commission on Civil Rights (Downs, 1970):

> Racism may be viewed as any attitude, action, or institutional structure which subordinates a person or group because of his or their color. . . . This is true of Negroes, Puerto Ricans, Mexican Americans, Chinese Americans and American Indians. Specifically, white racism subordinates members of all these groups primarily because they are not white in color, even though some are technically considered to be members of the "white race" and even view themselves as "white."

Another definition appears in *Portraits of White Racism* (1977) by David Wellman: "Racism can mean culturally sanctioned beliefs which, regardless of the intentions involved, defend the advantages whites have because of the subordinated position of racial minorities" (p. xviii).

Because they identify racism very clearly with attitudes, actions, or institutional structures that perpetuate *White* privilege and the subordination of people of color, these definitions elicit considerable anger and resistance. The same is true for parallel definitions of sexism. There are many reasons why people react with this intensity. In the case of men and white people, accepting the definition appears to involve accepting responsibility for the phenomena it points to and having a responsibility to change things. For working-class students who don't feel privileged, this responsibility and the implications that follow from it are particularly hard to swallow. They are difficult for women of color and men of color to accept because in many cases the reality they point to challenges their own strong belief in the American Dream, that in this land of equal opportunity anyone who works hard can make it. If they accept the definitions offered and acknowledge the existence of the phenomena, they may have to revise their own expectations about their future.

The implications of accepting these definitions are difficult for others to accept because many have a lot invested in believing that race and gender stereotypes are accurate reflections of natural differences that justify the unequal treatment and opportunity that they have observed and benefited from and, perhaps, participated in. And they are difficult for still others to accept because sex roles, at least, if not race privilege, are bound up with identity, and to acknowledge the existence of sexism, and perhaps racism as well, involves challenging one's own sense of identity, which may be too difficult or too painful or both. Finally, most students are very individualistic in the way they see the world. They have been taught to "blame the victim" and have difficulty recognizing problems as social in nature. The depth and breadth of the resistance generated by early attempts to reach consensus on definitions of key terms makes it clear that in race and gender studies, unlike in many other areas of discourse, arriving at mutually acceptable definitions is a goal of the undertaking rather than a prerequisite for it.

UNINTENTIONAL RACISM

An important task, then, is to persuade students that racism and sexism are powerful forces in today's society. I often use selections from Richard Wright's work to bring students face to face with their own powerful but dated image of what racism is about. My students are sickened by the experiences Richard Wright recounts in *Black Boy*, but they are also reassured, because, clearly, they can never be guilty of the cruelty carried out by the Whites in Wright's world. They are eager to embrace his experiences as a paradigm because if *that* is racism then clearly they are not racists, and racism (like sexism) is a matter of historical interest, not contemporary concern. Getting them to understand the more subtle operations of institutionalized and unintentional racism in themselves and in the society is much more difficult. Doing so requires introducing the idea that both racism and sexism can be either intentional or unintentional, either conscious or unconscious.

Most people like to think of themselves as fundamentally fair in their treatment of others. They believe that they would not, intentionally, discriminate against someone because of their race or gender. From this they mistakenly conclude that because they would not discriminate *intentionally*, they do not discriminate. It is difficult for them to understand that the simple policies and practices of our basic institutions are themselves "rigged" in favor of certain groups and result in racist or sexist consequences quite apart from the particular intentions of the individuals who carry them out.

The concept that unconscious attitudes and beliefs shape our behavior is even more difficult for many people to come to terms with. My own students have virtually no understanding of the concept of the unconscious that might be used to explore racism or sexism. Most of them reflect on their own beliefs and find, once again, that they believe that everyone should be treated equally and that it is wrong to discriminate. They find it difficult to understand what it might mean to hold unconscious beliefs to the contrary, which shape our behavior or color our perceptions. They believe that much of what I point to as examples of sexism is simply "natural." Examining a definition of sexism, such as the one offered by Jessie Bernard in *Women and the Public Interest* (1971), can help spark a reconsideration of their way of viewing the world:

> The unconscious, taken-for-granted, unquestioned, unexamined, and unchallenged acceptance of the belief that the world as it looked to men was the only world, that the way of dealing with it that men had created was the only way, that the values men had evolved were the only ones, that the way sex looked to men was the only way it could look to anyone, that what men thought women were like was the only way to think about women. (p. 37)

To illustrate the way in which unconscious gender stereotypes can influence behavior, I have my students read about a study of public school teaching that revealed significantly sex-biased instructional methods (Safran, 1983). They are surprised to find that even those teachers who were self-proclaimed feminists consciously striving for equity in their classroom were themselves shocked when videotapes of their teaching revealed markedly different treatment of boys and girls. This presents the opportunity to point out that an intellectual rejection of sexist stereotypes doesn't necessarily free one from the unconscious power of them.

To further underscore the point that no one is immune and to try to convey how powerful our unconscious beliefs can be, I share examples of my own unconscious and unintentional gender or race stereotyping. By doing so, I give my students tacit permission to be guilty of similar failings without feeling that they are terrible people. Using fairly trivial examples from everyday life is usually effective because such examples are less likely to make people feel defensive. Sometimes I talk about the year my daughter chose a blue Sports Billy lunch box and my son picked a Star Wars lunch box that happened to be red, and I regularly put her lunch in his lunch box because, after all, blue is for boys. The point is that writing books and articles and teaching race and gender studies for a long time doesn't make me immune to the power of what has been called unconscious ideology. In fact, recognizing the error one morning and understanding its source doesn't even mean I won't repeat it the next day. As it has for my students, it has been impossible for me to grow up in a racist and sexist society without internalizing some of that racism and sexism. Interestingly, sharing this with students and thereby giving them permission to acknowledge some of their own racism and sexism without feeling responsible for these, is often a necessary first step toward allowing students to take that responsibility. If good people with good intentions are capable of acting in a way that is racist or sexist, then they too can become self-critical without sacrificing their self-image as kind and caring people.

Encouraged to look for examples of the impact of this unconscious ideology in their own lives, students are often surprised by what they discover. I remember one student (I'll call her Karen) who consistently criticized everyone whose race and gender sensitivity did not match her own high standards. The other students consistently turned to Karen to give the "correct" perspective on difficult topics. Halfway through the course, Karen consulted her family physician about a medical problem and was referred to a specialist. The specialist turned out to be a Black man, and Karen, who was White, found, to her surprise, that she couldn't bring herself to be treated by him. When Karen shared this experience with us, both she and the class were badly shaken by this dramatic proof that unconscious attitudes can take precedence over consciously embraced beliefs and that even knowing that the reaction is ugly and irrational does not necessarily free one from it.

UNDERCUTTING RESISTANCE

Redirecting our attention from the lives of people of color to the lives of White people and from the lives of women to men's lives is another way of undercutting resistance to acknowledging the force and nature of both racism and sexism. Much of our early teaching about race and gender has focused on the pathology of racism and sexism and their crippling impact on White women, women of color, and men of color. But this exclusive emphasis leads to the sincere and seemingly appropriate rejoinder from White people that "My family didn't own slaves, what has this got to do with me?" or some variation on it that amounts to absolutely denying any responsibility for racial oppression. One value of integrating the study of race, class, and gender is that it provides an opportunity for White people to think about what it means to be White and to realize that, unlike people of color, they have, for the most part, taken their racial identity for granted. Instead of their focusing exclusively on the pathology of racism and sexism, White students can be asked to analyze the implicit privileges they enjoyed growing up White—class differences notwithstanding. They can be helped to understand that racist policies, practices, and attitudes are not less racist simply because they are unintentional or even well-intended. The issue is not whether their ancestors owned slaves or whether *their* sister happens to get paid more than their brother.

Learning what it has meant to grow up white in North America is learning that you have inevitably benefited from racism, just as learning what it has meant to grow up male in North America is learning that you have inevitably benefited from sexism. Putting White men in touch with their race and gender inheritance and how it differs from those of White women and women and men of color can illustrate how some of us profit from racism or sexism regardless of our intentions. I often make this point by talking about my own recent experience with breast cancer. I talk about the ways in which my position as a White, middle-class professional woman living in a large metropolitan area affected my diagnosis, treatment, and prognosis; and I use available comparative statistics on recovery rates to point out that quite apart from any intentions of my own, I have a significantly better chance of being alive 5 years after my mastectomy than, for example, a Black woman who underwent the same operation on the same day.

Introducing the impact of class differences on race and gender is important at this point because it helps explain why working-class students who are in fact privileged by virtue of their race or gender may not *feel* as if they are privileged. What we perceive as their race or gender privileges may well be experienced by them simply as the core of their sense of self and may be their only basis for feelings of self-worth. In fact, we know this to be true. We know that racism and sexism often serve to obscure or mitigate class exploitation either by allowing certain relatively powerless groups feelings of superiority over certain other groups or by directing attention toward race and gender competition and away from the class privilege that remains unnoticed and uncontested. No wonder our students find their race and gender privileges difficult to identify and painful to relinquish.

Carrying out our study of race and gender within the context of class is critical for a number of other reasons as well. Perhaps most important, introducing the idea of class domination, and talking about capitalism's need to reproduce it, takes what appears to be a personal dissatisfaction and exposes it as a political issue. When I talk about sexism, it's clear to me that some of my students, mostly men but a few women as well, think that I am simply bitter about some unfair treatment I have personally experienced in the past. I offer an economic-social analysis, and they hear complaints and bellyaches. When I talk about racism, it is harder to accuse me of raising my personal misfortune to a political plot, but they find other ways to discount the content. Some White students type me as "a liberal" or a "nigger lover" and then dismiss my perceptions on the grounds that they say more about my personal bias than about reality. That a White person would choose to empathize with the experience of Blacks or other people of color is proof positive for some of them that I have some nameless problem that entitles them to dismiss what I say. But when I show students that the racism and sexism we have been examining fits into a system of class domination and is used to perpetuate it, things begin to make sense to them on a whole other level.

MAKE CONNECTIONS

An effective way of beginning to make these connections is to recast traditional class exercises designed to uncover gender stereotypes so that they allow us to look at the race and class implications of such stereotypes as well. A fairly common exercise in women's studies classes involves dividing a blackboard in two and asking students to help compile lists of so-called feminine and masculine traits (as defined by the cultural stereotype). Once the lists are completed, students are asked to analyze the results of this survey. They notice that the characteristics assigned to women are largely negative in contrast to the positive connotations of most male-defined traits; they notice that women are often defined in terms of the absence of male qualities; they notice that women tend to be more dramatically defined by their biology than men and so forth. But wait. Who are these men that our culture describes as "breadwinners," "leaders," "protectors," "rational" movers and doers? Surely they are neither Black nor Hispanic nor working class. And who are these women who are "gentle," "patient," "nurturing" mothers and wives? Surely, as Sojourner Truth pointed out so long ago, this is not the cultural stereotype of Black or Hispanic or working-class women. We've asked our students to define men and women without making reference to class or race, and they believe that they have done what we asked. But, of course, it was never possible to define a cultural stereotype without specifying race and class, and the fact that some of us did it for so long simply shows how easy it is to inadvertently participate in the falsification of reality by rendering certain groups invisible. Once we approach our analysis of stereotypes from the perspective of race, class, and gender, our students can make many new discoveries that will help them make better sense of how reality is defined and whose interest this "reality" serves. They quickly realize that the stereotypes of White women, men and women of color, working-class men and women, and all children have many qualities in common, and that these qualities appear legitimately to deny them leadership roles in society as well as significant control over their own lives. Further, it becomes clear that the very qualities that are positive when attributed to White, privileged males can become negative when incorporated into the stereotype of women of color or working women. In fact, when someone other than a White, privileged male appears to manifest those previously positive qualities, the individual is often held up to ridicule or labeled pathological.

It quickly becomes apparent to them that prevailing stereotypes purport to merely describe, but really evaluate as well. Power becomes the ability to define difference as deficiency, as deviance, as pathology. Male qualities and behavior are the standard for appropriate or exemplary behavior. Women are described in terms of those masculine qualities or characteristics that they lack. The worst thing you can say about any man is that he is more like a female than a male.

And yet, it is not that simple: The ideology about sex-role differences encourages female schizophrenia. We are both different from men in the sense of being inferior and in the sense of being special. We can do things such as give birth to men's children and care for other people, things men tell us they are unable to do. Thus we are special. Yet those very capacities render us inferior, since no man in his right mind would want to do those things anyway. Embracing our culturally defined female image requires that we cooperate in the male-defined charade that we are different and better than men at the same time that we are worse than them. This double or triple bind that women learn to internalize as part of their self-definition explains why some women and men have difficulty recognizing language or behavior that is blatantly sexist. I'm thinking here of male behavior that supposedly shows respect for women, such as opening doors and lighting cigarettes. Such deference to women purports to be respectful by according them special treatment. Yet such treatment is actually used to define women as less self-sufficient and competent than men; it thus reinforces the schizophrenic nature of the cultural stereotype.[3]

The cultural stereotype of Blacks, which is unqualifiedly negative, manages to avoid this ambiguity while retaining a schizophrenic quality of its own. Here, differences are clearly portrayed as deviant, even pathological, regardless of whether they pertain to appearance or character. As we know, to say that the Black family has a different structure from the White family is not merely to describe differences but also to condemn them. For the most part, successful Blacks in our society, from business people to beauty queens, tend to be those who have managed to become "White." Every time a Black person succeeds in this way, his or her success reinforces rather than undermines the dominant ideology's insistence on equating difference with deficiency, or even pathology. I am reminded of a statue of Booker T. Washington that I saw on the campus of Tuskegee Institute almost 20 years ago. Washington, dressed in a suit and standing tall, is taking a blindfold off the eyes of a half-naked (read "savage"), crouching Black man whose large nose and swollen lips are in clear contrast to Washington's more Caucasian countenance. The schizophrenic nature of the message to Black people in the United States is clear: Blacks can become successful insofar as they emulate Whites, but since Black people can never actually become White people, their success requires that they participate in a maddening, because hopeless, charade.

To criticize stereotypes because they present women in a derogatory way will strike some students as trivial; and to expose the racist nature of stereotypes of people of color will only be persuasive to students who are prepared to reject, not embrace, their veracity.

But by offering an analysis of the way in which these stereotypes both reflect and perpetuate class, race, and gender domination, we raise the discussion to a whole other level, one that most students find fascinating and cogent. This framework is particularly meaningful for working-class students, since it begins to provide White, working-class males with information and analysis that can help them come to terms with the powerlessness they feel at the very same time that they are accused of privileged status in relation to all women and to men of color. Examining statistics that reflect the distribution of wealth, income, employment, services, and opportunity in the United States in light of the way class, race, and gender differences are defined and maintained by these stereotypes is the next logical step in showing how the combined use of these categories can explain the way in which society is organized and whose interests are served by this organization and distribution of resources.

IMPACT

For some students, being exposed to an analysis of contemporary society that raises issues of race, class, and gender will have a lifelong impact. Like those of us who already adopt a feminist, antiracist, class perspective, they will come to live in a different world from their peers. These students, however, will be in the minority. As time passes, most students will look back on their experiences in our classrooms with suspicion. They will again begin to wonder why we persisted in seeing racism and sexism everywhere. They will become increasingly critical of what they were taught and increasingly condescending toward what they will once again choose to portray as our subjective concern.

The problem cannot be solved by changing either our course content or teaching skills. The majority of students will continue to resist dealing with issues of race, class, and gender as long as those issues are raised in a few isolated courses. Who can blame them? We tell them that racism and sexism are everywhere, that they pervade our past and our present and shape our future, and yet these same realities go unmentioned in most of the courses that these students take throughout their undergraduate career. Given the powerful reasons these students already have for resisting this content, it is not surprising that they quickly revert to dismissing these issues. Until this content is integrated into the entire curriculum, students will continue to view it as the peculiar concern of a small group of faculty. The dramatic and empowering perspective to which we expose our students in courses in race and gender studies can only be sustained if that perspective is reinforced by what students learn throughout their college career.

Acknowledgment. This paper has benefited enormously from ongoing discussions with my colleagues in the Race and Gender Project at William Paterson College.

NOTES

1. In fact, a conference about women's studies research was held at the University of Pennsylvania in March 1986, with the title "Collaborations and Connections," which I have borrowed.

2. Two previous papers that I wrote during the initial stages of teaching this course may be of interest to readers: "Teaching 'Teaching Racism and Sexism in a Changing America'" and "Integrating the Study of Racism and Sexism: A Case Study." Both of these early papers were written during a time when a significant percentage of the students in each section of this course were Black and when most sections were team-taught by a mixed-race-and-gender team. This paper reflects our current experience where most sections have few students of color and where the majority of sections are taught by individuals, not teams.

3. For an excellent and more detailed analysis of such behavior, see Marilyn Frye's (1983) discussion of the male door-opening ritual in her book *The Politics of Reality: Essays in Feminist Theory,* pp. 5–7.

REFERENCES

Bernard, J. (1971). *Women and the public interest*. Chicago: Aldine.

de Beauvoir, Simone. (1952). *The second sex*. New York: Alfred Knopf.

Downs, A. (1970). *Racism in America and how to combat it*. U.S. Commission on Civil Rights.

Frye, Marilyn. (1983). *The politics of reality: Essays in feminist theory*. Trumansburg, NY: Crossing Press.

Lugones, M. C., & Spelman, E. V. (1983). Have we got a theory for you: Feminist theory, cultural imperialism, and the demand for the woman's voice. *Women's Studies International Forum, 6*, 573–581.

Wellman, David T. (1977). *Portraits of white racism*. Cambridge: Cambridge University Press.

Rothenberg, Paula. (1984). Teaching "Teaching racism and sexism in a changing America." *Radical Teacher, 24*, 2–5.

Rothenberg, Paula. (1985). Integrating the study of racism and sexism: A case study. *The Journal of Thought, 20*, 122–136.

Safran, C. (1983, October 9). Hidden lessons—do little boys get a better education than little girls? *Parade Magazine*, p. 12.

ABOUT THE AUTHOR

Paula Rothenberg is director of the New Jersey Project on Inclusive Scholarship, Curriculum, and Teaching and professor of philosophy and women's studies at the William Paterson College of New Jersey. Her interdisciplinary anthology *Race, Class, and Gender in the United States: An Integrated Study* (St. Martin's Press) is widely used in diversity courses around the country and is about to go into its fourth edition. She is coeditor of a number of other books, including *Feminist Frameworks* (McGraw-Hill), one of the very first women's studies texts, now in its third edition, and *Creating an Inclusive College Curriculum: A Teaching Sourcebook From the New Jersey Project* (Teachers College Press). She writes and lectures on gender and multicultural curriculum transformation and scholarship-related topics.

CHAPTER 12

Homophobia and Sexism as Popular Values

David Bleich

I wonder how much has changed since this was written in 1987, besides my place of work and myself.

The population at the University of Rochester is more diverse than it was at Indiana University. Yet, the apprentice teachers I supervise report students' sentiments identical to those I heard 10 years back in Indiana: The HIV positives should be placed on an island or exterminated. The topic of gender identity rarely refers to identities other than heterosexual. There have been several gay and lesbian teachers, but they dare not come out in class. If works by gay or lesbian authors are studied, the discourse is balanced, but the meanings of the literature's sentiments are not deeply understood. If I suggest that characters in films we study may be gay, students do not comprehend this, on the grounds that the characters are not clearly marked as such in the films (e.g., Artie and Judd in *Compulsion*). "Don't ask, don't tell" seems to be a classroom philosophy as well.

I teach "mixed genres" in the literary and identity senses. I have trouble getting nonfemale heterosexual people to understand the meaning of being "implicated" in the gender identity of others. I have trouble getting students to include the homoerotic in each person's sexual capability. The "mixed" is not welcomed by most men. I think that in the past decade, among heterosexual men, homophobia has gone further underground; among heterosexual women, homophobia has become more discussable. The most alarming sentiment I hear is that feminism and affirmative action have achieved their goals. Far too many students

This chapter originally appeared in *Feminist Teacher*, 1989, 4(2/3), 21–28.

The Feminist Teacher Anthology: Pedagogies and Classroom Strategies. Copyright © 1998 by Teachers College, Columbia University. All rights reserved. ISBN 0-8077-3741-0 (paper), ISBN 0-8077-3742-9 (cloth). Prior to photocopying items for classroom use, please contact the Copyright Clearance Center, Customer Service, 222 Rosewood Drive, Danvers, MA 01923, USA, telephone (508) 750-8400.

take this position, stifling discussion and threatening to cause disorder in the curriculum when this view is disputed. Because of the commonness of this view, I think nothing has changed.

When we consider common forms of domination—sexism, racism, classism, and homophobia—as they appear in popular ideology, we don't usually try to decide that this ism causes that ism, since the practical political purpose is to eliminate all of them. Yet, Gerda Lerner, in her recent book *The Creation of Patriarchy* (1986), offers the following observation: "The patriarchal family is the cell out of which the larger body of patriarchal dominance arises. Sexual dominance underlies class and race dominance" (p. 209). It is true that a direct, topical inspection of the characteristic forms of social domination might urge the belief that men and women share in them equally, especially insofar as both sexes use similar language to express ideological superiority. For racism, we hear, "people should stay with their own kind"; for classism, "the poor need to be responsible for themselves"; and for homophobia, "seeing two men/women kissing makes me want to vomit." Even nonfeminist women who accept the traditional arrangements in the sex/gender system often justify them by saying that "motherhood is the most important relationship." However, this similar language indicates not the free cooperation of men and women, but, in Lerner's terms, the unconsciously coerced collaboration of women, first in the underlying sexist social arrangements, and *consequently*, in their cooperation with other forms of domination. In other words, because sexism is the oldest, most established, and least questioned form of social domination, it permits men to gain the help of women to perpetuate masculine, economic, racial, and heterosexual domination. There is no human society in which, for the most part, this is not the case.

Of course, I will not try to give proofs, but only present thoughts that will support Lerner's view of the primordiality of sexism. By discussing the work of 115 first-year students at Indiana University (62 women and 53 men), particularly their essays on homosexuality, I think I can present a reasonably reliable picture of homophobia in America today, and show how the students' language suggests that sexism underlies homophobia in both men and women; and how in those cases in which women do not collaborate with sexism, they are not homophobic. Put still another way, I will try to show that the gender difference in attitudes toward gay men and lesbians helps to confirm Lerner's claim about the primordiality of sexism.

This is not, however, a statistical study in the traditional positivistic sense, where all variables are carefully counted and processed. A commonly used but traditional term, lately, for looking at what people are actually saying and thinking in social science is *empiricism*, and many socially oriented studies are now taking place with the assumption that mathematical authority can attach to such studies if the statistics are handled sensibly. Yet it is part of my argument that an exclusively quantitative approach to a problem of ideology such as this is just not enough and itself represents what Naomi Scheman (1980, 1983) has called "socially masculine" thinking. I therefore want us to use the term *experience,* to include both statistical information and qualitative, not rigorously counted, verbal formulations. In this way I will try to show what the experience of homophobia is among first-year students, and then to claim that we need not investigate every single community or even a "statistically significant" sample for us to believe that the values that these students hold are fairly general, that we may reasonably expect to find them in other groups of students and in other societies, and that, therefore, this is a problem that requires immediate attention. By substituting experience for empiricism, I want to help enlarge the scientific ideology of the academic community so that it is no longer dominated by masculine thought styles and by men. Right now, empiricism is too often an exclusivist thought style, in which the "hard" and countable data are assumed to be the best data; I think both countable and nameable information should gain authority together depending on whether any particular combination provides enlightenment for the issue under investigation.

THE QUESTION

In December of last year, I asked my class of about 150 first-year students the following question, to be answered in class in about 40 minutes:

> Describe a conversation with someone either of your own or another sexual preference (lesbian, male homosexual, bisexual, asexual, heterosexual) on the issue of homosexuality. Give as many salient details as you can about this conversation, particularly how attitudes about homosexuality were *expressed.*

In this course, no piece of work was graded, and so the students felt freer than in most classes to write their opinions truthfully, that is, without fear that their opinions had to agree with those of their instructors. About 20% of the class either themselves held or reported that parents or loved ones held opinions such as these:

> (1) Homosexuality is the only topic on which Mad Max [a campus preacher] and I have the same opinion. He says homosexuality is a menace to society and that the faggots should be stoned.

(2) We would talk about homosexuals and make fun of their gay rights marches when we saw them in the paper. When the AIDS thing started we suggested shooting all of the queers or putting them on an island like lepers.

(3) I feel homosexuality is an act *of sexual perversion* and gays all should be shot, but I guess we don't have to waste the bullets; they are going to die of aids [*sic*] soon enough anyway.

(4) I said the fag [Harvey Milk, the homosexual official of San Francisco who was assassinated] got it because this other dude didn't want any fags teaching his kids. Lori said, "The poor guy." I said, "the poor guy? they should all be shot." Lori said, "You sound like my dad, he can't stand gays, he always gets upset when he hears about them and probably would kill one or two if he had the chance." I said, "sounds good to me."

(5) I remember one comment made about how all homosexuals should be put in one building and have the building blown up.

All of these comments were given by young men. The first four writers themselves advocate the murder or extermination of homosexuals. None of them was joking. Although none was actually conspiring to carry out his wishes, the significant thing is that they all felt free enough to write such thoughts although knowing that their essays would be read by professors or other authorities in the university. Here is a related narrative:

(6) We drove off with me, Dave, and the two geeks in the back seat. Then suddenly one of the other "guys" asked Dave if he was gay like his brother. Dave was also stunned, while Steve and Al burst out laughing. Just when I was about to vomit, Steve pulled down a small street, came to an abrupt stop, and he and Al jumped out of the car. They both reached in and pulled the gay guys out and just started to nail on the fags. After they beat the hell out of them they took their wallets and watches, got back into the car, and took off again. Me and Dave sat motionless while Al took all the money out of the wallets, and tossed them back to me and Dave. . . . I felt kind of sorry for them while they were getting beat to hell, but I still have a hard time feeling any sympathy for them.

This is an instance of gay bashing, an activity of peremptorily assaulting any gay men who can be found, just for the fun of it. The writer apparently did not participate in the assault, but just sat by while it took place. He reports that he was "about to vomit" at the thought of the two gays becoming friendly (the four in the car had deliberately tried to "pick up" gay men to "make some money"), but the assault seemed to prevent the vomiting and shored up the heterosexual integrity of the four young men in the car. Another student, also male, reported that when a few guys in an informal bull session noticed a group of gays nearby, one suggested, "There are about six homos in the lounge next door. Let's go beat the shit out of them. I'm sure it will only take two of us." The writer apologized: "It's just the fact that homosexuality is such a disgusting and gross thing that I can't help being prejudiced. It just grosses me the fuck out. Take it or leave it, this is how I feel."

Whereas young Americans don't recognize such behaviors from a historical standpoint, those of us who are older, and perhaps European, have no trouble recognizing the fascist mentality in its characteristic beginnings. The last writer is himself Japanese American and has been the victim of prejudice; now, he is assimilated and participates in homophobia—the one form of mob hatred in which most members of out-groups close ranks with the dominant majority. Eddie Murphy, the successful Black comedian, is well-known for his long routines making fun of homosexuals and his skillful caricatures of them on the screen. About 60% of the essays from this class reported that homosexuality was disgusting and gross—the most frequently used adjectives—and many men who did not actually advocate either extermination or gay bashing felt that it was excusable to beat up gays or "throw them out the window" if one of them made a sexual proposal to them. Only one woman out of the whole class said she would "slam the bitch" if a lesbian proposed a sexual encounter. No women advocated mass extermination, though one said that bisexuals (who spread AIDS) "don't deserve to live." No women advocated gay bashing, though many reported joking about homosexuals among themselves. And one woman reported a kind of game of verbally "tormenting" gay men and lesbians by screaming at them from passing cars.

I think it is safe to say that the activity of gay bashing and the feeling that it is more or less all right to want all homosexuals to die, die off, or be killed adds up to an almost exclusively masculine value. It utilizes characteristic (but not exclusively) masculine social habits of getting together in groups and finding a suitable scapegoat. This habit starts in elementary school, where smaller boys or those who achieve success primarily through mental effort are often designated as the scapegoats and beaten up at every opportunity—a practice sometimes excused even by women as "boys will be boys." Sometimes the scapegoat is a retarded person or an impoverished one, but the gatherings of boys in violent causes is as common as rain. Having been socialized with this value, these boys soon grow out of the actual practice of scapegoating.

Those young men heading for the primarily masculine workplace—that is, those in my class—have already gotten used to woman baiting in private—the telling of jokes that degrade women and their bodies; used to the preference for transient sexual encounters, to the confident belief that the truly powerful are always other men. Now they come to college and work as colleagues with seemingly independent young women, and woman baiting is overtly inhibited (though not altogether eliminated) by their female instructors (my staff of six included only one male instructor). It is at this point that gay baiting becomes a widely shared way to continue the momentum of their masculine socialization. Their female teachers are heterosexual; only one male student admits to being gay, even though it is likely that about 15 of the 150 are either gay or lesbian. Plenty of women in the class have participated with the men in ridiculing gays and expressing nausea and a desire to vomit at the sight of two gays or lesbians making love. On top of this, the instructors have repeatedly promised that no student is to be penalized for his or her political opinions and all should go ahead and speak their minds. Mad Max has already issued a convenient formulation: Gay men should be stoned. At the historical moment when it looks as if gays and lesbians will be increasingly protected by the law, when the closet is no longer publicly considered the right place for homosexuality, the opposite real value also emerges: Homosexuals should be exterminated. (One student said that they should be put back in the closet.) The enabling value, however, is not Mad Max or fear of AIDS; the enabling value is sexism—the right of men to gather to take and exercise power and to organize themselves in violent causes—such as war—if they so choose, with the expectation that women will support them either out of love or necessity.

The writer of the third response on my list—I will call him Mr. F—the young man who thought that he did not have to waste bullets on gays, wrote the following, earlier in the same essay:

I probably sound really biased against gays but I feel that it is sacrilegious. If God wanted faggots on this planet he would have made Adam, Eve, and Mike [a homosexual acquaintance] so that they all could join in together and perform sexual acts together. Then I said: "I feel that gays are just the beginning of the end of the world." I don't feel that we are going to find a cure for the AIDS virus and that it is the beginning of the eventual doom of the human race. This may sound very far fetched and eccentric, but consider this. In the bible the end of the world is to come at a time where disease runs rampid [sic] and earthquakes and volcanos come to life. In the past couple months a lot of this had been happening.

Of course, this young man does indeed sound eccentric. Nevertheless, almost 20% of this class—about half men and half women—reported that homosexuality was either against their religion, if they were Roman Catholic; or that it was against God and the Bible, if they were Protestant. Among these students, Christianity emerges as one of the protectors of homophobic feelings. One Catholic student took the trouble to explain how one of his teachers gave the following rationale: Sex is only for reproduction; any kind of sex that is only for pleasure is wrong. Protestant students stressed more that the Bible "forbids" it. Historically, in both Catholicism and Protestantism, those who hold religious power are men. But this is also true for Judaism and every other world religion. Gerda Lerner (1986), in fact, reports that long ago, goddesses were eliminated from the heavenly population, so that gods and priests were men only.

In his essay, Mr. F cites the Apocalypse—the end of the world—the sense that AIDS is one of a series of events adding up to the Judgment Day. Norman Cohn's (1970) 1957 study, *The Pursuit of the Millennium*, documents how medieval chiliasts—peripheral, evangelical con men, working for sex and money—also routinely cited the end of the world in order to gain the sexual attention and the money of women whose men were at war or otherwise missing. These chiliasts, like the evangelists of today in America, some of whom have already been revealed as frauds pursuing these same ends, utilize the psychology of the charismatic and homophobic gang leader, one of the boys yet above them, to play out the familiar predatory theme song that enables men to enact not-so-unconscious wishes for sex, violence, and violent sex, and deprives women, the poor, the dependent, of a decent livelihood, personal dignity, and sometimes their lives.

Insofar as religion depends on a central icon who is a masculine scapegoat, someone who "willingly" bears the guilt of the community and in whose name a group of men serve as intermediaries to salvation, it maintains both a psychological and institutional system of approval for the seemingly outrageous opinions of the young men in my class, while at the same time *implying these students' partial, but likely, participation in homosexual feelings*. From this perspective it looks as if the ease with which people use religion to support homophobia is made possible by the sexist functions of religious values to begin with. Furthermore, the fact that the *same percentage* of my group—though not always the same individuals—say that they use religion against homosexuality as report advocating mass extermination, suggests how "normal" the scapegoat psychology really is. Many students in my class were outraged by Shirley Jackson's story, "The Lottery," in which one person (a woman) is arbitrarily picked by lot to be stoned in an annual ceremony; perhaps half or more of the class, however, was more concerned with whether the victim had a right to complain (which she did) than with the fact that such a practice was stipulated to begin with.

Of course, in our explorations, we teachers could have "told" the students just which issues to discuss, but since we left it to the students to say what the issues were, we can observe how their values are consistent across the board, however depressing such discoveries may be. Though I will not go into it here, every inquiry we made into class, race, sex, and so on disclosed that at least half the class claimed that victims are generally responsible for their own misfortunes. With regard to sexism, some women accept this mendacious principle: If a husband cheats or is alcoholic, the loyal wife feels that it is either her shortcoming that brought it on or her responsibility to stop it and "save" the husband.

Some men seem to have reacted to this issue in less panicky ways, but consider this: Only one male student in this class, whom we'll call Mr. R, was willing to offer the following thought: "I feel that if I am seen with homosexuals, most people will think I am one too. It's just the way society is about most things." Only one young man had enough courage to announce that he is afraid of being thought to be homosexual, even though it was clear that every heterosexual young man in the class had the same fear. Only one other young man, Mr. S, was willing to apply the class term *homophobia* to himself:

> The conversations I've had about homosexuality have always been brief. I think this is probably true because of my strong homophobia. . . . I am very very closed minded about homosexuality. . . . We seem to look at homosexuality as some sort of disease. . . . I say this is a stereotypical view because the United States is generally a homophobic society. Homosexuals are looked down upon and discriminated against greatly. I think one major reason we are so against homosexuality is that it threatens our own sexuality.

No other student, man or woman, came out and said that the United States was a homophobic society. Many students said that they were closed-minded or prejudiced, but even Mr. R used the word *society* as an abstract noun to state the source of the values. Only Mr. S was willing to relate these values to the specific society he lives in, implying that there may be other societies with different values, a thought not entertained by any other student.

I bring in these two masculine views because they represent the exception, the rarity of willingness to announce personal responsibility, to admit to fear, and to think in terms of America as having national values.

Just as in international relations, no diplomat ever says that his or her country "feels threatened," saying, rather, that this or that country "poses a threat to our national interest," men attack homosexuals physically and verbally because their "sexual interest" is threatened by homosexual invitations. To traditionally socialized men, the possibility of homosexual sex *threatens to sever the comfortable connection of sex and power* and presents a model of two socially "equal" partners, the very possibility denied by the tradition of patriarchal family life. One student reported that "many of my friends said that homosexuals give a bad name to the male species; that men are tough and strong, not little pee wee's with a high voice and a sexy walk like a girl." Although most heterosexual men don't actually feel any likelihood of suddenly becoming homosexual, it seems, at least in part, that they invent the fantasy of being homosexually seduced in order to conceal the social anxiety produced by the contemplation of equality with women. Notice how the following essay demonstrates a real fascination with homosexual life, a willingness to actually use heterosexual language in contemplating homosexual sex, all done in a group of young men only. Mr. D:

> Basically I'd have to say that the issue of homosexuality is made fun of by my friends and I. A little "come here baby" or "looking good in those jeans" would have to be some common phrases used by practically every guy on our floor. But when it comes down to really talking about it people take a very different view, at least the ones that I know.

> There was one time we were just messing around saying stuff like "you're mine tonight baby" and other much more vulgar phrases, when we all kinda stopped talking, looked at each other and said "Yuck!" Then, Mike, a good friend of mine, said, "Man, I don't see how anybody could do that . . . it's sick as hell." We all agreed by making grotesque faces at the thought of it. Then another guy, Rich, started telling us about a gay guy he used to know. "If that guy got too close to me I would hit him upside his head," Rich told us. Then I began telling them about a gay guy . . . he was a pretty nice guy. But I swear I would be scared to change in the same room because I thought he would jump me. They sort of laughed at that, but then after I told them that he asked me to go out with him sometime everybody got grossed out. Another guy in with us said they all should be lined up and shot. Our conversation ended pretty much there as Miles bent over and said "Do me."

I'd have to say that our attitude was pretty hostile and very antihomosexuality. Our conversation was along more vulgar lines than what I wrote too. But I'd have to say that nobody who was there actually would "line up and shoot" any of them. And there is really no telling who is and isn't. A friend of mine from high school always seemed pretty normal. But when I went home for break I found out that he got going at a party with another fellow in the woods! But then again I can't say that I agree with it all. I guess what I'm trying to say is that the people are OK but the act is not.

It is fairly common knowledge that when young men such as these are set off by themselves, they often do function very well under egalitarian principles and mutual affection. The writer feels that the violent views definitely would not be enacted, even though he admits to great "hostility" to gays. On the other hand, the universality ("every guy on our floor") of making joking homosexual remarks and the physical imitation of homosexual sex (bending over and saying "do me") demonstrates a feeling among men that is more overt among women—both a curiosity and an *ultimate lack of discomfort with homosexuals behaving as they wish*. As this student moves toward the end of his essay, he is obviously more thoughtful and conciliatory as he realizes that homosexuals are "OK," and settles on the quiet rejection of homosexual sex. It seems to me that only coercive collectively held values could account for the strong habitual and conventional denunciation of homosexuality among men. One aspect of these values is perpetuated by religious power and tradition, whereas various other cultural practices perpetuate the general and secular social tradition of men as a class maintaining power over women as a class.

GENDER DIFFERENCES

Often, in the women's essays, which also generally reject homosexual sex, some version of "I don't understand" is used to describe the women's attitudes toward homosexuality. The difference between the women's and the men's use of this thought points up the difference in attitude between the two genders. Here are two fairly characteristic "middle-of-the-road" masculine recognitions that homophobia comes out of ignorance.

Mr. W: I never understood homosexual or lesbian behavior and because it is a topic not many others understand I never really discussed it much. The times I've heard it mentioned were when it

was used as a put down method or a way of making someone feel
bad.

    Mr. K: I know that Bill really hates homosexuality but not
homosexuals. I guess because he sees that they're real they're in his
town and they have needs. Maybe that's why some people hate 'em
some hate the idea and others hate the idea and the people. Ignorance.

Although these statements seem reasonable enough, neither writer expressed any wish to enlighten himself or speculated that if he knew more,
his overall attitude might be different. The ignorance is given as a fact that
does not really pose either a personal or social conflict. The fact that they
as individuals don't understand homosexuality is to them neither a personal nor a social problem. In contrast, consider the following two responses
from young women in the course. Ms. B, the first student, tells of her reaction to news that two women were discovered in a room at 2 A.M. expressing their love and engaging in oral sex. She reports on what happened when
four women started discussing this event:

> We agreed that all of us would probably feel ill at first, especially
> under the conditions that it was revealed. . . . We also agreed that a
> good next move would be for the two girls to move into the same
> room. When I think about it, I realize I would never assume the
> same thing in a heterosexual relationship. . . . I also think it would
> take me a lot of time to understand and feel completely comfortable
> being close with these girls. . . . I hope as I go through college I will
> learn more about homosexuality so I can be more open minded. At
> this point, I have far too many stereotypes.

It seems as if in this instance Ms. B used the essay occasion itself to work
out a new opinion, first when she notices that she would respond differently to a heterosexual "discovery" and then when she appropriates her
sense of being "in college" to serve the need of being just as close with lesbians as with other students. Understanding is seen as part of the larger
growth process rather than an "either-I-understand-it-or-I-don't" situation.
Here now is a student who writes that she actually has begun the process
that Ms. B hopes will take place. Ms. H:

> The one thing I noticed about life on campus was the importance of
> people's sexuality in daily conversation. . . . the topic of homosexu-
> ality was never so prevalent as it is here. . . . One of my dorm
> buddies said Bloomington has the third highest percentage of gays

in the country. I was shocked!!! If I had known this before I applied, I probably would not have come here simply because of my lack of understanding. . . . I brought up the fact that I didn't like gay people . . . when I first got to campus . . . I was attacked and called closedminded and stupid. . . . I mean do *I have* to like gay people? . . . I didn't make any generalizations about them. I just didn't understand them and they scared me in a way because I used to think of them as being unstable people who have had bad times before in relationships or in life or something. . . . Anyway, I have come to know now at least a half dozen gay people and my feelings have somewhat changed. I'm not afraid of them any more . . . and they seem to lead nice quiet lives. I guess I had a lot of learning to do. I'm glad I came to Bloomington after all.

This was the only student in the class who explored her fear of homo-sexuals and gave the reason that she had heard that they led unstable and troubled lives. But she also reported that she knew from the beginning that she did not understand homosexuals, and she remarked in uncited parts of the essay that she was irritated at the hypocrisy of others who also didn't know about homosexuality. The key to her change of view, however, is not any abstract understanding but just the experience of relating to gays and lesbians. In our class, we had in a few speakers from the Gay-Lesbian Alliance in order to respond to the students' views in this set of essays, and like Ms. H, several of the women in the class sub-sequently reported that meeting gays and lesbians was the key to reduc-ing their fear and ignorance as well as to finding out the fundamentals of homosexual lifestyles. As one of the previously cited essays suggests, many students think that "performing sexual acts" is the principal be-havior of homosexuals. Social contact with them simply defeated this fantasy immediately and taught that sex for homosexuals plays more or less the same role as it does for heterosexuals.

Ms. H said that she thought that some kind of interpersonal misfor-tunes had occurred in the lives of homosexuals that had something to do with their being homosexual. By the end of the essay, she seems to have disabused herself of this idea. Nevertheless, among other women in the class, but not among men, there was a clear concern for the other circum-stances in the lives of gays and lesbians that might shed light on what, to heterosexuals, is a peculiar set of sexual desires. A good instance of this is the essay by Ms. J, who starts it off by reporting that "in the past two years, there has been an increase in the number of lesbian relationships at my high school." She discusses the situation on the volleyball team, which had at least one lesbian member, but one who caused no trouble; that is, "Here she was standing in the middle of 20 naked girls in the locker room and not once did she take a second look at any of us or make any type of advances. She was only attracted to her partner." The writer reports that she and her friend approached this young woman about her lesbianism, and found out, as a result,

> that the girl was sexually abused by her father when she was a child. Therefore she became involved in a lesbian relationship because of her father's negative influence and because of the care and love the other women showed her after the terrible experience. So my friend and I came to the conclusion that she probably would have never gotten mixed up in such relationships if she would not have had to go through what she did. She told us that she was ashamed of her decision but that she couldn't feel comfortable around males. She felt as though she was being used as her father used her. She is now going through therapy and trying to piece her life back together. My friend and I consider her a very good friend and also respect her. She taught us that most lesbian and male homosexual relationships come about because the persons involved are very confused and their emotions are easily played upon. I still feel that such relationships are wrong but hopefully we can come to understand them better.

Even though this writer implies that lesbianism is an emotional disorder, the tone of understanding and sympathy is much more characteristic of female than of male responses. Ms. J does not envision some outcome in which lesbianism is eliminated. She expresses no hostility for her friend. Her attention seems mainly to be, on the one hand, on the fact of lesbianism, and on the other, on the family situation in the girl's life that she assumed from the girl's comments to be connected with the lesbianism. It is noteworthy that Ms. J was the only student who mentioned paternal sexual abuse—incest—in any connection with this topic. Considering the matter in broader social terms, this kind of sexual abuse is common and increasingly reported. Just as lesbians often have had to suppress or deny their sexual identity, many women who were sexually abused in childhood (and in adulthood too, for that matter) have had to keep silent about their experience. Because of this suppression, they may share with lesbians a conscious fear of male violence and power, as well as a special vigilance against possible rapists.

Writers such as Adrienne Rich or Barbara Smith are at pains to distinguish their situations from both male homosexuals and female heterosexuals. Even though Ms. J wrongly assumed that the father's sexual abuse "caused" the friend's sexual preference (thus protecting her [Ms. J's] own heterosexist assumption that lesbianism had to have been caused at all), the fact that her essay brings the two issues out at once suggests (to those of us still learning about sexism) how abuse victims and lesbians are both victims of sexist ideology in a way that male homosexuals are not, though, obviously, both lesbians and gays have a great deal to fear both from collective heterosexist values and from gangs of heterosexual men. The habitual sexual abuse of daughters by their fathers (and the concealment of this practice) is probably one of the least acknowledged results of heterosexist ideology. Only an ideology supported by a masculine power structure would permit such practices to be perpetuated throughout history. Despite Ms. J's error, her essay provides an occasion to think about how sexism and heterosexism are related.

A RANGE OF VIEWPOINTS

Several students used the occasion of this essay to begin thinking about these wider differences between male and female homosexuality. The range of views here is again instructive, particularly the women's speculations, as they continue to point up the likely roots of homophobia in male sexism. Among those students who tried to compare male and female attitudes toward homosexuality—about 18% of the total—all but three (two women and one man) of them agreed that men reject male homosexuality more violently than women reject lesbianism; they also agreed that women are generally more accepting of all kinds of homosexuality. The one male student who was the exception to this pattern claimed that he and his girlfriend agreed that homophobia was stronger against members of one's own sex. One of the female students who gave this opinion wrote another essay on the same topic some weeks later, after hearing class discussions:

> Ms. W: Most of the men express sick feelings in addition to hostility toward gay men. Perhaps a reasonable explanation for this could be gender. Ever since we were young we have been establishing the values for our particular gender. It is interesting to note that girls are more likely than boys to be allowed to engage in both roles of the boy and girl. There is really no evidence of a "Tom Girl." It is easy to visualize a father becoming upset because his son plays with dolls. From the other perspective, a little girl playing baseball is not as crucial an issue.

Ms. W notes here the relatively common fact that childhood gender role socialization is more flexible for girls than for boys. She notes later in her essay that because male flight attendants are often both attractive and homosexual, it did not seem to her that homosexuality came about because they were rejected by members of the other sex. Although she admits her own seemingly spontaneous rejection of homosexuality, the bulk of Ms. W's essay is the citation of reasons why it is hard to keep an open mind on the topic. The importance of this essay, I think, is that it details all the factors—the Bible, AIDS, parents—that keep this young woman in ignorance of why she feels "very bigoted and narrow-minded." As a result of discussion, of my lectures on the topic, of her female teacher's lengthy explanation of her friendships with lesbian women, she senses that something is wrong with her attitude toward homosexuality. What she does not see is that with the acquisition of female sexuality, she came under the aegis of sexist ideology, which has made her feel that her (patriarchal) family-oriented values force her to deny the sense of flexible sex roles that she experienced in childhood. Her first essay on the topic reported that she was very close friends with a very religious young man "who never passed judgment on anyone." But when she walked the streets of Washington, D.C. with this fellow and they saw two men holding hands, and this religious friend then said, "If there is one thing I cannot stand it is faggots," she reported being unable to continue the discussion with him. She found the young man's attitude hypocritical and otherwise objectionable, yet she could not finally oppose him, because she also opposed homosexuality! She could not identify the fact that she was collaborating with his male sexism, and thus was unable to challenge this peremptory expression of bigotry by her respected male friend.

Here is an excerpt from another essay by a young woman, Ms. N, on a theme similar to Ms. W's, but the element of hypocrisy is missing, because the young man makes no religious or moral pretenses.

> I remember a conversation with a male friend who . . . sees females as physical objects, and he asked me how I viewed males thinking all females looked upon men as chunks of flesh to be in awe of. So I suggested that he try viewing women as friends first—just like he would any guy he just met, as opposed to seeing a girl in the stereotypical sexual object sort of way. This led to me asking him a question. "When you see a guy do you ever think of saying 'oh—he's nice looking' or 'I like his hair.'" Well of course this brought immediate rejection—he would never do that because that is how 'fags'" act. I told him that girls comment on other females' personal appearance without meaning anything sexual. . . . Yet my friend would not admit to even thinking that another man is nice looking or even dressed well.

Instead of ending this essay with an ideological speculation or a guess as to why her friend holds these views, Ms. N chose a much friendlier path, noting that all men weren't like this one, who was "just behaving so immaturely at times." Even though she herself cited compelling evidence for the derivation of homophobia from sexism, Ms. N did not identify either of these forms of prejudice in her essay. Among the 60 or 70 women in this class, only perhaps 6 or 8 consistently were able to identify specific behaviors as sexist. The vast majority of women thought as Ms. N did—not attempting explanation but hoping, in a sense, that the peculiar behaviors that they encountered were local and not symptomatic of a threatening situation in society at large—and this in the face of strong opinions by their outspoken female feminist teachers.

MORE COMFORTABLE?

Some students reported the familiar fact that pornographic films of lesbians making love seem erotic to men, but corresponding films of men are disgusting. This fact led to the opinion of one man that "society is more tolerant of lesbianism than of male homosexuality." Obviously, what this response to homosexuality on film actually shows is that men are sexually interested in lesbian sexuality sometimes, but that this interest is naturally translated into the principle that "society" is more tolerant. One female student did catch this fallacy. The student I cited previously, who expressed her wish that college would help change her stereotypes, also reported that "we all feel more comfortable with the idea of two men together than two women." Although this opinion was a minority one in the class (and it is certainly not true of men), her explanation was a fact that lesbian critics are at pains to emphasize: "Maybe this is because male gays have had more exposure and publicity lately than females. Lesbianism is not as often discussed or dealt with in society." This was the only reflection in the class on the relative amounts of public attention received by gay men and lesbians. Yet her observation is undoubtedly true. When Blacks began getting White attention, it was Black men who were listened to at the expense of Black women; when homosexuals began getting attention, it was the gay men sooner than the lesbians. Ms. B is trying to explain her response, correctly, I think, as having been socially conditioned by the sexist response to homosexuality. She explains, in other words, her own strong responses to lesbianism as the result of the social repression of lesbianism. She is one of the few students who was able to begin at least thinking of her private feelings as related to larger problems in society.

COERCIVE IDEOLOGY

After studying these many essays and sorting through the bewildering variety of expression and opinion, I found one simple formulation that clearly expresses the condition of homophobia as being derived from the underlying coercive ideology of male sexism. Ms. M writes, at the conclusion of a second essay of hers, on homosexuality:

> It seems like we bring up this topic all the time, but I do think this topic is gender related again. I think girls find it easier to have homosexual males as friends because they don't have to worry about getting "hit on" all the time. Guys like to get "hit on" so they don't want homosexual friends, especially not guys.

Getting hit on is slang for a relatively peremptory request or expectation of sexual activity. It strongly implies that it is just one occasion that the "hitter" is after, and that all the preliminary talk in the conversation is geared to the final aim of winding up in bed with the "object." More specifically, this means that the hitter almost certainly does not consider women (or the men) as likely partners in a relationship that includes the whole range of human exchange, but is only sweet-talking (flattering and urging) the other person into a brief sexual assignation. In this passage, Ms. M discloses what is an undoubtedly generic feeling among women—that they are eligible regularly to be asked to engage in the kind of sex that they generally don't want—transient sex, without continuation or responsibility. If they wanted it, and if they did not fear they could be coerced or raped, Ms. J would not be using the phrase *worry about* in regard to a sexual encounter. Thus, getting hit on is a common, even banally familiar gesture that is almost always a symptom of a sexist ideology. To Ms. J, having homosexual male friends means to her being able to do something really important— relating to men as friends without there also being an area of emotional and possibly physical threat in the friendship, without, that is, sex being related to power. Men, she observes, like to get hit on as well as hit themselves, which means, of course, that men with a sexist attitude attribute it to women without question, as Ms. N reported (her friend thinking that women were in awe of the physical flesh of men). Because sexism is an ideology or a cultural paradigm, men behave as if it were a structure of "how things are." Homosexuals of both genders remind them all too insistently that this is not how things are, and so they do not wish to be associated with homosexuals, "especially not guys" (that is, gay men), who, in their ideology, represent a fifth column, a group of men who inherently subvert an otherwise male privilege. What does one do to traitors? In the

United States, the penalty is death: "Line them up and shoot them." Lesbians, in addition to being suppressed just because they are women, do not require as much worry on the part of sexist men, because, in part, many heterosexual women participate in male sexist ideology, and, in part, they (lesbians) are more obviously not members of the hegemonic group to begin with.

I am writing about these topics in this way—with the purpose of sharing a lived experience—mainly in the service of the issues themselves, but also to demonstrate just how important the classroom is as a place to discover existing ideologies and as an appropriate place to change them. Both quantitative and qualitative information was necessary in these causes, and I am hoping that if we in the academy, an institution with an overwhelmingly male population, can pay more flexible attention to our own ways of doing business, our population will be vastly enriched with new colleagues from a variety of genders, freer, hopefully, of those dangerous isms and phobias.

REFERENCES

Cohn, N. (1970). *The pursuit of the millennium: Revolutionary millenarians and mystical anarchists of the Middle Ages* (rev. ed.). London: Maurice Temple Smith.

Lerner, G. (1986). *The creation of patriarchy*. Oxford: Oxford University Press.

Scheman, N. (1980). Anger and the politics of naming. In S. McConnell-Ginet et al. (Eds.), *Women and language in literature and society* (pp. 174–187). New York: Praeger.

Scheman, N. (1983). Individualism and the objects of psychology. In S. Harding and M. B. Hintikka (Eds.), *Discovering reality* (pp. 225–244). Boston: D. Reidel.

ABOUT THE AUTHOR

David Bleich teaches writing and other subjects in English, women's studies, and Jewish studies at the University of Rochester. Forthcoming from Heinemann in 1998 is *Know and Tell: Disclosure, Genre, and Membership in the Teaching of Writing and Language Use.*

CHAPTER 13

Breaking the Silence

SEXUAL PREFERENCE IN THE COMPOSITION CLASSROOM

Allison Berg, Jean Kowaleski, Caroline Le Guin,
Ellen Weinauer, and Eric A. Wolfe

Not long ago, Allison gave a copy of this essay to a colleague, who
returned it the next day with a pained expression on her face. "This
was excruciating to read," she moaned. (Not the hoped-for response.)
"It's such a teaching nightmare," she continued, "I almost couldn't bear
to keep reading." To her, the only thing more remarkable than our
collective pedagogical blunders was our willingness to publish such an
unflattering description of them.

Looking back on this essay, we see it as the product of a particular
moment when the issue of sexual orientation as a pedagogical concern
was relatively new to the academy, as were we. The pedagogical
decisions we made in 1987–1988 certainly reflect the inexperience of
beginning teachers, but they also reflect the lack of institutional context
for addressing sexuality in the classroom. Since 1989, when this essay
was written, so much excellent scholarship has appeared—on the politics
of coming out in the classroom, on making space for lesbian and gay
student voices, on confronting the heterosexism of the academy and the
larger culture—that our early attempts to broach this topic seem, in
retrospect, woefully uninformed.

At the same time, there is still relatively little written on the role of
the straight teacher in gay/lesbian/bisexual studies, though one might
find helpful analogues in recent scholarship (by Toni Morrison and

others) that asserts the necessity of interrogating Whiteness as a racial identity. We still believe that the dialogue begun in the late 1980s deserves more voices. The importance, and the risk, of "breaking the silence" has become even more apparent to us as we have left the relative safety of graduate school to begin teaching careers at a private high school in Michigan, large state universities in Mississippi, a community college in Oregon, and a liberal arts college in Maryland, where we struggle to find ways to continue the conversation begun here.

In a session titled "Writing, Teaching, and the Politics of Sexual Preference" at the 1989 Conference on College Composition and Communication in Seattle, Paul Puccio argued for the importance of breaking the silence surrounding the issue of sexual preference. Though many composition classrooms are increasingly devoted to examining the ways in which social membership can shape and construct our identity, we as teachers tend to consider that membership as limited to gender, race/ethnicity, and socioeconomic class. We overlook sexual preference, and, in so doing, replicate a societal and institutional silence that is destructive to ourselves and to our students. As Puccio indicated, this situation "will never change unless there is more of a 'coming out'—a coming out not only of lesbian and gay academics but also a coming out of the subject itself." Implicit in Puccio's statement is the suggestion that dealing with gay and lesbian issues, and confronting homophobia in the classroom, must be more than a lesbian or gay teacher's concern. This coming out must involve many voices—those of gay, lesbian, and straight academics, teachers, and students. But we must also recognize that each of us will face the responsibility for breaking the silence in different ways, confront different problems, and find different solutions. Our goal in this essay is to explore our own experiences as straight teachers introducing sexual preference into a first-year writing course at Indiana University. Through this exploration, we carry on a dialogue with other voices working to break the silence.

At the conference session mentioned above, we presented papers that grew out of our teaching experience, and this panel was our first substantial entry into just such a dialogue. Our experience as the straight members of a mixed gay and straight panel addressing a largely lesbian and gay audience forced us to reexamine our teaching, to question the values and assumptions implicit in our classrooms, and to recognize the ramifications of the ways that we had approached the topic of sexual preference as teachers. The papers we gave at the conference were largely scholarly; we examined excerpts from our students' writing and attempted to account for and categorize their responses, which ranged from expressions of disgust to calls for violence. With hindsight, it seems clear that in our conference papers we approached the issue first as scholars, and only second-arily as teachers. By describing the patterns we saw in our students' writing—in effect viewing our students' virulent homophobia as a phenomenon to analyze—we were distancing ourselves from what was perhaps too painfully obvious: We had raised an issue that we as teachers were unprepared to deal with. Thus, our papers focused on how students responded to the topic of sexual preference and omitted the ways in which we, as teachers, approached the topic. Significantly, the responses to our panel centered on the dynamics of our classrooms and *not* on our interpretations of student writing. This response forced us to reassess critically our practice as teachers addressing the topic of sexual preference. From this reassessment comes the newfound understanding that as we teach we must not exempt ourselves from the process of learning about this issue, or fail to recognize that we are laboring under the same sorts of silences that our students experience—silences that are directly reinforced by the profession in which we work. Given these silences, it is important to provide some context for our own decision to broach this topic. During the 1987–88 academic year, six Indiana University graduate students—Allison Berg, Chris Iwanicki, Jean Kowaleski, Caroline Le Guin, Ellen Weinauer, and Eric Wolfe—served as teaching assistants for Professor David Bleich's first-year composition course, Studying One's Own Language. This two-semester course met three times a week: once a week in general lectures that all 144 students attended, and twice a week in discussion sections led by us, the teaching assistants. During the first semester of the course, both students and instructors wrote biweekly, in-class essays in which we described a remembered conversation dealing with the current topic of discussion: family, gender, education, class, race, or sexual preference. The 2nd semester brought literature into the course, and the biweekly essays were written as responses to literary texts corresponding to the same general topics that structured the first semester. Throughout the year, these "lecture essays," copied and distributed to class members, became the text for class discussion and the basis for further analytical writing. Ultimately, the aim of the course was to understand the ways in which our language situates us in terms of social group membership and reveals and perpetuates ideological values.

In conceiving of the course, we—David Bleich as well as the associate instructors—participated in the same kind of silencing that Paul Puccio argued against. We did not originally include sexual preference as a topic for the course; it came as a kind of afterthought. When the syllabus was put together in the fall, the final few weeks were left open, and it was only as the semester moved toward its end and the necessity of settling on a sixth topic became pressing that we decided definitely to include sexual preference. Our decision was based in part on our observation that when students discussed the other topics of the course, they seemed to have no language with which to discuss sexuality. Our goal was to elicit concrete examples of how students talked about homosexuality; through discussion and analysis of students' everyday language, we hoped to begin unravelling the complex power dynamics inherent in sexual and social relations, and to explore the connections between sexual preference and the other topics of the course. Because the topic was not listed on the syllabus at the beginning of the course, however, students no doubt got the message that the issue was a kind of afterthought, and inferred, therefore, that sexual preference was not a significant social issue, or, at least, that it was less significant than the earlier topics. This may have allowed our students to believe that homophobic attitudes would be sanctioned.

The assignment followed a format similar to all the previous lecture essays, and read:

> Describe a conversation with someone either of your own or another sexual preference (lesbian, male homosexual, bisexual, asexual, heterosexual) on the issue of homosexuality. Give as many salient details as you can about this conversation, particularly how attitudes about homosexuality were expressed.

We tried to design the assignment in such a way that no writers would need to risk identifying their own sexuality. Yet, we realize, in retrospect, despite this attempt to attend to the needs of gay and lesbian students, our question was, first, speaking primarily to our heterosexual students and, second, allowing students to be homophobic. For gay and lesbian students, the question must have seemed horribly ironic, because the phrase *attitudes toward homosexuality* implies that the expected audience is clearly heterosexual; our question presents homosexuality as something "other," something that the writer should have an attitude "toward." For a gay or lesbian student to attempt seriously to answer the question in the terms we provided would call for a level of personal disconnectedness inimical to the goals of the course. Indeed, the one student who had already come out to his class could only comment that the question did not fit his perspective.

The phrasing of the question also allowed our heterosexual students to remain disengaged, uninvolved; because we asked them to discuss only homosexuality, our heterosexual students could treat sexual preference as an issue that applied to *others,* and not to themselves. In other words, the question invited them to respond with no sense of personal stake because they were not asked to reflect on their own sexuality, and the degree to which it represented a choice. In contrast, the essay question on the topic of race asked students to describe a time when they were made aware of their *own* race or ethnicity; thus, it tried to interrupt the common white tendency to think that only people of color have a racial membership. One result of asking students to focus on homosexuality, then, was that we supplied a means for our straight students to keep the topic on a level safely outside of themselves. From the beginning, then, we set terms that would allow for homophobic student responses: We brought in the topic of sexual preference too late, we spoke not to lesbian and gay but to straight students, and we let those straight students remain personally distanced from the topic itself.

Many of our students responded in kind. Their responses ranged from violence to disgust (often linked with violence) to "it's OK as long as they stay away from me" to "I never think about it and I don't want to." Coupled with this was an assumption of consensus; despite the fact that students knew they would share their writing with peers and teachers, many seemed to feel that it would be acceptable to advocate "shooting all the gays." This perceived consensus prevailed even in the responses of students who knew one of their classmates was gay. In part because we were not prepared for them, we allowed students' homophobic responses—and our indignation at these responses—to dictate our teaching of the issue.

Since this topic came at the very end of the first semester, the first opportunity that we had to deal with our students' essays was in the first class meeting of the second semester, a general lecture. During this lecture, Bleich, who has a rather confrontational teaching style, was able to use the lecture format and his own strong personality to give voice to his anger and, by extension, ours. In this extraordinary lecture, he confronted students directly with his feelings about the violent homophobia expressed in their writing and told them, essentially, that such expressions amounted to fascism, were unacceptable, and that those who voiced such attitudes must be responsible for the implications of what they chose to say.

All of us felt that Bleich's confrontation was important—indeed, necessary. In many ways, in fact, Bleich simply brought to the surface the tensions that our question and student responses to it had engendered. The expression of his—and our—anger and the impassioned denunciation of student attitudes came, however, at a price: the creation of a classroom atmosphere fraught with conflict and alienation. Many students felt betrayed by and angry toward Bleich, believing that he had asked for their honesty and then condemned them. Some students were angry at other students, feeling that they all had to suffer as a result of the more overtly homophobic members of the class. We were involved in these oppositional tensions as well: We were Bleich's surrogates, in part, and also the conduits through which student-student conflict could flow. Further, we were personally angry, disturbed by the students' homophobia. The classroom had thus become completely polarized: It was now a tangle of "us versus them" relationships.

The polarization of the classroom further deflected our attention away from the topic of sexual preference. Our students' emotional responses to Bleich's lecture became primary: Was he being unfair? Was he taking away their right to express their opinion? We needed to attend to those responses to some degree; but in allowing them to dominate the classroom dialogue, we perhaps collaborated with our students' unwillingness to engage the topic itself. In addition, since many students felt that Bleich was taking away their right to express their "true" feelings, they responded by claiming their homophobia even more strongly. For many students, it became an issue of free speech and free thought. Ultimately, then, the polarized classroom dynamic perpetuated the already developing focus on homophobia.

We seemed to be caught in a vicious circle. Our question engendered (or at least did not do enough to prevent) homophobic responses; our opposition to those responses only consolidated students in their position and kept us on the topic of homophobia. Clearly, teaching in terms of homophobia has problematic ramifications: It reinforces social sanctions against homosexuality by establishing heterosexuality as the standard from which homosexuality is "judged." Perhaps even more important, it silences gay and lesbian students. Paradoxically, by trying to break the silence surrounding issues of sexual preference, we were reinforcing it for our gay and lesbian students, rendering them voiceless, recreating their sense of invisibility, and heightening the risks of coming out. In addition, we were cutting ourselves off from the possibility of hearing them and learning from their perspectives.

We see now that only when we moved toward talking about sexual preference in concrete terms—resisting abstract and distanced statements about "homosexuality"—did we shift from this destructive focus on homophobia. We realized early on that our students had a propensity to objectify sexual preference in their lecture essays: Few students talked about gay or lesbian people they knew personally; many students removed themselves completely from the issue by recounting conversations they had only "overheard"; and few, if any, depicted heterosexuality itself as a choice. At the beginning, we added to this tendency toward abstraction by not talking about these essays in the same ways that we had discussed students' previous writing. Whereas we usually selected a single essay to distribute to the students, so we could focus on specific language features and patterns, this time—in an attempt to impress students with the enormity of their own homophobia—we excerpted bits and pieces from several essays, thus taking them out of context and distancing the "language of homophobia" from the writers themselves.

Yet we did try several strategies that we hoped would make the issue more concrete. First, in an attempt to give students a context in which to explore emotionally authentic ways of talking about sexuality—whether homosexual, bisexual, or heterosexual—we distributed Audre Lorde's love poem "On a Night of the Full Moon" to our students. We did not, however, reveal the author. We assumed that most students would read the poem as a heterosexual love poem and that once we had discussed the issues it brought out—emotional need, intimacy, and trust, as well as physical eroticism—we might reveal who the author was and talk about heterosexuality and homosexuality in more concrete and human dimensions. Yet even before students learned that the poem was a lesbian love poem, many of them found its explicit eroticism disturbing and "disgusting," once again demonstrating the difficulty they had in finding an authentic language for sexual experience. The usefulness of our approach was further limited by the element of trickery implicit in our lesson plan, which now seems a clear reflection of our own discomfort with this issue. Using the poem anonymously allowed us to assume a kind of knowledge that set us apart from our students, rather than giving them the message that we too were engaged in the struggle to think about sexual preference in a social context, to deal with homophobia, and to find a more human language for sexuality.

Of course, the move to bring gay and lesbian literature into the classroom could have been very useful. Our experiences have taught us that we, as straight teachers, need to listen to different voices so that we can discuss gay and lesbian issues from as informed a perspective as possible; similarly, we need to provide our students with the opportunity to hear voices other than heterosexual ones. Ideally, we would hear from gay and lesbian students in the classroom; but although we must work to make our classrooms safer spaces for coming out, the number of gay and lesbian students who will come out to their classmates is most likely small, particularly when the teacher is straight and while the culture remains heterosexist. Texts by gay and lesbian writers can provide some new voices and new angles of vision. Yet the teaching potential of gay and lesbian writings will be limited as long as we read them only in relation to gay and lesbian issues; using texts in this way will only enhance our students' perception that gay and lesbian people are defined primarily in terms of their sexual preference and so can only speak on this, "their" issue.

The most successful approach we took in concretizing the topic was to invite a woman from the Gay and Lesbian Alliance's Speaker's Bureau to come to our classes. The speaker, a senior at Indiana University, talked a little about homosexuality and homophobia in general, and then specifically about her own life experiences—coming out, dealing with her family, her relationships. She devoted the rest of the time to answering questions. The responses that we heard from our students following this session were uniformly positive. Our heterosexual students seemed relieved to meet, albeit in a controlled environment, a lesbian student, and to realize that a gay person could be a perfectly "ordinary" and likable human being. It was at this point that previously very homophobic students began saying that "gays are people too." Though such a position is a long way from an understanding of the systematic and institutionalized oppression of gays and lesbians (not to mention a recognition of their unique life experiences and culture), it was an important and positive first step for many of our students, and our first step toward countering the abstraction that we, as well as our students, fell prey to. Perhaps, too, for our gay and lesbian students, this experience provided a positive role model, someone who was open about and proud of her sexual preference. Yet straight teachers who invite gay and lesbian speakers to their classes must do so not in order to foist responsibility onto the shoulders of gays and lesbians (i.e., it's your problem, not mine), but rather as a way of engaging other voices in their attempts to raise the issue of sexual preference.

Overall, we worked to counter the polarization and abstraction that we faced—and to a degree recreated—in our classrooms by searching for ways to bring in lesbian and gay voices and break the silence that surrounds them. The risk involved here is that focusing exclusively on gay and lesbian voices allows straight students and teachers to consider themselves exempt from the issue of sexual preference. It was perhaps all too easy for us as straight teachers to perpetuate the normative silence that surrounds heterosexuality, and thereby to protect it from critique and questioning. Although we sought ways to encourage a concrete human understanding of "homosexuality" by inviting our students and ourselves to learn from our own language use, from gay and lesbian texts, and from a lesbian speaker, we missed one immediate and concrete means of understanding sexual preference—our own and the majority of our students' choice of heterosexuality. We never really put ourselves as teachers in a position where our own sexual preference would be subject to questioning, nor did we invite heterosexual students to do the same for themselves.

In retrospect, it is possible to see what we might have done to begin problematizing heterosexuality. Certainly, the whole issue of "coming out," of announcing one's sexual orientation, might be made a topic of class discussion. When students assume, as in our case they did, that their teacher is heterosexual, that teacher might ask students what it would mean to them if she were lesbian, and why heterosexuals in general tend to assume other people are straight until proven otherwise. We could then begin to explore the ways heterosexuality is made to seem inevitable, a given.

It is telling that this most immediate way of teaching about sexual preference—problematizing our own heterosexuality—didn't become clear to us until we had the opportunity to enter into a dialogue with gay and lesbian teachers at the Conference on College Composition and Communication (CCCC) panel session, mentioned at the beginning of this essay. This was the first time any of us had been aware of being in a sexual minority in a professional setting, and the experience forced us to recognize the importance of acknowledging our sexual preference when dealing with this issue. At the same time, the conference created opportunities for gay and straight teachers to talk with each other and exchange perspectives about our classrooms and teaching methods. Ultimately, this coming together was an important learning experience, without which our insights would have remained limited.

In spite of all the problems we faced, then, raising the issue of sexual preference provided an important learning experience for us as teachers as well as for our students. The slow process of unlearning heterosexist assumptions and fears is one in which we as teachers participated and in which we are still engaged. Our classroom experience was a first step, an initial breaking of the silence that surrounds sexual preference and perpetuates institutional and social homophobia. Our experience at CCCC was another step for us, one that made us talk about and ultimately reexamine our teaching. Now that we've started talking, we need to keep talking, to straight teachers, to lesbian and gay teachers, above all to our students. We need to continue the dialogue into which we have entered, to continue making this issue speakable in our professional lives as well as in our classroom.

ABOUT THE AUTHORS

Allison Berg is an assistant professor of English at St. Mary's College of Maryland, where she teaches American literature, composition, and women's studies. She has published essays on William Faulkner, Pauline Hopkins, and Marita Bonner and is currently finishing a book-length project on representations of race and maternity in U.S. fiction.

Jean Kowaleski recently completed her PhD in English at Indiana University and is now teaching English literature and composition at Detroit County Day School, an independent high school in Beverly Hills, Michigan.

Caroline Le Guin teaches composition and literature at Blue Mountain Community College in Pendleton, Oregon. There, when she is not teaching the displaced timber workers, teen mothers, grandmothers, cowboys, cowgirls, and occasional budding feminists who pass through her classes to find their own voices in writing, she raises chickens.

Ellen Weinauer is an assistant professor of English at the University of Southern Mississippi, where she teaches courses in early American literature and gender studies. She is completing a book on antebellum property law and American fiction.

Eric A. Wolfe currently teaches American literature and culture, critical theory, and composition at the University of Mississippi. He is at work on a book titled *The Lure of the Voice: Constituting the National Subject in the Early United States.*

CHAPTER 14

A Discourse on the Care and Handling
of Feminist Administrators

Lynette Carpenter

The thinking that went into this article was the crystallization of what I had learned from my years as a women's studies administrator, living in the war zone between two enemy camps and trying to negotiate with both. It began as a response to a Modern Language Association Women's Caucus session in which a feminist administrator was attacked in a way that made me uncomfortable. The attacker is herself an administrator now, and I suspect that she might hold different views from those that she held then. What goes around comes around.

I wrote the article almost 10 years ago now. Often, that kind of distance makes rereading painful. Yet I remember quite well what I wrote then, and 10 more years of experience in universities have done nothing to alter my views. Over the years, I've had many requests for the article from beleaguered women administrators and the women who love and support them. I doubt that it can "stop one heart from breaking," but if it makes people think, makes women administrators feel better understood, and makes everybody laugh, I'm content.

Recently, I had occasion to be on the job market. (Yes, Gentle but Suspicious Reader, behind these words lies a story, but not the one I am concerned with here.) As my stack of rejection letters for teaching jobs overflowed the corner to which they had been consigned and threatened to take over my study, I took drastic action: I began to apply for administrative positions. After 7 years of administration in one of the largest women's studies programs in the country, I was eminently qualified for a host of what are termed "midlevel" administrative positions. My luck began to change. But wait.

One day I was informed that I had survived the first cut for an associate vice presidency at a large urban institution. A friend of mine tried to explain to me, over long distance, why I should want this job. "I know you don't like the city," he said, "but in this kind of job you will travel a lot." From across the room, I could feel the hackles rising on my only-child cat. "I know you don't like the city," he said, "but you can stay there a year or two, and move on." *Move again in a year or two?* My feline housemate glared at me; we are both too old for this. "Anyway," he said, "it's a great job to move up from." Ah, there's the rub. Move up to what? Did I really want to be a vice president? A president? To my mother, who lives in the city in question, I said, "If I moved up to any of these positions, I would earn lots of money, work very hard, travel a good deal, compromise my principles at every turn, and lie awake at night worrying about these compromises. And everyone would hate me." I do mean everyone; my cat, by this time, would have moved in with the neighbors.

I wish to address something that has happened to the women's liberation movement on college and university campuses, where many movement leaders, no doubt to their astonishment and ours, have become administrators—not just assistant and associate deans, but department heads, deans, and occasionally, vice provosts, provosts, and presidents. What *are* they doing there?

I am going to begin with an observation that has probably occurred to most of you: Most of them are not in it, first and foremost, for the money. Nor are they, if they are true feminists, likely to be in it for the heady sense of power, the glamour and prestige, the expansion of their suit wardrobe, or the endless parade of lunches at the faculty club. Now, each and all of these may play some role in their decision to take on administration; a woman with two children in a private school, a father in a nursing home, or merely a vision of a comfortable retirement may well consider trading her faculty salary for an administrative one. And there are other factors I haven't mentioned, the most likely of which are faculty burnout and departmental infighting. But I would still contend that most feminists take on administration primarily for the purest of motives: They believe that they can make a difference. They want to make the institution more humane, more responsive, more effective, more feminist. And they believe that they can push it, or pull it, or drag it in the direction in which they want it to go.

Unfortunately, for all their efforts, feminist administrators, with no exceptions I can think of, remain an embattled minority functioning within

an essentially patriarchal system. Therefore, they are asked to compromise
their feminist principles every day. To adhere unswervingly to those principles is to announce one's imminent departure from the administrative
"team." So what's a feminist to do? Those who last out the week are the
ones who learn to pick their battles, to concede defeat and move one, to
weigh their defeats against their victories and assess whether the price they
have paid is too dear. Should they resign over the hiring of another man in
an all-male department or stay on to safeguard funding for the women's
center? Should they resign over the nonpromotion of a women's studies
scholar or stay on to prevent the consolidation of women's and men's athletics? Should they depart when the administration resolves to fight a sexual
harassment suit, or should they stay on in order to provide the plaintiff
with the kind of inside information and advice to which the defense has
access?

These are difficult questions, and most of us would not like to be called
upon to answer them. Most of us prefer to opt out of such decisions. We
are uncomfortable with, if not downright hostile to, compromise, and especially the kind of daily, hourly compromise required of an administrator. In the best of all possible worlds, the feminist administrator would
resign in any of these cases, found her own university by a consensus decision of her feminist educational cooperative, and we would all go and
teach there—and be paid enough to keep our children in private schools,
our father in a nursing home, and our cats in kitty litter and caviar. But
this scenario is not a likely prospect for most of us. Most of us will spend
our professional careers working in patriarchal institutions—institutions
that will not change unless we help to educate our students to expect and
then demand something better, and then provide both the faculty and the
administrative leadership necessary to respond to that demand.

BREAK RANKS?

While we are waiting for that change to take place, we have some choices
to make. As individual feminist educators, we can choose to remain in the
faculty ranks, where we are most directly involved in the educational process, and where we are called upon to make fewer compromises. Or we
can choose to become administrators in the hope that, at best, we can
effect significant and structural change and, at worst, influence small-scale
budgetary and policy decisions and represent a feminist viewpoint in policy
debates; in exchange, we agree to pay the price of compromise. If we choose
to remain faculty members, we have other choices. We can choose to support those of our feminist colleagues who make the choice we didn't make,

or choose not to. That is, we can choose to accept the conditions of compromise under which they serve as administrators, or we can hold them strictly to feminist principles they cannot hope to meet. The implication of the latter course is clear: We prefer to work with an administration devoid of feminists and feminist principles.

As someone who has chosen the path of lesser resistance, as someone who does not aspire to be a dean, provost, or president, and as someone who has benefited greatly from a feminist presence in the administration at my institution, I urge that unless we want to give the game back to the old boys and live with the consequences, and unless we are willing to give up our own research and teaching, not to mention our scruples and our summer vacations, we must support feminist administrators on our campuses.

But I do! some of you are saying; I took one to lunch only last month! Or you are saying, this woman is nuts if she thinks I'm going to support every decision our affirmative action director makes. So let me clarify what I mean by support.

I do not mean that we should agree with every decision an administrator makes just because she's a feminist. We have a responsibility as feminist faculty to make our opinions heard, and we have a special responsibility to do so where feminist administrators are concerned. Depending on the circumstances, we may wish to voice strong disagreement. At the same time, the divisiveness of bitter public disagreement only serves interests foreign to our own, and undercuts the position not only of an individual feminist administrator but often of all feminist administrators. We need to recognize that some disagreement is inevitable. We need to be willing to understand that decisions are made within contexts of which we may be inadequately informed, and that although a willingness to listen may lead to a more thorough understanding, it may not do so in circumstances of confidentiality. We need to be willing to extend some trust that feminists for whom we have regard are doing the best that they can do within the constraints imposed upon them. And we need to allow them a margin for error. Sometimes they will be wrong. But then, sometimes, so will we.

LOOKS LIKE A JOB FOR . . .

Supporting a feminist administrator also involves some understanding of other constraints imposed by the rigid hierarchical structure of the institution. In my experience, feminist administrators are often expected to solve every problem related to women and minorities on campus, whether it falls within their purview or not. Have you a worthy returning woman student who has been unable to obtain financial aid? A dean who has refused to increase the budget for Black studies? An international student whose country has had a revolution and whose visa expires in 6 days? A flood in the women's locker room? A merit dispute with a department head who has never heard of the National Women's Studies Association? A shortfall in the women's studies budget? Inadequate nighttime security in the area of the women's dorms? Call in Our Woman in the Administration; surely *she* can do *something*. If she is a bright woman who has figured out how to do what her male colleagues do—circumvent the hierarchy—frequently she can. But frequently, she can't. The last miracle she worked was getting herself into her present elevated position. You may have to settle for information, such as the name of the person you should have contacted to begin with, and advice.

What most concerns me is a tendency to punish disagreement or inaction with silence. When a feminist administrator is cut off from the rest of the feminist academic community, both parties suffer. The administrator is left without guidance and without the base of support that strengthens her position in policy debates. The feminist academic community is deprived of a valuable resource, as well as of a source of information. Meanwhile, the administrator wonders why she is there, what she is doing; she envisions all her accumulated earnings going toward an early funeral, which feminists will picket and other administrators boycott.

For many if not most administrators, feminist and nonfeminist alike, the realities of administration are disheartening. Real change is by no means as easy to achieve from the inside as it appeared to be from the outside. The university is a leviathan that swims in accustomed currents, a feminist administrator merely a single mutation, the effects of which may take years if not centuries to become visible. Small but important achievements are often more visible to others than to the administrator herself. Of some accomplishments to her credit, she is not even aware; after awhile, the right decisions begin to be made even when she is not present—on a day when her daughter is sick or her son is in a school concert. The men who make the decision have heard her voice so often that they hear it now, even when she is not there, and they allow her voice to persuade them. Meanwhile, she knows her name is on lists; her services are in demand. She serves on the YWCA board. She chairs a community task force on teen pregnancy. She judges the local newspaper's "Woman of the Year" contest. And she is the administration's token woman—on committees X, Y, and Z, at the head table of the annual awards banquet, and in the institution's publicity photographs. But is she contributing to the real change she set out to instigate? She would ask a psychotherapist, but she doesn't have time.

We, who are like her but not like her, owe her a great deal. We owe her for the many small changes in our work lives and work environments, many of them changes we will never know she had a hand in creating. And we owe her for the sacrifices she has made in pursuit of that larger change that is our common goal.

ABOUT THE AUTHOR

Lynette Carpenter, an associate professor of English at Ohio Wesleyan University, is still in recovery from 7 years as a women's studies administrator. Part of her therapy is to write the Cat Caliban mystery novels under the pen name of D. B. Borton. She has published critical essays on literature and film, and has written for *Ms.* magazine. To practice humility, she studies pottery and aikido, a Japanese martial art.

CHAPTER 15

The Hand and the Hammer

A Brief Critique of the Overhead Projector

Eloise Knowlton

Time rolls on. In the years since writing "The Hand and the Hammer,"
I have regularly lectured to large groups of students in dauntingly
immense halls using, precisely, an overhead projector. Years of practice
have somewhat altered my theory. I stand by the dynamics sketched in
the article below, but I am no longer so strongly convinced that they
don't ultimately work to the feminist teacher's advantage in one important respect: the dissolution of the body. My students, dominated as
they are by their eyes, preoccupied with their own and others' appear-
ances, caught up in the ultimately videocentric economy of the visual,
are, I begin to believe, set free into a different, and not entirely Pla-
tonic, space of the visual. No longer distracted by this or that seen
detail, they can focus their gaze (and it is also the Gaze) on an idea
rather than a woman (me). Although I maintain my suspicion of source-
less Knowledge, I've come to appreciate the leveling that occurs between me and my students when the focus moves to the light show.
Undertaking this essay in a fervor of annoyance, I failed to pay enough
attention to one condition of the overhead's space: that my students
and I are in the dark, together. Freed from seeing that it is me (the
woman, the grader, the authority figure, the professor, the ersatz mom,
the older sister, the intellectual, the punisher, the pedagogue), they, I
think, begin to listen.

Things which are ready-to-hand and used for the body—like gloves, for example, which are to move with the hands—must be given directionality towards right and left. A craftsman's tools, however, which are held in the hand and are moved with it, do not share the hand's specifically "manual" movements. So although hammers are handled just as much with the hand as gloves are, there are no right- or left-handed hammers.
—Martin Heidegger, *Being and Time* (1962, p. 109)

If critical theory has done anything for us in the past 20 years, it has made us aware of the ways in which, in our using signs, signs equally use us. It is cause for deep concern that we as teachers can find ourselves in complex and subtle ways continuing rather than displacing the signifying practices of sexism, racism, classism, heterosexism, and authoritarianism. In their social configuration, and in their instability, signs do their own work, apart from our good or ill will.

Even before what is now called critical theory, even before we discovered that Europe had gone on thinking and writing without us, new critical formalism taught us that the *form* of the statement is inextricably central to the *content* of it: that *what* we say is aided or diminished by *how* we say it. Critical theory strengthens this: The means of a message are not merely an ornament to meaning, a secondary corroboration of the matter, but actually constitutive of it. To shout angrily, and with raised fist, "I love you!" is, especially in this age of the hegemony of sarcasm, to see the sign system of the word quickly overcome by the sign system of the raised fist. Too often, we as teachers mix our messages in precisely this way. Our words say one thing; our actions (and words, too: How different are these?) framed in a certain context can only signify something quite different. All of this places increasing pressure on those signifying practices that the *means* of teaching employ. The manifest content of the course (French, calculus, social studies) can be seen to cloak another and just as real set of lessons that pedagogical practices themselves convey: lessons in power and authority, lessons in order and disorder, lessons in what counts as knowledge, who counts as a source of knowing, what is thinking—in short, what we might call the epistemological underpinnings of the lived experience of teaching and learning. None of this is any news: A certain liberal concern for the implicit messages of classroom practice is so well accepted as to be almost de rigueur; this is the fashion that assures us that we are not fascist. We do our best to sit in circles, decentering the implicit messages of teacher as sole knower and controller. When we can, we avoid lecturing and opt instead for peer review and group work in an effort to suggest alternate validations of knowledge and to deemphasize individual competition. Learning, we try by these means implicitly to convey, is not solitary, not monologic, not simple-minded containment and regurgitation, not a means to avoid punishment or to gain power over others.

To what extent these efforts in themselves cloak the cynical possibility that this is precisely what learning may indeed be largely about (at least right now, in this culture) is a thought we would rather not entertain. It is unsettling to suppose that despite our most sincere efforts not to capitulate to what we see as the abuses of a certain power structure (the ordering of the classroom, the institution of the "school"), we may yet convey what is still most urgent for our students to know: how to shut up, how to obey, how not to get in trouble. Are these not indeed the skills they will find most useful? Is there anything else to be read in the teacher-student dynamic other than confrontation? Are we, as some would suggest, best advised to accept and foreground overtly a relation accepted intrinsically as conflict (see Strickland, 1990)?

Or, conversely, we might argue, what is so *bad* about order, and specifically that kind of order? Isn't there a strong romantic idealist fantasy at work in our saying that we can or ought to be embarrassed by our practices of constraint? Or that we could escape *all* orderings? "The worst thing we can do is pretend we don't have power," writes Mary Rose O'Reilly (1989, p. 146).

If we are to resist either cynic's voice—already too ready to gloss our practices, our results, even our best intentions—we must trust not only to a rather less rigidly Darwinist sense of what counts as and leads to "success," but to the very baselessness of the signifying structure. Surely we need not choose between the leftist's admission to the inevitability of class(room) conflict, nor the rightist's wholesale embracing of the project of an authoritarian order (two options by the way, with an eerie resemblance). To accept the arbitrary (the changeable) in language is to find a place to resist its differential (conservative) workings. All is written, but in sand, not in stone. Alternative practices in the classroom can implicitly teach an expectation of a different sort of order, and a different sense of what counts as order, while admitting that *some* order, some grammar, will exert its dynamic on the practices of any group. And thus a continued revision of the practices of the classroom can take place: an attempt at resistance through trying somehow to notice the way our hands conform to the shape of our tools.

By way of qualification, I add that the call for revision here is no intended repetition of the humanist narrative of authorial control of signification, in this case of author/teacher on text/class. By altering classroom semiotics, the altered dynamic itself effects the revision, and the revision of the position and place of the instructor as well as that of the students. The anthology of teacher–student interactions mimics that of reader and text; but we are simply not in a place to say who does what to whom when all are equally positioned in discourse. In the same way that it is dizzyingly difficult to undertake to fix or trace the precise contribution of one morpheme in one word in one phrase in one context to what we call "meaning," it is equally dizzying to try to predict what one alteration of classroom practice might ultimately mean. But just as texts are in constant revision, so too are classes, students, teachers, and institutions, and to engage that mutability is precisely the stuff of reading, of teaching, and this, it seems to me, cannot be obviated or ignored. But I have vamped long enough. Here then, my critique, offered as one example—there might have been many others, simpler or more complex—of reading classroom grammar by way of one element within it: the overhead projector.

THE SCENE OF THE OVERHEAD PROJECTOR

What is the scene of the overhead projector? It is a room, dark, or at least darkened, with a single illuminated square, a focal point toward which all gazes orient themselves. A voice, attached to a body less visible than what full light might afford, glosses what an invisible hand (or a hand visible only as shadow) writes on a transparency. The writing is enlarged, diffused, bodiless as all writing. The instructor stands to the side. In this restaging of Plato's cave, the clear focus of attention is on the play of light and dark.

The semiotics of this scene play themselves out according to the very persuasive dichotomy of light and dark: Knowledge (or simply the aim of student desire) is literally enlightenment; they sit in the gloom of ignorance. Their task is to transfer into their own dark script the diaphanous message *above* them (the up/down dynamic fits in nicely too). In its direct quotation of television, the overhead projector positions its viewers as viewers, passive and somehow removed, caught up in a dominance of the scopic over the aural, even as the spoken word only glosses the more manifest written word before them.[1] It is the visuals that count here, with all the masculinist implications of both passivity and control that the visual implies. Knowledge becomes the object of a gaze, in the pejorative Sartrean sense.

The ultimately neoplatonic light/dark binarism is enhanced by the one/many split between mass of students and singular illumined visual. Singularity's implication of identity, selfhood, and efficient control is associated in rather a divine way with the semiotics of the enlightened. On the one hand is knowledge, which is here divine clarity itself; on the other, the muddied and muddled plurality of students—diverse, teeming, disordered and, by implication of the inefficiency of the many, disempowered.

They sit, at least in theory, silently: This is a visual space, and the aurality of even the teacher's voice is on the margin.

And so is the teacher herself. One of the most devastating repercussions of the semiotics of the overhead is the way in which it dispenses with the teacher, rids her of her body and the knowledge of its source. What counts as important exists in a way made far more credible (in the logic of this neoplatonism) by the expunging of physical materiality. Female instructors, especially, can gain important points in credibility if they, as women who are semiotically bound to the body, can perform this miraculous transformation, from physical, aural, and visual presence, to bodiless commentator on a distanced central concern.

A woman with an overhead projector is a man: objective, rational, disassociated from the physical[2]; the fitting hierarchical role of god is played aptly by the illuminated text for which s/he serves as exegetist. This sex change is no real threat to this order: The presence of the central light—the conveyer of knowledge—ensures the stability of the hierarchy. As long as the positions of god and man are filled, the system is intact. And seeking their natural level underneath, are, of course, woman and nature.

Even as the instructor is both marginalized and masculinized, the students are both feminized and naturalized, made part of a dark, fecund, teeming plurality, a dangerously untutored mass, subjects of an initiation into a knowledge system that relegates them to the outside. In this signifying system, students, like women, count as untamed nature: a tribe to be colonized, a jungle to be mapped. I remember my sixth-grade teacher (a man, as it happens) calling out above the din, "It sounds like feeding time at the zoo in here." That a discourse of the animal (physicality) and of the wild (a place outside language) circulates widely among students as a privileged term (party animal, animal house) underscores the way in which they have learned their place and are willing to use it as a form of resistance, albeit merely oppositional. They can read the writing on the wall.[3]

With all positions in the system filled, learning can happen. Information, delivered in a bodiless state, is not qualified by the intervention of a medium, such as a person, who would be expected to have a particular limited "perspective" on the message, a limitation that would qualify its credibility. The language of the overhead is a transparent one and, again like god, encompasses all perspectives. Indeed, the flatness of the presentation—its lack of perspective or three-dimensionality—eschews any single focal point.[4] By its very indifference to where the viewer is, the overhead image imparts a bland impartiality, a disinterestedness which, at least since Matthew Arnold, has been the hallmark of objective truth.

In its strict focus, in its demonstration of the chiaroscuro binaries of this mode of signification, there is much that can, in the name of efficiency, be avoided. I have seen teachers hide from their students, and their students' questions, in the shadow of the projector. For the overhead has a logic of its own and a time of its own. It has a crank. In the same way that the overhead's hegemony of the visual teaches us to cut out "distractions"—such as bodies, voices, physicality, limited perspectives—it likewise teaches us to cut out anything that might threaten to slow the linear progression of information rolled like credits (in more than one way) over the screen. The prominence of the overhead image as the real business of the class defines any sort of two-way communication (discussion, question and answer) as luxurious, tangential, fatty excess, a disturbance of the temporal economy, a waste of time. In the keen necessity to get done what is important, the logic of the overhead projector selects, reduces, and clarifies a product that can then, achingly necessary in this world of the bodiless, count as the material and countable result of the class's efforts: five pages of notes, x amount of genuine, laboratory-tested, extravirgin knowledge, economy size.

WHAT ELSE MIGHT BE DONE?

To the extent that one agrees with my reading of the scene of the overhead projector, the critique itself suggests some means of resisting it, without junking the equipment altogether. Leaving on as many lights as possible ensures that the physical presence of the instructor remains a visible force. Shutting the projector off to discuss and take questions breaks up the tunnel-visioned focus, and disturbs the temporal push toward completion that the overhead often institutes. Finally, limiting use of the overhead as much as possible, or using another mechanical means, might be a good idea. (Handouts, for instance, are a little more work, but avoid many of the problems outlined above.) It is a symptom of the pervasiveness of what I have called neo-platonic semiotics that it is difficult to imagine any mechanical classroom medium about which similar difficulties might not be raised: the film, the slide projector, the increasingly appealed-to vcr, which manages in another and even more complete way to do away with the body of the teacher.

My intent in this brief essay is not to design (market? sell?) a new piece of classroom equipment, and one that is more ideologically correct. My intent is rather to articulate why and how we as teachers must stay conscious of our tools even and especially when they are working well, when they are efficient. What model of knowledge is ensuring their credibility? What lack is their efficiency supplying and at what price? It is not that we are in any way wholly in control of the classroom space. Signs do their own work, apart from us. But we can read the signs, stay aware of them, and try to notice how the ready-to-hand is sometimes rigid against us and our students. Then stir the pot.

NOTES

1. This is in direct contradiction to Jacques Derrida's suggestions regarding a traditional association between presence and the oral, but with all the resemblance that opposites always bear. Although television's medium is clearly passive, it institutes several subject positions for the viewer. For instance, during shows, the fourth wall is up. The conceit is that the actors do not know the viewer is there. Like Shelley's definition of the lyric poem as not "heard" but "overheard," television shows are a medium of eavesdropping or, more fashionably, voyeurism. Commercials, however, often direct themselves to the viewer in the most overt way. The result is a sort of metaphysical flickering: you are, you aren't, you are . . . The cultural implications of our television-tutored ability to make such a radical shift in subject position—without noticing—are still to be looked for.

2. Naomi Wolf's *The Beauty Myth* (New York: Morrow, 1991) describes well the politics involved in the body of the working woman.

3. There is also a concomitant discourse of teacher as lion tamer or missionary: the necessary differential.

4. A good deal of work has been done regarding the implications of Renaissance perspective, and what it does to the viewing subject. See, for instance, Burgin (1982).

REFERENCES

Burgin, Victor. (1982). Looking at photographs. In *Thinking photography* (pp. 142–153). London: Macmillan.

Heidegger, M. (1962). *Being and time* (J. MacQuarrie and E. Robinson, Trans.). New York: Harper and Row.

O'Reilly, Mary Rose. (1989). "Exterminate the brutes": And other things that can go wrong in student-centered teaching. *College English, 51*, 142–146.

Strickland, Ronald. (1990). Confrontational pedagogy and traditional literary studies. *College English, 52*, 291–300.

ABOUT THE AUTHOR

Eloise Knowlton comes from a long line of feminist teachers, beginning with George Furse (b. 1830), who thought it not a waste of time to teach his daughter Margaret to read. Knowlton holds a PhD in English and textual studies from Syracuse University; since the 1991 essay for *Feminist Teacher*, she has published mainly on James Joyce. Her *Bordering Joyce* is due out this year (1998) from the University Press of Florida. Knowlton is married and has a daughter, Clare, who is learning to read.

CHAPTER 16

Lesbian Instructor Comes Out

THE PERSONAL IS PEDAGOGY

Janet Wright

I have been coming out as a lesbian in my social work and women's studies classes now for 6 years. Since I use personal narratives in my teachings and I expect my students to honestly examine themselves, their histories and cultures, and their values as they become social workers, I feel strongly that my ability to talk honestly and openly about myself and my family is a necessity. However, I am more aware now than I was when I originally wrote this article of the emotional toll that coming out in the classroom takes on me. In this article I emphasize the positive effects of coming out both on myself and on my students—who so clearly benefit from authenticity. I remain convinced that the benefits outweigh the costs for me, as well. However, I am struck and challenged by the fact that it hasn't gotten any easier for me over the years and that the initial experience of coming out still leaves me feeling raw and too vulnerable. My thinking now is focused on how to renegotiate and transform this experience of fear and vulnerability for myself.

In the fall of 1990, when I had been a full-time instructor at the University of Wisconsin-Whitewater for one year, I decided to come out as a lesbian during the section on sexual orientation in my Human Behavior and the Social Environment class. I had been nervous for over a week before

This chapter originally appeared in *Feminist Teacher*, 1993, 7(2), 26–33.

The Feminist Teacher *Anthology: Pedagogies and Classroom Strategies.* Copyright © 1998 by Teachers College, Columbia University. All rights reserved. ISBN 0-8077-3741-0 (paper), ISBN 0-8077-3742-9 (cloth). Prior to photocopying items for classroom use, please contact the Copyright Clearance Center, Customer Service, 222 Rosewood Drive, Danvers, MA 01923, USA, telephone (508) 750-8400.

this class was to take place. But as I looked out at the 25 faces that had grown familiar in 6 weeks of classes, my fear became nauseatingly cold. Why is coming out always so hard, I later wondered. Perhaps because I fear that the other(s) will cease perceiving me as an individual and instead lock me into a category they label perverse or sick or immoral.

During my first year of teaching, I had brought in gay and lesbian friends to be the "dyke/gay for a day." This was the protocol I learned as a teaching assistant in women's studies elsewhere. The technique aimed at "normalizing" gay/lesbian life without risking tainting the women's studies department with a confirmation of the rumors—that we were all lesbians anyway, so there was no need to take our words seriously. The professor had suggested that if I wanted to come out, I do it when *I* was the instructor of the course, not as a teaching assistant.

I was accepting the challenge. I was tired of the evasions. I felt dirty during class discussions of sexual orientation, as if I were eavesdropping on conversations not meant for me. In order to teach in the way that I was most comfortable—using dialogue and narrative—I had to be able to model self-disclosure. There was no longer a choice. It was a risk I had decided to take.

I began that class by illuminating my fears, and then explaining why I decided to come out. The students were silent. I discussed the myths about gay men and lesbians, especially the myths I find most offensive—that lesbians hate men and that homosexuals molest and recruit children. The students were silent. I told them my own story of coming out as a lesbian. The students were silent. I dismissed class early, with instructions to bring any question they had about gays or lesbians, written with no name, to the next class (see Appendix A). They filed out silently.

I sat dejectedly in my chair in the classroom, trying to breathe, trying to calm my jumbled thoughts and feelings. Interrupting my thoughts, one of the students walked back in. I braced myself. She said, "I just wanted to tell you that I am a lesbian, although I've never really said that before, and I have never felt so validated in all of my life. Thank you for your courage."

That comment was the first of a stream of feedback from students that has almost without exception validated and confirmed my decision to come out in that and in subsequent classes.

"I don't understand why you had to come out in class," a student commented once in a discussion on sexual orientation. "That seems like something too private to talk about in classes."

Self-doubt flooded up within me as I attempted to answer the question. The familiar scornful comment, "I don't mind if people are homosexuals. I just wish they wouldn't *flaunt* it," was repeated in my mind. I had decided to come out in classes because it felt right, but clearly the time had come for a more logical, critical analysis with which to expand on my empathic understanding. Why did I feel it was a good strategy to come out in my classes—and a *strategy* for exactly what?

There are at least three possible targets or receivers of the act of coming out in classes: the instructor herself or himself, the students, and the university community. What are the ramifications of coming out for these different receivers?

THE IMPACTS ON THE INSTRUCTOR

Secrecy, the closet, is a shell often worn by gay men and lesbians to protect us from violence and from biased judgments and unfair treatment. Secrecy can be used to enhance and protect life and is an indispensable tool in protecting and maintaining identity (Bok, 1983). But secrecy can also damage those who are attempting to "pass." "Passing" prevents building a liberation movement. It prevents us from fighting back, from attacking the myths and superstitions. As Kantrowitz (1984) said about passing as a Jew, "Anyone who has heard, as I have, Jew-hating remarks said to her face because the speaker thought she didn't look Jewish knows both the survival value and the knife twist of passing."

Empowerment comes from acting on one's own behalf. "If I am not for myself, who will be?" (Kantrowitz, 1984). If I cannot stand up for myself and articulate my own concerns, then how can I help others to understand and care about them? Coming out is one step on the road to acceptance and liberation.

The argument that one's sexual preference is something private and intimate ("I don't talk about *my* sexuality!") does not apply to coming out. Coming out is not a discussion of intimate sexual details, it is a discussion of identity. This is what keeps it from being a narcissistic attention-seeking ploy. The Personal Is Political was a powerful political slogan because "it insisted on the primacy of the personal, not in a narcissistic way, but in its implied meaning of the self as a site for politicization, which was in this society a very radical challenge to notions of self and identity" (hooks, 1989). Naming and giving voice to one's experience is the first step in learning about domination and how it functions. The key for the instructor is to link discussions of personal identity to knowledge of how to work towards changing and transforming the oppressive parts of society. Coming out, then, becomes part of the struggle against dominant/subordinate thinking.

Secrets also isolate and distance us from others, leading to inauthenticity in relationships. Both radical educators (Freire, 1989) and feminist pedagogists (Noddings, 1991; Belenky et al., 1986) emphasize the importance of the relationship between the teacher and the student. Solas (1990) found that social work students perceived that the most important component of overall teaching effectiveness was the relationship between the educator and themselves. The best teachers, they felt, were willing to help students and were approachable. Both Gordon (1974) and Rogers (1969) emphasize the teacher–student relationship. Rogers identifies three qualities that facilitate learning:

1. Realness in the facilitator of learning.
2. Prizing, acceptance, and trust—prizing the learner.
3. Empathic understanding.

Gordon argues that there are five traits in a good teacher–student relationship:

1. Openness or transparency, so that each is able to risk directness and honesty with the other.
2. Caring, so that each knows that she/he is valued by the other.
3. Interdependence of one on the other.
4. Separateness, to allow each to grow and to develop her/his uniqueness, creativity, and individuality.
5. Mutual needs meeting, so that neither's needs are met at the expense of the other's needs.

Effective teachers, then, are authentic and willing to self-disclose as a means of reducing hierarchy and of sparking dialogue.

Freire (1989) refutes what he calls the "banking concept of education," in which "knowledge is a gift bestowed by those who consider themselves knowledgeable upon those whom they consider to know nothing" (p. 58). This type of education simply perpetuates a system of domination and subordination. Instead, Freire calls teachers to teach through dialogue, practicing "co-intentional" education that minimizes hierarchy between teacher and student and emphasizes partnership in the pursuit of knowledge.

An authentic relationship between the instructor and the students benefits the instructor by decreasing the distance between them. The instructor is able to teach using her/his own life experiences as examples and as case histories. There is less need to guard oneself, and the instructor can more easily build a sense of shared humanity. Heterosexuals, who don't have to guard this core part of themselves (who, for example, speak candidly about partners and celebrations and holidays) may have difficulty understanding the guardedness and sacrifice of spontaneity that accompanies the closet. Being oneself, being real, makes the art of teaching more comfortable and more relaxed. As Uribe and Harbeck (1992) write, "A major aspect of hiding is the ever present need to self-monitor" (p. 15). We can concentrate our energies on the lessons at hand, unencumbered by the fear of discovery, if we are out to students. This authentic relationship not only benefits the instructor but also benefits the students.

THE IMPACTS ON THE STUDENTS

The relationship between the student and the instructor creates the climate in which learning takes place. Creating an atmosphere of acceptance and mutual caring may predicate the ability to think critically, especially for women students. Nofz (1990) writes, "The inevitable result of criticism without positive affirmation is a great reluctance to share ideas that one holds worthy of examination."

When a teacher can be open and honest about her/his own life, even the difficult parts, students feel safer, more respected, and trusted. This relationship is the fertile ground where learning can take root. As Greene (1991) puts it, "It may be that education can only take place when we can be the friends of one another's minds." When the teacher offers the students stories of her/his own struggles with identity, with overcoming oppression, the students can discover connections with themselves and "penetrate barriers to understanding" (Witherell, 1991). Stories, Witherell continues, enable us to imagine "the experience and the feeling of the other" (p. 94).

In some classes over the past 2 years, I have distributed an additional evaluation form along with the anonymous end-of-semester evaluation (see Appendix C). This form explores the effects of my coming out in the classroom. The first question asks, "In this class, as part of the section on sexual orientation, the instructor 'came out' as a lesbian. What effect did this have on you?" Students choose to check one of the following categories:

- No effect
- Positive effect; I learned something from it
- Negative effect; it wasn't helpful
- Should have kept it to herself

Out of 56 questionnaires, no students have checked the last two responses. Forty-nine students have checked that it had a positive effect on them and seven said that it had no effect. Of those seven who checked the "no effect" line, several went on to explain that they had already had considerable exposure to gay/lesbian issues.

On the second question, "Did this enhance your learning and your ability to understand the issues involved in sexual orientation and homophobia?", 53 students checked "yes." All of the three students who checked "no" cited that they already understood the issues. Some of the student comments are illuminating on the value of coming out in establishing an open classroom atmosphere.

> I think it took a lot for the instructor to come forth and tell us she's a homosexual. I have a lot of respect for her because she's not pretending to be someone she's not.

> I have plenty of friends that are homosexuals/gay. But I do feel that it helped a lot of other students and *made the atmosphere a more sharing one* [my emphasis].

> I realized that the stereotypes are so inaccurate that you hear. It was good for the class to hear a personal story which is very normal and not odd.

> I got a greater understanding of the myths and stereotypes surrounding homophobia in our society and had more factual, personal experience material to absorb—I got to *feel* [my emphasis] what gays and lesbians have to endure and as a result am much more tolerant.

Although positive affirmation and encouragement are important in a classroom, they are not sufficient to create a comfortable dialogue. If we expect students to share life experiences, to examine them critically in light of new knowledge, then we are encouraging them to take risks. If, as Nofz (1990) says,

> we as professors refuse to take similar risks, we set a powerful example of disassociating one's life from one's education.
> We need to share more of our own struggles with inquiry, not just the end results of what we have learned. Each time we allow our students to see that we, too, sometimes face uncertainty, or have a nagging personal experience that cannot be fitted neatly into the disciplinary wisdom, we invite our students to join in that struggle.

MacDermid et al. (1992) concur:

> Separation (between learners and educators) is emphasized when learners are asked to use their personal experience as bases for building knowledge but the educator does not do the same; the learners are being asked to take

risks (by revealing personal information) that the educator does not take. Personal stories revealed by educators allow learners to see them from a human perspective, enhancing the felt connectedness between them and minimizing the gap between the personal and the political.

Feminist educators (Noddings, 1984; Witherell, 1991; Belenky et al., 1986) emphasize that most women (and perhaps most men, too) learn best through a pedagogy that emphasizes connectedness between learner and educator, among learners, and between learners and experience. Dialogue, which necessitates a genuine interest in the other, is an important key to learning (Grumet, 1981). Self-disclosure opens the possibility for true connected, respectful, critical dialogue.

Another way that an instructor's coming out can be beneficial to students is that it provides a model. Providing models of gay/lesbian teachers is important for both gay/lesbian students and for heterosexual students. It helps to break the sense of isolation, hopelessness, and fear experienced by gay and lesbian students. Gay and lesbian students, like any other oppressed group, need their elders as models and guides. But gay and lesbian teachers feel especially constrained. Coming out may cost us our jobs. We could be accused or suspected of molesting or recruiting young impressionable students. A major component of every oppression is isolation, but it is overwhelmingly potent in the oppression of gays and lesbians because we can't always even identify each other.

Recent estimates by the Department of Health and Human Services suggest that of the more than 5,000 suicides annually of young men and women between the ages of 15 and 24, more than 30% of them may be directly related to emotional turmoil over sexual preference issues and societal prejudices surrounding same-sex relationships (Harbeck, 1992). Uribe and Harbeck (1992) believe that gay, lesbian, and bisexual adolescents may be at higher risk of dysfunction, partially because of a lack of positive role modeling influences and experiences and their dependence on parents, peer groups, and educators who may be unwilling or unable to provide emotional support. In their study of homosexual adolescents, Uribe and Harbeck found that: "One of the most significant facts was their feelings that they existed in a box, with no adults to talk to, no traditional support structures to lean on for help in sorting out their problems, and no young people like themselves with whom to socialize" (p. 15). Recognizing that some gay/lesbian people have genuine and terrible constraints on coming out at work, those of us who can, must. The lives of young lesbians and gay men are depending on our strength.

For heterosexual students, the presence of an openly gay or lesbian teacher can provide them with an important model, too. Many heterosexual students may believe that they have never known a gay man or lesbian. This invisibility allows the stereotypes and myths to persist. One student commented on her/his class evaluation:

> I guess I was extremely prejudiced toward homosexuals before I took this class. I have never had contact with a homosexual before, at least not as far as I'd known. I realized that I have to accept people for their individual characteristics and attributes, rather than for their sexual preference. I'm no longer homophobic at all. I think Janet did a great job. She was very open and honest.

Harbeck (1992) notes that several psychological studies have demonstrated that if a heterosexual individual knows a homosexual, then acceptance increases as stereotypical responses decrease.

Bias is not only an intellectually learned process, it is also emotional. Therefore, unlearning bias must have an emotional component. When a teacher comes out as lesbian or gay, the student must confront bias and oppression on a personal level. The out lesbian/gay teacher who can dialogue with students about the oppression she/he experiences will help students personalize the issues—oppression can take on a new, more personal meaning. Students may be freed to more critically examine oppression in their own lives. For example, one student spoke about her experience with being hospitalized for phobias in high school, the stereotypes people held about mental illness, and the effects of this on her life. Students have, after the teacher's disclosure, examined experiences with eating disorders, being a Jew in a Christian society, rape and sexual abuse, child abuse and woman abuse, alcoholism, and so on. The students' abilities to critically examine these experiences in an accepting classroom atmosphere have been empowering and, in some instances, healing. Secrets tend to foster feelings of shame. Openness can dissipate these feelings.

Student comments on my class evaluation forms support the idea that they learned about oppression from the instructor's coming out:

> I am glad you came out in class. I feel some of those same fears. I am anorexic/bulimic. People have a lot of misconceptions on this.

> I want to thank you for your respect for us. My dad is gay and he never hides it. He is proud.

> I had no clue nor ever thought of the sexual orientation of the instructor. It made me realize that anyone can be gay/lesbian and it doesn't make them any less of a person.

I had a negative attitude toward gays and lesbians, probably because I never knew any. But now I realize that they are just people
too.

I used to be very against homosexuals because I didn't understand
them. The information given helped me understand what these
people are about.

I—not to my knowledge—have never met a homosexual person. I
guess I was a little homophobic—but I have an open mind. I'm glad
I know.

It's better to see people who represent the stereotypes in our society
in order to disprove them. I think it is easy for people to hold bias
until they are confronted by a person who presents an image of fact.

You once said in class that we are all prejudiced because we are
raised to be, and that sometimes we are too "liberal" to admit our
prejudice and at first I wanted to be defensive. But yet, when I went
with my friends, some of whom are gay, to various bars and felt
uncomfortable, I was angry with myself for feeling uncomfortable. I
realized that my feelings had no basis and that you were right.

Modeling as a visible gay or lesbian teacher takes on other meanings,
too. By being out, we model honesty. We validate difference. We show that
individuals have choices—choices to be the men and women that they are,
regardless of societal prescription. At a time in their lives when traditional
students are just beginning to listen to their own voices over their peer
group, over parents—we model the values of being oneself, authentically
and without reserve. And this is one of the most important lessons of life.

IMPACT ON THE UNIVERSITY

When instructors and other staff are openly gay and lesbian, the university and their respective departments will no longer be as free to operate
under the assumption of heterosexuality. A struggle between conflicting
values on lesbian/gay issues at Oberlin College illustrates this. On the one
hand, the institution was among the first to adopt nondiscrimination clauses
for sexual orientation. On the other hand, there is a strong emphasis and
focus on heterosexual orthodoxy—that traditional heterosexual roles for
men and women are the only truly acceptable ones. Gay men and lesbian

women, for example, are not supported in political activities. However, if administrators are aware of gay and lesbian faculty and staff, they may realize that the topic is "on the table" and their actions and policies can be and will be challenged.

Identified gay and lesbian faculty and staff will also be used by the university and the department as consultants. Although there is danger of tokenism ("Let's make sure there's a lesbian on the committee"), even tokenism can be progress. On the one hand, it is insulting to think that one person can even attempt to speak for as heterogeneous a group as gay men and lesbians. On the other hand, at least the topic is addressed. And, the modeling takes place on a collegial level as well—administrators and colleagues are forced to see and acknowledge a gay man or lesbian woman. Stereotyping becomes less viable.

SUGGESTIONS FOR DEPARTMENTS

The fear of backlash is well-founded, of course. It occurs as any oppressed group advocates for its own equal rights, and homophobia consists of a unique blend of hatred, fear, and moral indignation. There will be violence, both physical and emotional, against gay men and lesbians, their supporters, and those wrongly suspected of being gay or lesbian. However, some academic departments will choose to contribute to an atmosphere of acceptance rather than ignore the struggle. It is not necessary to wait for a faculty member to come out or to recruit a gay or lesbian faculty member in order to begin this process. Following are some suggestions for departments and faculty.

1. Adopt a resolution on sexual orientation (see Appendix B). A resolution makes very clear the attitudes and intentions of the department around sexual orientation. This resolution can be included in the student handbook, distributed and discussed in classes, and pointed out to every potential faculty and staff member. This is a crucial step in structuring a safe environment for gay men and lesbians.

2. Posters, decorations, pamphlets, and handouts in and from the department can project a positive image of gays and lesbians and an accepting departmental attitude.

3. Examples of gay and lesbian couples and families as well as counseling issues such as coming out should be common in role plays and practice classes. Policy and research classes can incorporate gay and lesbian issues. Most important, faculty can use inclusive language, such as *part-*

ners instead of *husband and wife*. Lesbian and gay reality is thereby integrated into and validated by the curriculum.

4. Departments must recognize and discuss the possible ramifications of a colleague coming out to students. Heterosexual students may seek information and understanding from heterosexual faculty on gay/lesbian issues. Are faculty sufficiently prepared and comfortable with their own views? How will the department handle extremely homophobic students? Is there an attempt to screen such students out of the profession? How? What if students refuse to have the lesbian/gay instructor as an advisor? How will the department respond to a sudden drop in student evaluations? When faculty grapple with these issues, they acknowledge the unique oppression they are confronting.

Department chairs need to be aware of the dangers and opportunities that open to an out faculty member in the university. An identified gay/lesbian faculty member may be seized on by university administration, leading to the dangers of tokenism and overextension.

On the other hand, an out faculty member can enrich the perceptions of and discussions on oppression for departments as well as for university administrations.

5. Heterosexual faculty members can come out as strong supporters of gay/lesbian rights by discussing their own participation in a gay rights march, by relating their own experiences with gay brothers, sons, and lesbian daughters, and sisters, gay/lesbian friends. Faculty members might attend and later discuss a meeting of P-FLAG (Parents and Friends of Lesbians and Gays)—or better yet, plan a field trip and take the students along.

Faculty members could try wearing pink triangle buttons for a day and discussing their own personal reactions and fears, as well as the reactions from others.

Faculty members can write letters to the school paper, protesting homophobic statements or events or supporting gay/lesbians rights.

Perhaps most important, faculty members could discuss in classes their own processes in shedding their homophobia. Students desperately need heterosexual models who can honestly discuss their homophobia and their methods for combatting it.

CONCLUSION

Coming out in the classroom is not the only strategy for fighting homophobia and heterosexism. It is not appropriate for all classes or for all les-

bian/gay faculty members to come out to students. "Each teacher has her
or his individual methods of teaching, of reaching the students, of creating
a rapport that permits some learning to occur" (Khayatt, 1992, p. 173). The
labels can be uncomfortable—*straight* or *queer; heterosexual* or *homosexual*—
because they once again reinforce dualistic and simplistic thinking. Sexuality, gender roles, and identity are complex concepts that cannot be adequately
or comfortably pigeonholed into rigid labels. An instructor who teaches a
graduate level course on sexuality, for example, might consciously reject
the notion of identifying her/his present place on the continuums. Coming
out may not make sense for instructors of certain large lecture classes or
certain topics. Context is always an important factor in decision making.

However, there is an important function for those educators who are
willing and able to self-identify as lesbian or gay. Societal hatred, fear, and
misunderstanding are focused on the stereotyped images of gay and lesbian. One way of diffusing the potency of those labels is by redefining them,
refraining them, so that they lose their negative power. Coming out in the
classroom opens the dialogue on sexual orientation and on oppression on
the personal level. This can be empowering for the faculty person as well
as the lesbian and gay students. But it can also model an authenticity and
acceptance that challenges, empowers, and honors all the classroom participants who, regardless of sexual orientation or preference, are unique
and diverse individuals.

REFERENCES

Allen, Katherine R., & Crosie-Burnet, Margaret. (1992). Innovative ways and con-
    troversial issues in teaching about families: A special collection on family
    pedagogy. *Family Relations, 41*, 9–11.
Belenky, Mary Field, Clinchy, Blythe, Goldberger, Nancy Rule, & Tarule, Jill.
    (1986). *Women's ways of knowing*. New York: Basic Books.
Bok, Sissela. (1983). *Secrets: On the ethics of concealment and revelation*. New York:
    Vintage Books.
Freire, Paulo. (1989). *Pedagogy of the oppressed*. New York: Continuum.
Gordon, Thomas. (1974). TET: *Teacher effectiveness training*. New York: Peter H.
    Wyden.
Greene, Maxine. (1991). Foreword. In Witherell, Carol, and Noddings, Nel (Eds.),
    Stories lives tell: Narrative and dialogue in education (pp. 83–95). New York:
    Teachers College Press.
Grumet, Madeleine R. (1981). Conception, Contradiction and Curriculum. *Jour-
    nal of Curriculum Theorizing, 3*, 292.
Harbeck, Karen M. (Ed.). (1992). *Coming out of the classroom closet*. New York:
    Haworth Press.

Hegel, Georg Wilhelm Friedrich. (1967). *The phenomenology of mind*. New York: Harper and Row.

hooks, bell. (1989). *Talking back: Thinking feminist, thinking black*. Boston: South End Press.

Kantrowitz, Melanie. (1984). *Anti-Semitism, racism, and coalitions*. Speech given in Minneapolis, MN.

Khayatt, Madiha Didi. (1992). *Lesbian teachers: An invisible presence*. New York: State University of New York Press.

MacDermid, Shelley M., Jurich, Joan, Myers-Walls, Judith A., & Pelo, Ann. (1992). Feminist teaching: Effective education. *Family Relations, 41*, 31–38.

Noddings, Nel. (1991). *Caring: A feminine approach to ethics and moral education*. Berkeley: University of California Press.

Nofz, Michael. (1990). The classroom and the "real world"—are they worlds apart? *Teaching Forum, 12* (pp. 1–3). Undergraduate Teaching Improvement Council, University of Wisconsin System.

Pharr, Suzanne. (1988). *Homophobia: A weapon of sexism*. Little Rock: Chardon Press.

Postman, Neil, & Weingartner, Charles. (1969). *Teaching as a subversive activity*. New York: Dell.

Rich, Adrienne. (1980). Foreword. In J. P. Stanley & S. Wolfe (Eds.), *The coming out stories* (pp. xi–xiii). Watertown, MA: Persephone Press.

Rogers, Carl R. (1969). *Freedom to learn*. Columbus, OH: Charles E. Merrill.

Solas, John. (1990). Effective teaching as construed by social work students. *Journal of Social Work Education, 26*, 145–154.

Uribe, Virginia, & Harbeck, Karen M. (1992). Addressing the needs of lesbian, gay, and bisexual youth: The origins of PROJECT 10 and school-based intervention. In Harbeck, Karen M. (Ed.), *Coming Out of the Classroom Closet* (pp. 9–28). New York: Haworth Press.

Witherell, Carol. (1991). The self in narrative: A journey into paradox. In Witherell, Carol, & Noddings, Nel (Eds.), *Stories lives tell: Narrative and dialogue in education* (pp. 83–95). New York: Teachers College Press.

Witherell, Carol, & Noddings, Nel. (Eds.). (1991). *Stories lives tell: Narrative and dialogue in education*. New York: Teachers College Press.

APPENDIX A
QUESTIONS FROM STUDENTS

What follows is a sampling of anonymous, written questions that students have given me in Human Behavior and the Social Environment classes. This format of asking students to hand in anonymous questions that the instructor takes home to consider and answers in the next class period has been very successful.

What brought about your change in behavior, or what made you realize your true feelings?

When did you know? Who did you tell?
Did you know when you were married?
How does one know that one is gay/lesbian?
A homosexual student wrote an article on how homosexuals need more
    effort on coming out of the closet, standing up for their rights, etc.—
    then signed it "anonymously"—why would they do this and totally
    contradict themselves?

Family

How did your family handle your homosexuality—first your parents
    and then your children—after you were previously in a heterosexual
    relationship?
How do your parents feel? Brothers, sisters?
How did you explain to your family (children and parents) about your
    sexual preference?
How does having and/or growing up in a household with a homosexual
    parent(s) effect children?
Do your kids get teased or beat-up, are they afraid to bring friends home,
    or embarrassed to be seen in public with you?
What were your children's first reactions?

Dating/Relationships

Where do lesbians and gay men go to meet other homosexuals, other than
    gay bars? Do you have a partner at this time?
Is it the same kind of love if you were "in love" with a man?
What is it that you like about your partner? Are you currently involved
    with someone? Are you and your partner sexually involved? How do
    you introduce your partner?
Do you go places (bars, etc.) where you interact with other lesbians?
How did you approach your first lesbian relationship? Was it awkward?
    Did you make a date like everyone else?

Friends

How do men treat you when they find out you are a lesbian?
How did the other professors react?
Are your previous boyfriends offended?
Are other women afraid of you, or afraid to touch you normally, because
    of your sexual preference?

Marriage/Husband

Are your biological children from your ex-husband?
The book says that most people know their sexual preference before age
   20. If that is true, why do many homosexual people enter into hetero-
   sexual marriages?
What does your husband think and what happened in your marriage?
Did your ex-husband know?

Sex

What do lesbians do for sexual arousal or stimulation with each other?
Do you still have heterosexual desires?
Has anyone expected that you were into every other kind of thing (like
   group sex, or whatever)?

Causes

Do you think homosexuality could be genetically linked?
Do you think people are born gay?
What was the reason for you becoming a lesbian?

Legal issues

Is it legal for lesbians and gay men to marry in Wisconsin? In any state?
On what grounds would child custody be granted or not to the gay/les-
   bian parent?
Have you ever been discriminated against because you are a lesbian?

Religion

What are your religious beliefs and how does it effect your sexual
   orientation?

Miscellaneous

Do lesbians still feel "feminine"?

Comments

I think it took a lot of courage for you to tell our class about this—I think
it's cool that you're not ashamed of who you are and if anything, I think it

makes one a better person admitting to oneself and others about who you
are and what you believe. I don't see you any differently than from the first
day of class.

I applaud your openness. Many students never knew a gay or lesbian
and just heard stories. You are giving them an excellent example.

APPENDIX B
RESOLUTION REGARDING SEXUAL ORIENTATION

Whereas discrimination against gay men and lesbians is still legal in most
states and is widely practiced and accepted throughout the United States;

Whereas there is no known cause of homosexuality and it appears to
be a naturally occurring human diversity which is present in at least 10%
of the human population;

Whereas gay men and lesbians are as psychologically and emotionally
adjusted as the rest of the population;

Whereas no harm comes to other peoples as a result of a homosexual
orientation;

Whereas the social work profession has historically committed itself
to the goal of social equality and the elimination of oppressions; and

Whereas the National Association of Social Workers Code of Ethics
prohibits discrimination on the basis of one's sexual orientation;

We, the faculty and staff of the Department of Social Work, University of Wisconsin, Whitewater, are resolved:

To educate and raise awareness in social work students about the oppressions of homophobia and heterosexism and their harmful effects on
society as a whole;

To work against the discrimination of gay men and lesbians wherever
it exists in the University community;

To improve the University climate for the gay men and lesbians who
are faculty/staff, classified staff, and students, and

To work for the acceptance of gay men and lesbians as full-fledged
members of society, entitled to the same rights, responsibilities, and respect
as any other citizen.[1]

APPENDIX C
EVALUATION FORM

In this class, as part of the section on sexual orientation, the instructor "came
out" as a lesbian. What effect did this have on you?

- No effect
- Positive effect; I learned something from it
- Negative effect; it wasn't helpful
- Should have kept it to herself

Did this enhance your learning and your ability to understand issues involved in sexual orientation and homophobia?

Why or why not?

How do you think the instructor could have improved your learning experience on the issue of sexual orientation?

NOTE

1. This Resolution was adopted by the University of Wisconsin–Whitewater, Department of Social Work Faculty, January 1991.

ABOUT THE AUTHOR

Janet Wright has a PhD in Social Welfare from the University of Wisconsin–Madison and is presently the Chair of the Social Work Department at the University of Wisconsin–Whitewater. Her book on lesbian step families is expected to be published by the Haworth Press in 1998.

CHAPTER 17

Would You Rather Be a Goddess or a Cyborg?

Suzanne K. Damarin

The increasing presence and pressure of information technologies throughout society and in our schools and colleges require that committed feminist teachers find standpoints with respect to these technologies in our lives as individuals and as teachers. In the past decade, feminist analyses of the ways in which technologies operate in the social construction of gender (and, conversely, the ways in which gender operates in the construction of technologies) have grown in number, depth, and complexity. But the very complexity of the relations uncovered between and among gender, technology, and numerous other factors can be almost as overwhelming as the technologies themselves. These analyses certainly open feminist eyes to a multitude of "hidden" relationships. As Sandra Harding (1991) points out, however, one cannot achieve a standpoint, a position from which to understand and act, simply by opening one's eyes. A standpoint must be constructed; and constructing a standpoint requires sustained attention and hard work.

This chapter represents some of my work on constructing my own standpoint as a fiftysomething White feminist educator schooled in mathematics and information technologies. In it I try to integrate my enduring feminist values and guidelines with my analyses of technology, and it reflects my struggle, not only for a personal understanding of the ways in which gender and technology are entailed in the social construction of each other, but also for a feminist place to stand and for a sense of how to act.

This chapter originally appeared in *Feminist Teacher*, 1994, 8(2), 54–60.

Two years after writing it, I am still fairly comfortable with its goddess/cyborg/witch/laughing mother/alone standing woman, largely because she is so multiple, complex, proactive, and provocative. But the hot air of "technological progress" blows stronger—and there are new issues to deal with. The increasing use of surveillance technologies in schools, the growing impact of information ownership on our right to know, the politics of the information superhighway, are looming as areas of concern. I have perspectives (mostly negative) on each of these, but have yet to develop a standpoint from which to work both with and against these pervasive technological issues in all their social ramifications.

The rampant growth of postmodern information and communications technologies throughout society and the increasing pressure to incorporate these technologies into education create new and uncomfortable situations for feminist educators. The patriarchal roots of these technologies, together with a multiplicity of traditions, beliefs, issues, and practices that have separated women from technology leave us with little in the way of direction or insight for appropriate feminist responses to the demands of these pervasive technologies. It is urgent that we find new and creative modes of being and acting in this high-tech world.

Cultural theorist Donna Haraway (1991) recognizes the powers of technologies as they operate on the society at large and on individuals. In much of her writing, she challenges feminists and other radicals to create new ways of being in postmodern society and new relationships with postmodern technologies. Her cyborg figure, first described in 1985 to stimulate socialist feminists to rethink feminist politics, embodies this potential. As described in "A Manifesto for Cyborgs,"[1] the cyborg is a subject in search of radical strategies of survival in the face of multiple impositions of command, control, communication, and informatics. To survive, the cyborg must find new feminist consciousness and political savvy. Having described the exigencies of cyborg life in some detail, Haraway ends her paper with the provocative statement "though both are caught in the spiral dance, I would rather be a cyborg than a goddess." The dilemma, to be a goddess or a cyborg, seems to me to be a central issue for teachers as they dance a spiral inscribed by politics, science, and the lives of children who are emerging in this time and space of postmodern technologies.

In this article, therefore, I elaborate (and celebrate) the goddess and cyborg mythologies in the contexts of teaching. The cyborg-versus-goddess dichotomy is not unrelated to other lopsided binary choices we make. ("Do you teach subject matter content? Or do you teach 'the whole child?'") The spiral dance of education can be viewed as movement among the various positions offered in the evolving economies of hyperspace, virtual reality, and post-Fordist capitalism. A spiral, however, requires three dimensions in order to exist and be danced; it cannot be reduced to binary questions of goddess versus cyborg or to any other dichotomy. Therefore, like Haraway in all of her writing, like the goddess and other religious myths with their trinities, and like the deconstructive move in postmodern philosophy, the spiral dance invites and requires the search for a "third term," in this case, positionalities for teachers who are neither goddess nor cyborg, but who are always already both.

THE MYTHOLOGY OF THE GODDESS: LEGENDS OF TEACHING

Goddess myths have existed in many cultures; the stories and powers of the goddess are recorded in texts and artifacts ranging from earthen vessels used to transport the water that sustains earthly life to tombs that signify transport from one life to another. David Kinsley (1989), in his study of the goddess as she is represented in the literatures and artifacts of both Eastern and Western cultures, describes her universal attributes and responsibilities. The goddess,

> although undoubtedly possessing a variety of functions and characteristics insofar as she reigned for so long and over such a large area, was primarily the mother of all life. . . . Images of the goddess, pregnant, giving birth, or holding infants are not uncommon. But she was not just the mother of human beings, she was the mother of all, the spirit that imbued all creation with life and vitality. She was not, in any important way, a warrior goddess, although she was associated with death. Her association with death . . . suggests her second major aspect, "the Taker of All," a form in which she was responsible for transformation, metamorphosis, regeneration, rebirth, and so on. (p. xiv)

Responsible for the nurturance of life and vitality, for transformation and metamorphosis, she was/is surely at least partly a teacher. It is teachers who are charged with the transformation of humans from childhood play and innocence through adolescent self-construction to burgeoning adulthood.

The discourses of the goddess as nurturing and maternal, the idea of "Goddesses in Every Woman" (Bolen, 1984), and Catharine Beecher's 19th-century construction of teaching as "woman's true profession" come together in the discourse of the teaching profession as the continuation of mothering and the nurturance of the individual child. If this discourse is sometimes muted by the cacophony of political demands for accountability, computerization, and professionalization, it is not obliterated but continues to flourish within the context of teachers' lives and desires.

The emergence, within the past decades, of an extensive discourse of caring as the guiding ethic of teachers (Noddings, 1984) appears to be an effort to re-reify the goddess within the teaching profession. Grounded in the examples of maternal nurturance and godly theories of Martin Buber and other theologians, the discourses of the one who is caring, the cared for, and the maintenance of the caring relation have no truck with postmodern technologies, information explosions, or cyborgian enigmas of identity and subjectivity. The one who is caring, the teacher attentive to the cared for, is "taker of all" . . . accepting of the whims and foibles of students, yet responsible for their metamorphosis, their shedding of childish attitudes and ignorance as they adopt new forms of adolescence and adulthood.

Reading the goddess as metaphor for teacher, the teacher is inscribed in goddess myths, myths that prevail in both prescriptive and dialectic forms. In the rules for teachers codified a century or more ago, and in the media portrayal of teachers, we find reflections of the mythology of the goddess—one who is generous of her love and nurturance, responsible to her roots, and eschewing of sexuality. In love, the goddess/teacher is agape, not eros. Writing of the teacher as she appears in the texts of novels, films, and TV, media theorist George Gerbner (1973) notes: "Typical is Miss Dove, who is so devoted, so selfless, so excruciatingly good" that she passes up the opportunity to marry (p. 78).

Retired schoolteachers interviewed by Green and Manke (1994) express similar themes of selfless devotion that is intrinsically rewarded when they see "with their own eyes" that students are indeed transformed, metamorphosed, and reborn. Preservice teachers are drawn to the profession by the allure of this mythology. Indeed, like members of religious orders, many feel that teaching is a calling. It is not uncommon for future teachers to have felt the call while in the early grades and to have begun teacherly activities by playing school. For those who receive it, it is a call to responsibility for nurturance and transformation of students; in the words of one preservice teacher:

> I want to be able to shape children's lives, giving them hope for the future and instilling a sense of confidence in each one. Teachers may be the hope for changing our society for the better.

Like (some of) the media teachers described by Gerbner (1973) and others, these former and future teachers eschew worldly satisfactions and save their most critical remarks for others in the profession who seek such extrinsic rewards. Summarizing their interviews with retired teachers, Green and Manke observe that "one of the worst things these teachers could say about a teacher was 'she's in it for the money'" (p. 107). Thus, even as these teachers speak a discourse of teacher as goddesslike paragon of devotion and commitment, they also reveal a counterdiscourse of (some/other) teachers' materialism.

Discourses notwithstanding, in a very real sense teachers are not goddesses, but earthly creatures who must negotiate their sustenance and positionalities in the material world. Contradictory discourses emerge at the interstices of myth and reality. Green and Manke's (1994) retired teachers, for example, speak not only of the moral failings of teachers who "are in it for the money," but also of the insufficiency of the monetary remuneration for themselves. Generally speaking, teachers "conceive of money as tainted" (Joseph & Burnaford, 1994, p. 11); yet they invoke future financial success as motivation for the students whom they teach. As Joseph and Burnaford observe, in this and in other regards, "teachers' moral callings reflect their own values but not the values or aspirations of those whom they teach" (p. 11).

Conflicts between goddess-inspired images of teachers and the realities of the classroom emerge in other domains as well. On the one hand, teachers see themselves as leaders and as powerful; but in practice, they are seen (and often see themselves) as "pawns in a game . . . we don't even know . . . is being played" (quoted in Efron & Joseph, 1994, p. 72).

Media portrayals of teachers reflect and extend this ambivalence; not every media teacher is the good Miss Dove mentioned earlier. Indeed, negative images of teachers predominate over positive ones in film and televised portrayals. These images range from buffoon to tyrant to witch. Although the frequency of male teachers is much greater among the media teachers than among actual teachers, female teachers are especially subject to TV and movie ridicule, a pattern that has remained constant for 2 decades (Joseph & Burnaford, 1994; Gerbner, 1973). According to Gerbner, teachers are "outstanding among all TV occupations in being the 'cleanest' and the 'kindest.' But they were also rated the 'weakest,' the 'softest' and the 'slowest'" (p. 83). If media teachers are most often men, they are men with characteristics most often associated with "the good" as perceived in (i.e., written into) the "feminine." Gerbner offers the following observation:

Giving teachers a messianic mission and having schools soak up all the dreams and aspirations citizens have for their children dooms the enterprise to failure. No social order can afford to make good on such a promise. The illusion itself contains the seeds of the noble-but-impractical image. It becomes only reasonable and realistic to show teachers full of goodness, but sapped of vitality and power. Turn on the power and the impotent figure becomes a monster, only confirming the doubts and suspicions inherent in the ambivalent image. (p. 91)

The power of the goddess as described by Kinsley (1989) is feminine power realized and practiced through birthing, nurturance, and transformation. Classroom teachers accept the calling to this goddess power. In the media teacher, however, this power is stripped away in patriarchal skits and texts. The power "turned on" in Gerbner's (1973) analysis is a more patriarchal version. As when the electricity of lightning strikes an electrical transformer, there is danger, darkness, and confusion . . . the breeding ground for monsters. Through the media of modern and postmodern technologies, the goddess emerges de-deified and one of many monsters, a figure adopted by Haraway (1992) in her discussions of the "inappropriate/d others."

(IN)APPROPRIATION OF TEACHERS:
THE HIGH-TECH VERSION

In recent years, some feminists have sought in the literatures of goddess worship a history of matriarchal societies, and in the re-turn to goddess mythologies, a move toward, if not a female-dominated society, at least one that is more hospitable to women and to the valuing of them. Kinsley's (1989) analyses do not encourage this move, however; he observes that goddess worship prevailed in some patriarchal and misogynist societies. He warns his readers to be wary of those accounts in which goddesses are portrayed as subservient to men. In this time of the large-scale educational adoption of computers, arguably the surrogates of men (and of hyper-capitalist men, at that), Kinsley's warning is one that teachers (and teacher educators) must heed. Literatures of re-inscription of the goddess/teacher within the evolving economies of distance education, computer-based learning, multimedia-based instruction, and the teaching of students to navigate the information superhighway, assign to her those (sub)service tasks required to establish and continue the hegemony of man-machines in the redefinition of education: facilitation, troubleshooting, and monitoring.

Recognizing Kinsley's (1989) warnings and these developments, teachers might join Haraway in electing to choose as "role model" some figure other than the goddess, but teacher education provides slim pickings in this regard. There is a sense, of course, in which postmodern teachers can no more elect *to be* cyborgs than they can elect *to be* goddesses. This modern realist issue is not what concerns me here; instead, my concern is with the possibilities of cyborgian myths and legends as metaphors or simulacra through which we might build a new construction of teaching and of teachers in postmodern times. To my knowledge, the concept of cyborg is not yet represented in teacher education, nor in the discourses of teachers, though some educators have begun to look at the ways in which cyborgs are constructed within educational domains. Insofar as teachers must be cyborgs, then what kind of cyborgs should they/we be?

The educational literatures that address the relations between and among teachers, students, and machines are dominated by the technocentric narratives and exhortations of educational technology; patriarchal institutions of the BUGOMIS (BUsiness, GOvernment, MIlitary, Science) feed and are fed by these literatures. Voices of dissent can be found in a relatively small number of works by Bowers (1988), Noble (1991), and others who reveal the roots of educational technology, its past and current failures, and its threats to current concepts and practices of education. Beyond these dedicated praises and critiques, the literatures of teaching and teacher education seem to be silent with respect to information technologies; new works and theories on teacher ethics, image, and practice emerge regularly with nary a mention of technology in the classroom—or, for that matter, outside it. By refusing to recognize technology, these literatures seek to deny its effects. Strategies of denial can be powerful moves on the part of hegemonic leaders (as any marginalized person can attest), for they render politically invisible that which is being denied. But silence in the face of huge investments by the BUGOMIS, not only of dollars but of "political capital" as well, is arguably dysfunctional behavior—a strategy of hiding in cyberspace and hoping the monster will go away. Silence is not effective as counterhegemonic politics.

(Parenthetically, I wonder: How many of these texts of denial have been written on word processors? How many have been desktop published? How many use data that are organized and analyzed through SAS or SPSS? How many postmodern qualitative researchers have eased their scholarly burdens by using Ethnograph? Of these, how many recognize the computer as a presence in the classroom described? . . . And, were *your* data scanned into an electronic database? Did you use a library search system? Computer graphics? The Internet? To write/research/submit/present your AERA paper? Did you teleconference with your cosymposiasts? Fax your abstract to the panel of referees? Are you a cyborgian educational researcher?)

Oppositional educational writers, and some educational technologists (e.g., Knupfer, 1993) recognize that what we are dealing with is the imposition of change by well-financed and politically powerful elites. But this is not the only story. *We also elect and enjoy* the "bennies" of the technologies imposed, the benefits that we call savings of time, increased productivity, control of our own manuscripts, and so on, as well as the Benzedrine "down" as we move from the political cacophony of faculty lives to solitary communion with computer screens. Everywhere, people are opting in, even as they are opting out; opting in and opting out become indistinguishable. Are we being co-opted, corrupted, colonized?

Would you give up your laptop?

It's interesting that you might think here that I mean a computer, and not that comfy place where a child might seek a teacher's love.

The mythical cyborg of Haraway denies the denial of technology in the world and invites all of us to seek new and metaphorical resources and polyvocal, multicited politics of survival in the face of command-control-communication-intelligence, the C³I of the power orgy that fathered and fathers postmodern technologies.

THE MYTHOLOGY OF THE CYBORG: NEW ROLES/RULES FOR TEACHING

Haraway's "Manifesto for Cyborgs" (1991) "is an argument for *pleasure* in the confusion of boundaries and for *responsibility* in their construction" (p. 150). Like the goddess, the cyborg is a mythological creature: as described by Haraway,

> The cyborg is resolutely committed to partiality, irony, intimacy, and perversity. It is oppositional, utopian, and completely without innocence. No longer structured by the polarity of public and private, the cyborg defines a technological polis based partly on a revolution of social relations in the *oikos*, the household. Nature and culture are reworked; the one can no longer be the resource for appropriation or incorporation by the other. . . . The main trouble with cyborgs, of course is that they are the illegitimate offspring of militarism and patriarchal capitalism, not to mention state socialism. But illegitimate offspring are often exceedingly unfaithful to their origins. Their fathers, after all, are inessential. (p. 151)

In Haraway's version/vision, the cyborg has sprung the lock of its subservience to military masters and roams at will the networks constructed for patriarchal control. No longer constrained by these constraints, she seeks out spots in which there is a residue of vulnerability, an interstice, to use Foucauldian terminology, in which knowledge might accrue and power might be constructed. Analogous to the aquatic animal, itself part water and swimming in a sea made not only of water, but also of micro- and other organisms, the cyborg—part nature, part machine—is not essentially different from her environment—part nature, part machine. The cyborg is not in any necessary way a robot, a mechanical pseudoman that follows the directions of a pre-inscribed program with faithfulness to its father. Instead, the cyborg seeks sites for resistance to the naturalizing of machines and to the mechanization of culture.

Cyborgian teachers roam among us today; they are cousins of computer hackers and of data entry operators and of other intrusions of the computerized panopticon workplace. Cyborgian teachers accept computers into their classrooms only to divert the effects of C^3I; like the teachers described by Olson (1988), they subvert the intentions of machine donors and use computers to reproduce and magnify their own personalities. Some, like those described by Apple and Jungck (1990), deny, through their (in)actions, the importance of the machine to themselves and to their students.

Because they need not be faithful to their human or machine-theoretic roots, cyborgian teachers take pleasure in ironies and reversals unthinkable for their precyborgian mentors. They mess with the machines to create ficts and factions from socially constructed facts and fictions. Like the Barbie Liberation Front, they switch the tapes in Barbie and G. I. Joe . . . and they bring the dolls to school and see what the kids make of a Teen Talk Barbie talking gruff and tough and a G. I. Joe that squeals about wanting to dance and math being hard.

Cyborgian teachers play with the anthropomorphism of machines . . . their students unpack the grammar and meanings of adjectives and nouns: *computer anxiety* and *computer capability;* they diagram the visual grammar of screen displays and write poems about the machine anxiety over humans. Metaphor and metonymy are the methods of their daily lesson plans. If, as Andrew Ross (1991) claims, the language and discourse concerning computer viruses is derived from the discourses of sex and AIDS, then the cyborgian teacher reverses it back; in the teaching of the cyborg, the mandatory computer lessons on preventing computer viruses become an advance organizer for a new and subversive curriculum of sex and AIDS education.

The cyborgian teacher may be unfaithful to the fathers, but she does not forget what they have done. While the BUGOMIS worry about the problem of extending copyright and other capitalist and patriarchal legalities to the age of electronic text, the cyborg-teacher fills the electronic bookshelf with slave narratives and the diaries of farm women, texts too unimportant to have been copyrighted in their time. Students, mandated countless hours of keyboarding instruction, use this classroom time to enter these and other narratives of resistance and survival. Within the domain of command and control, cyborgian classes around the world create an excess of texts that escape control.

Recognizing technophilia and technophobia as the love-hate binary that sustains technocentrism, the cyborgian teacher is suspicious of them both and frames her teaching in the deconstruction of this pair. A cyborgian reading of research texts concerning educational technology requires different questions than does a reading framed by educational effectiveness or by ideas of goddess-good teaching.

A THIRD TERM: POSTMODERN WITCHES, MOTHERS, LONERS

Although Haraway (1991) frames the choices available for living (and, ipso facto, for teaching) in the future around the binary, cyborg versus goddess, there are other choices available for elaboration, construction, and just trying on to see how they feel. Radical feminists of the past 2 decades have sought, for example, to reclaim the power of the witch, the crone, and the hag. Under the name of the w.i.t.c.h., a *Wild Independent Thinking Crone and Hag*, we might imagine these much maligned women as teachers. *Witch* is, after all, an appellation hurled at teachers from time to time, not only by rebellious students, but also through portrayals in children's books, rock songs, and other media.

In *Websters' First New Intergalactic Wickedary of the English Language* (1987) Mary Daly includes the following definitions:

> **Witch:** . . . an Elemental Soothsayer; one who is in harmony with the rhythms of the universe: Wise Woman, Healer; one who exercises transformative powers: Shape-shifter;—averting disaster, warding off attacks of demons and Magnetizing Elemental Spiritual Forces. (p. 180)

> **Hag:** . . . Witch, Fury, Harpy who haunts the Hedges/Boundaries of patriarchy, frightening fools and summoning Weird Wandering Women into the Wild. (p. 137)

> **Crone:** . . . Great Hag of History, long-lasting one . . . who has survived the early stages of the Otherworld Journey and who therefore has Dis-cov-ered depths of Courage, Strength, and Wisdom in her Self. (p. 114)

The witch/crone/hag is, thus, like the goddess in her transformative powers and like the cyborg in that she is a haunter of hedges and boundaries. Unlike the cyborg, whose milieu is surface and boundary, however, the witch is at home with depth and duration; the witch is an old hand with elemental forces.

The women of Greenham Common are modern-day witches whose understanding and use of elemental forces intersect technology and the findings of science in ways that allow crossings of the high-tech boundaries separating women from (the off-switches of) machines. On one occasion, they use "women's technology" to capture border guards policing the fence around the Greenham nuclear plant; they imprison the guards, motorcycles and all, in a web woven of high-tech cord. Later, the women turn elemental singing into sound waves of precisely the right amplitude and frequency to set swaying and "sing down" the chain-link fence. Feminist fantasy writing is full of similar women/witches who, like Gael Baudino's harpster turned high-tech rocker, use an elemental understanding of science and technologies to cross patriarchal divides.

The postmodern witch-teacher, a mythical creature who adapts the methods of the witch/crone/hag both to the classrooms and to the technologies of today, is neither goddess nor cyborg, but always already part goddess and part cyborg. Like the witch-women of Greenham Common, she seeks the elemental aspects of technologies that make them vulnerable and invokes elemental powers against them. In her computerized classroom, this cyber-witch pays no heed to the patriarchal "don't worry your pretty little head about it, dear" discourse that positions teachers and students as "not needing to know" about the elemental stuff of which technologies are made—zeros and ones and programs and control. She studies it out and shares it with her students; she reads a row of ones in computer memory as a row of dominos and knows that another "one" in the right register will cause a "domino effect," "zeroing out" the data, and with the data, the control. In these days of magnetic storage and retrieval of data, the concept of "Magnetizing Elemental Spiritual Forces" (Daly, 1987, p. 114) takes on new meaning for her; magnetizing and de-magnetizing go hand in hand.

Demystification is her motto. The cyber-witch teacher is dedicated to engaging students in "roboticide, the process of shedding of false selves manufactured in the State of Robotitude, releasing the Wild within" (Daly, 1987, p. 224). She teaches them to find routes of escape from this state: On a Disneyland field trip, they seek out the secret passages to the inner workings underground, and they take pictures with their shoes not touching the painted footprints marked Stand Here for Photo Opportunity. They learn to scramble their Internet messages and to shortcut the structured programs of computer-based instruction. They learn vocabulary forbidden from the Dolch list, and they speak it with courage, strength, and wisdom.

The witch, of course, is not alone in the space of the third term. In response to Haraway (1991), Susan Suleiman (1989) suggests two other mythical order figures; she writes: "Sometimes it is politic to 'be' a goddess, at other times a cyborg—or at still other times a laughing mother or 'alone standing woman' who sweeps the detritus of civilization" (p. 205). Suleiman does not theorize or describe the "laughing mother," but we can (still, today) imagine her, laughing as she reties the shoes that her daughter has shed at least 30 times a day, laughing as she watches the children enjoying the backyard technologies of swings and seesaws, laughing as she watches the children negotiate an Escher castle in a hologram game. She is laughing because she exists outside the world of Freud, Lacan, and even Chodorow and Dr. Spock. She can laugh because she is not weighed down measuring "quality time" and providing "cognitive growth experiences." She is a free spirit who can laugh as she dances with the children on a cyberspace dance floor, together tracing four-dimensional shapes and patterns with their bodies. Each day, she gathers her brood of children, and, like the cyborg, she runs along the networks of informatics until she finds a place where they can dance and laugh in the warm simulacrum of the sun.

Can we imagine a "laughing teacher" continuing the joyfulness of the laughing mother? A teacher unconstrained by cognitive learning theories and IEPs (Individualized Education Programs)? A teacher laughing as she splashes with her students in the simulated seas of an unnamed planet, as they feel the warm equatorial waters on their bio-cyber bodies still back in the wintry Midwest? Like the goddess, the laughing teacher is unconstrained by the worldly search for good sex and for an income reflecting her "comparable worth." Her laughter is undiminished by the "real world" of children dying from drive-by shootings, of child abuse, and of preparing children for careers that have obsolesced, given way to the economies of postmodern technology. In her classroom, students, too, escape these worldly cares . . . they make joyful noise, tell tall tales, and play hide-and-seek in the electronic garden. No Norman Rockwell teacher is she, with tightly drawn hair, pointer/punisher in hand, and on her desk an apple, fruit of the tree of knowledge of good and evil. The laughing teacher's hair blows free; in her hand she holds a magic wand, and the fruit on her table is a jar of Tang, simulated postmodern sustenance for long excursions into exciting worlds unchartable and as yet unknown.

The "alone standing woman who sweeps the detritus of civilization" is a figure introduced by novelist Christine Brooks-Rose (Suleiman, 1989); in bringing her to our attention, Suleiman muses over whether the alone standing woman is sweeping *away* the detritus of civilization, or sweeping new *patterns in it*. We can imagine this alone standing woman as a postmodern statue of liberty holding not a beacon but a broom. But, where does she stand in the "global village," this postmodern place where everyone is equally and intimately connected with everyone else? To be alone standing, she must have one foot in and one foot out of the border. She is as grounded in the network as is the cyborg, but, goddesslike, the alone standing woman escapes the dimensionality of the society that she sweeps. Hers is a teacherly position in the sense that teachers share the humanity of their students, but escapes humanness as it is understood by the youngsters in her class. For the alone standing teacher, her sweeping is her teaching.

If the cyber-witch teacher is an agent of demystification, the alone standing teacher is a mystery, always sweeping, but sweeping how? Sometimes she is a feminist pedagogue sweeping new patterns, sweeping the margins into the center of educational practice and attention; sometimes she is a multicultural teacher sweeping away the detritus of scientific racism. Perhaps she can sweep new patterns into the detritus we call technological determinism, and with the new patterns sweep recipes for new and differently balanced technologies. She sweeps "unthinking of educational technology" (Damarin, 1991) into the curriculum of teacher education and of schools, and she sweeps new situations in which situated learning can occur. School children play in the piles that she sweeps; they find new treasures in them and build castles of the detritus in the piles. She sweeps spirals in the piles, and together (students and teacher and the ever present broom) they dance a ceremonial good-bye when she finds and sweeps away a racist controller chip, a patriarchal mindcop, or a shackle meant for them.

CAN WE DANCE THE SPIRAL DANCE?

Speaking of the goddess and the cyborg, Haraway (1991) notes that "both are caught in the spiral dance" (p. 181)—dancing with us, and dancing as fast as they can, I expect, along a spiral path in three or more dimensions. The spiral might have been a circle, were it not for the hot air of the discourse of technological progress always blowing, pushing the circular arcs up and away in an extra dimension. The spiral is held in to its center by a centripetal force, a pull toward the elemental principles and rhythms of the witch women, toward the spirit and transcendent power of the goddess, the part-human of the cyborg, the joyfulness of the laughing mother, and the firm footing of the alone standing woman. But they/ we are, none of us, faithful to the center; the centrifugal forces that send us packing off in all directions might be as innocent as curiosity or as densely coded as the serpent in the garden. Pushed and pulled—in, out, and up—*we cannot not dance.*

But, what kind of dance is the spiral dance? The ballet of a Greek goddess? A postmodern march of the toy robot-soldiers? A do-si-do as we circle each other back to back? A clog dance of an alone standing woman? The back and forth of a jitterbug danced with broom in hand? A witches' circle (double, double, toil and trouble)? . . . And whom will you choose for a partner? a goddess? a cyborg? an alone standing woman? . . . And who might choose you? a witch? a laughing mother?

It is this spiral dance that our schools must teach our children to enjoy. If they are to escape the C³I of the Informatics of Domination, they must learn to dance on the borders of human and machine. Goddess teachers are no longer enough, if ever they were. The cyborg, the laughing mother, the witch, and the alone standing woman must all be invited to teach in our schools, not to "facilitate" efficient achievement of cognitive objectives and oxymoronic job skills, but to help our youth to see possibilities for living fully in the electronic moment and the information age. Teacher education programs must offer apprenticeship in witchcrafty sweeping, alone standing laughing, cyborgian spell casting and, yes, the grace of goddesses unfaithful to their fathers. Border teachers/creatures, trained like the goddess to be "takers of all" and like the cyborg to find "pleasure in the confusion of boundaries and responsibility in their construction," must be invited into our schools. Only they can assist our youth in the ironic creation of themselves as ever more human, even as they are constructed as ever more machine.

Acknowledgment. This article was originally presented as part of the Symposium on Cyborgs in Education at the annual meeting of the American Educational Research Association in New Orleans, April 3, 1994. I am grateful to Marilyn Hegarty for conversations about some of the ideas in this article.

NOTE

1. Haraway published "A Manifesto for Cyborgs" in *Radical America* in 1985; with minor revisions, this paper is reprinted in Haraway's collected essays *Simians, Cyborgs, and Women* (1991). Quotations and page references to "Manifesto" within the present chapter refer to the 1991 edition.

REFERENCES

Apple, Michael W., & Jungck, Susan. (1990). You don't have to be a teacher to teach this unit: Teaching, technology, and gender in the classroom. *American educational research journal, 27*, 227–251.

Baudino, Gael. 1990. *Gossamer axe.* New York: Penguin.

Bolen, Jean Shinoda. (1984). *Goddesses in every woman: A new psychology of women.* New York: Harper and Row.

Bowers, C. A. (1988). *The cultural dimensions of educational computing: Understanding the non-neutrality of technology.* New York: Teachers College Press.

Daly, Mary (conjurer, in cahoots with Jane Caputi). (1987). *Websters' first intergalactic wickedary of the English language.* Boston: Beacon Press.

Damarin, Suzanne K. (Winter 1991). Feminist unthinking and educational technology. *Educational and training technology international, 27*, 111–119.

Efron, Sara, & Joseph, Pamela Bolotin. (1994). Reflections in a mirror: Teacher-generated metaphors from self and others. In P. B. Joseph & G. E. Burnaford (Eds.), *Images of Schoolteachers in the Twentieth Century.* New York: St. Martin's Press.

Gerbner, George. (1973). Teacher image and the hidden curriculum. *American Scholar, 42*, 66–99.

Green, Nancy, & Manke, Mary Phillips. (1994). Good women and old stereotypes: Retired teachers talk about teaching. In P. B. Joseph and G. E. Burnaford (Eds.), *Images of Schoolteachers in the Twentieth Century.* New York: St. Martin's Press.

Haraway, Donna J. (1991). *Simians, cyborgs, and women.* New York: Routledge.

Haraway, Donna. (1992). The promise of monsters: A regenerative politics for inappropriate/d others. In Larry Grossberg, Cary Nelson, & Paula Treichler (Eds.), *Cultural studies* (pp. 295–337). New York: Routledge.

Harding, Sandra. (1991). *Whose Science? Whose Knowledge?* Ithaca, NY: Cornell University Press.

Joseph, Pamela Bolotin, & Burnaford, Gail E. (1994). *Images of schoolteachers in the twentieth century: Paragons, polarities, complexities.* New York: St. Martin's Press.

Kinsley, David. (1989). *The goddesses' mirror: Visions of the divine from East and West.* Albany: State University of New York.

Knupfer, Nancy Nelson. (1993). Teachers and educational computing: Changing roles and changing pedagogy. In R. Muffoletto & N. N. Knupfer (Eds.), *Computers in Education: Social, Political, and Historical Perspectives* (pp. 163–180). Cresskill, NJ: Hamden.

Noble, Douglas. (1991). *The classroom arsenal: Military research, information, technology, and public education.* London: Falmer Press.

Noddings, Nel. (1984). *Caring: A feminine approach to ethics and moral education.* Berkeley: University of California.

Olson, John. (1988). *Schoolworlds, microworlds.* New York: Routledge.

Ross, Andrew. (1991). Hacking away at the counterculture. In Constance Penley and Andrew Ross (Eds.), *Technoculture* (pp. 107–134). Minneapolis: University of Minnesota Press.

Suleiman, Susan R. (1989). *Subversive intent: Gender, politics, and the avant-garde.* Cambridge: Harvard University Press.

ABOUT THE AUTHOR

Suzanne K. Damarin is a professor in the School of Educational Policy and Leadership at Ohio State University, where her research and teaching bridge mathematics and educational technology, on the one hand, and cultural issues in education on the other. She has considered herself a feminist for as long as she can remember; in the 1960s she thought that her graduate work in mathematics and her feminism were mutually irrelevant. Today she finds her feminism central to her work in technology and mathematics education.

CHAPTER 18

Educating the Living, Remembering the Dead

THE MONTREAL MASSACRE AS METAPHOR

Jennifer Scanlon

I write this reflection on "Educating the Living, Remembering the Dead" in the aftermath of the Oklahoma City bombing, as the country reels from the shock that "it," namely terrorism, can happen here. Many of us already knew that. From the Ku Klux Klan to attacks on abortion clinics to the unnamed but ever present fear of male violence that keeps women from living fully active lives, terror and terrorism are present. The Montreal Massacre is a horrific example of this terrorism and of the ways in which our sound bite approach to violence prevents lasting analysis and eclipses opportunities for making connections.

Educators and activists must continue to name these acts of violence, to make connections between them, to work toward a society in which any and all acts of hatred and violence are condemned. The bombing of the federal building in Oklahoma City is related to the Montreal Massacre; the racism of the criminal justice system is related to the lack of money for drug rehabilitation programs; domestic violence is related to the political Right's plan to take poor children away from their mothers. Violence comes in some fairly spiffy boxes. It seems to me that a job of feminist teachers is to assist our students—and ourselves—in doing the unpacking.

To be sure, in the world of male fantasy, woman's body serves as the ideal site for the crime.
                        —Alain Robbe-Grillet (in Malette & Chalouh, 1991, p. 19)

This chapter originally appeared in *Feminist Teacher*, 1994, 8(2), 75–79.

The Feminist Teacher *Anthology: Pedagogies and Classroom Strategies.* Copyright © 1998 by Teachers College, Columbia University. All rights reserved. ISBN 0-8077-3741-0 (paper), ISBN 0-8077-3742-9 (cloth). Prior to photocopying items for classroom use, please contact the Copyright Clearance Center, Customer Service, 222 Rosewood Drive, Danvers, MA 01923, USA, telephone (508) 750-8400.

On December 6, 1989, fourteen women were murdered at the University of Montreal's Ecole Polytechnique. The murderer, M. L., walked into a classroom at the engineering school and demanded that the women move to one side of the room. When people stared but did not move, he fired two shots into the ceiling. "You're all a bunch of feminists," he shouted, "and I hate feminists" (Silverman & Kennedy, 1993, p. 136). Once the men left the room, M. L. opened fire, killing six women. He then roamed the school, targeting women and eventually shooting 27 and killing 14 before he killed himself (Silverman & Kennedy, 1993, p. 136).

The Montreal Massacre received media attention across North America and the world. M. L. gained notoriety as the worst mass murderer in Canada in modern times. Although he was a serial killer, and although most women victims of violence are not victims of serial killers but rather of people they know, this case nevertheless provides an important metaphor both for the violence women face and for the media and social scramble not to hold men accountable for male violence. In this chapter, I outline the way in which I use the Montreal Massacre in the introductory women's studies classroom to introduce a section of the semester that deals with violence against women. This chapter provides a description of this particular day's activities, including the small-group exercises in which students participate. By using a feminist pedagogical approach that emphasizes discussion and relational thinking, and by remembering the women who died on that day, we can at once pay tribute to a specific group of victims and name the larger social pathology—misogyny—that shows no signs of disappearing.

INTRODUCTION: TRIBUTE AND SONG

We begin by reading a list of the names, ages, and occupations or courses of study of the women murdered that day in Montreal. We talk about why it is that most people remember the name of the murderer (Marc Lepine, in this case, or Ted Bundy, in another famous case), but the women's names are forgotten. I explain why I will use only the killer's initials but have us read the women's names and a brief description both at the beginning and end of the class. Naming the victims is one way to keep their memories alive. Having the students read—and attempt to pronounce correctly the women's names—brings students into the discussion from the start. It is an attempt to make the women real, to explore the reasons why they died, to see education not only as informational but also as part of a process of healing (Bricker-Jenkins & Hooyman, 1987, p. 37). These 14 women were killed at the Polytechnique on December 6, 1989:

Genevieve Bergeron, 21, was a 2nd-year student in civil engineering.

Helene Colgan, 23, was a senior in mechanical engineering.

Nathalie Croteau, 23, was a senior in mechanical engineering.

Barbara Daigneault, 22, was a senior in mechanical engineering and held a teaching assistantship.

Anne-Marie Edward, 21, was a 1st-year student in chemical engineering.

Maud Haviernick, 29, was a 2nd-year student in engineering materials and a graduate in environmental design.

Barbara Maria Klucznik, 31, was a 2nd-year student in engineering materials.

Maryse Laganiere, 25, worked in the budget department of the Polytechnique.

Maryse LeClair, 23, was a 4th-year student in engineering materials.

Anne-Marie Lemay, 27, was a 4th-year student in mechanical engineering.

Sonia Pelletier, 28, was to graduate the next day in mechanical engineering.

Michele Richard, 21, was a 2nd-year student in engineering materials.

Annie St. Arneault, 23, was a mechanical engineering student.

Annie Turcotte, 21, was a 1st-year student in engineering materials. (Malette & Chalouh, 1991)[1]

The second part of the introduction is a song by Australian women's music performer Judy Small, called "Montreal, December '89" (1990). The song's setting is the memorial service for the dead women: "Seven thousand came that day to pay their last respects / to fourteen women slaughtered for no reason but their sex." One woman spoke aloud as she stood in the line, trying to make sense of the fact that it is "always men who resort to the gun, the sword, and the fist / Why does gunman sound so familiar, while gunwoman doesn't quite ring true?" she asks. "What is it about men that makes them do the things they do?"

Music is a powerful tool in the classroom and an effective way to open up or close a discussion. "Montreal, December '89" both touches the students and provides us with a basis for compiling a list of questions that individual students and the class as a whole will contemplate as they consider male violence against women in the following weeks. Why are women more likely than men to be assaulted or killed by spouses or lovers; and men, by strangers? Why do men resort to violence to solve their problems? What responsibility do all men have for any male violence? After we listen to the song, we put a list of these and other questions on the board. I provide the students with a few statistics about men's violence against women to add credibility to the questions, but I do not attempt to provide answers to these questions. These questions should guide their thinking as we talk about all means of violence against women—rape, domestic violence, sexual harassment, and murder—in the coming weeks. Although we will come back to the questions again and again, I caution, we may not answer them. I express my hope that everyone in the class will grapple with the questions and with her/his answers; if indeed there were one expert answer, perhaps we would have solved the problem by now. Although discussion of women's victimization is disempowering, posing questions and placing the students in the role of contributors can be empowering. A pedagogical approach, in this case, can help students deal with what they may find very depressing about women's studies classroom information.

Judy Small's (1990) song inevitably brings out some of what I want to counteract: our society's reluctance to blame men for male behavior. This murderer in Montreal was sick, some students argue, but he has little to do with everyday men or even with the other forms of violence women face. I consider this one of the social pathologies that prevents us from taking action on violence against women—we bend over backwards in order to be "fair" to men. One of my long-term goals is that over the course of the next few weeks the Montreal Massacre will be seen for what I believe it to be, part of a continuum of violence and hatred rather than an aberration that will never be repeated.

GROUP EXERCISES

After we listen to the Judy Small (1990) song and list our questions on the board, students divide into small groups, each with a separate exercise. By this time in the semester, students are familiar enough with group projects to start right in with their task: discuss their assignment within their group, choose a person to present their findings to the class, and decide if there are any ways in which their assignment sheds light on the questions we have on the board.

Group I: The Modest Proposal

This group reads "A Not So Modest Proposal for Safer Streets," a humorous piece by Judy MacLean. MacLean (1993), tired of being fearful every time she goes out after dark, proposes an "obvious solution": "What this country needs is a federal law forbidding men to go out on the streets unless accompanied by a woman" (p. 1). Such a move would cause an immediate drop in rape, street harassment, and gang behavior, MacLean argues, since men are much less likely to engage in such practices "when they have to bring their mothers or girlfriends along" (p. 1).

This group's assignment is to discuss MacLean's modest proposal both as humor and as social commentary. They are to determine where they think MacLean speaks in jest; where she may be perfectly serious. The goal here is that they will see what is too often invisible and unspoken; they will realize that women operate under a curfew, most often without comment and often without even their own recognition. They can connect that issue to the questions on the board—or propose that we add another question to the list.

Group 2: The Continuum

This group starts off its discussion by reading the following quotation from Nicole Brossard's (1991) "The Killer Was No Young Man":

> All things considered, M. L. was no young man. He was as old as sexist, misogynist proverbs, as old as all the Church fathers who ever doubted women had a soul. He was as old as all the legislators who ever forbade women enter the university, the right to vote, access to the public sphere. M. L. was as old as Man and his contempt for women. (p. 33)

Students are asked to juxtapose two arguments. First, M. L. was a sick young man who went off the deep end; his action is nothing more than the action of a psychopath removed from all social rules. Like all serial killers, he was "a very different kind of individual" (Silverman & Kennedy, 1993, p. 131). The second argument is this: Why do we understand pornography, women earning less money than men, beer advertisements, and men hitting their wives, but not M. L.? (Baris, 1991, p. 66). M. L. is part of a continuum, not removed from society but part and parcel of our woman hating. Laws may have changed about men's violence toward women, but attitudes have not kept pace.

This group must assemble supporting evidence for both sides, feel out their own position, and present their arguments to the class. They too can add new questions or propose amendments to the questions we already have in place.

Group 3: Language

This group will analyze the language used to discuss the Montreal Massacre by focusing on a letter sent to two Montreal newspapers but not published in either (Trudeau, 1991, pp. 73–74). This letter asks why the French-language press was so reluctant to use the feminine form for *victim*, even though all the victims were women. Students in this group also discuss other language uses, in search of connections. They discuss hate crimes legislation, which does not include gender (Heinzerling, 1994, pp. 102–104); athletic coaches insulting boys by calling them girls; the term *crime of passion*, which is often used when women are murdered by their spouses or lovers. This group is asked to make any connections between these issues, loosely grouped under *language,* and the questions on the board.

Group 4: Connecting Racism and Sexism

One of the strongest media responses to the Montreal Massacre was that the issue was that of exploiter and exploited, not that of gender. Feminists were accused of taking advantage of the situation by talking about misogyny. The killer was crazy, many argued; his actions had nothing to do with women and everything to do with his psychosis. "Yet if the killer had picked out a visible minority," argues Elaine Audet (1991), "everyone would have cried racism and remembered the Holocaust. Crimes against women have no history. This history, swept aside, has only begun to be written" (p. 44). This group has to decide for themselves if they agree with Audet. What did the killer's actions have to do with misogyny, and how does the press deal with issues related to any "minority" group? Would the media have responded differently, for example, if all the victims were white, the killer Black? Students can discuss several fairly recent crimes in the United States in which race, gender, or both were at issue: a White Boston man murdered his wife and placed her body in an African American neighborhood to locate the blame there; a group of African American and Latino youths raped a White woman jogger in Central Park; a Black man targeted and killed White and Asian passengers on a Long Island Railroad train in New York. My goal here is that students begin to examine critically the ways in which the media alternately highlight or ignore race and gender or pit *race* against *gender* in a false hierarchy that glosses over root causes of social hatreds.

Group 5: Space and Behavior

This group must examine a quotation and a poem about who takes what space and who does not. "Streets, sidewalks and other spaces, where men roam freely, become zones of hostile space for women" (Leach, Lesink, & Morton, 1986, pp. 10–12).

This group also examines Pauline Bart's (1993) poem "Prior Restraint" in its entirety; the following is an excerpt:

Every day I censor myself
Pinning my blouse so "nothing" shows
Checking my clothes so I don't look vulnerable
Thinking of putting up my hair
So I don't resemble a mark
Putting out trash in the morning
So I won't be in the alley at night
Parking in well-lit places (p. 4)

Students then must discuss the impact of the Montreal Massacre on all women in Montreal, all women college students, all women at the University of Montreal, all women studying engineering. They must attempt to make the connections between those women and all women who, because of fear of men, restrict their behavior. The job of this group is to place male violence in a context, a physical and geographic context.

Group 6: Strict Definitions of Female and Male Behavior

Contrary to what the media repeated again and again, M. L. himself argued that he knew exactly what he was doing. He even called the massacre a "political" act. In a suicide note, he stated, "Even if the Mad Killer Epithet will be attributed to me by the media, I consider myself a rational erudite" (Malette & Chalouh, 1991, p. 181). M. L. had no tolerance for female behavior that did not match his limited and limiting expectations. The job of this group is to outline traditional expectations of female behavior and discuss the costs when women transcend the boundaries. They can talk about the college context and then go outside the college realm. Do they see any strict definitions or delineations on our campus, in athletics, or with fraternities? When groups such as fraternities are vitally concerned with masculinity, how do they define femininity? Is that also part of a continuum? The group can add contemporary examples: Hillary Clinton, for example, or Anita Hill. Are men threatened by women, I ask them, when women earn more money, show greater intellect, attain higher levels of education?

GROUP PRESENTATIONS

Each group takes about 5 minutes to present their findings and arguments to the class. This approach works very well because students spend some time exploring one issue in depth but then hear about the arguments and discussions that other groups had concerning other aspects of the problem. In this way they receive the overview but also spend some time exploring and clarifying their own feelings and formulating their own arguments. To avoid stagnant groupings, I ask the students to form groups with people they have not worked with before, and I make a rule that the presenter at the end must be someone who has not presented before or, at least, not recently. I have found that even the quiet students participate in groups, and group solidarity—or even dissension—can provide them with the confidence to present to the class as a whole. This provides a space for the male students in the class, who generally feel uncomfortable when men as a group are held accountable for male violence. However, although some men in the class react the way the male does in the Judy Small (1990) song, by "getting steamed," most feel sufficient horror at the massacre to let down their guard and think about the implications of socially acceptable as well as unacceptable male behavior.

After the group presentations, we read the names of the 14 women once again. I ask them to keep our list of questions in their minds as they do their reading on violence against women; we will come back to the questions as they wish and certainly at the end of this segment of the course.

CONCLUSION

The Montreal Massacre is an appropriate metaphor for the violence that women face every day. Women's bodies are the site for many men's crimes, and until we name the connections, little will change. Feminist analysis of the Montreal Massacre at the time was "ignored or ridiculed or rejected with hostility" (Malette & Chalouh, 1991, p. 9). As a result, the women killed did not receive the respect they deserved, the attention their lives as well as their deaths warranted, or the analysis that can provide the means for changing the future so that other massacres, large and small, can be prevented. In the most recent book published in Canada to address crime, the wrong date is given for the massacre, and the authors speak ambiguously about how activists in Canada "used" the event to draw attention to the problem of violence (Silverman & Kennedy, 1993, pp. 136–137). No one, however, speaks about how the press used madness to obscure misogyny, the psychologists and talk show hosts used mother blaming to exonerate the self-proclaimed political actor, the society uses all means possible to avoid blaming men for male behavior.

By using the Montreal Massacre as a metaphor, women's studies faculty can open an honest, and revealing, dialogue about violence against women. By engaging students in a process that is respectful of feminist process, women's writings, and student ability, we can further student understanding of women's struggles to survive, to make their way in the world, to flourish. Only when students understand the continuum will they be able to hold others, and themselves, responsible for their own positions on that continuum of woman hating obscured by media, politics, the law, religion, education. Perhaps then they will understand better what they really fear when they tell us, "I'm not a feminist, but . . ."

NOTE

1. Malette and Chalouh (1991) draw together the words of activists, academics, journalists, and concerned citizens. Chapters address the media responses to the massacre in the French and English language press, present a feminist analysis of the murders, and make connections between the massacre and the larger social forces at work in Canada today.

REFERENCES

Audet, Elaine. (1991). A matter of life or death. In Louise Malette & Marie Chalouh (Eds.), *The Montreal massacre* (pp. 44–45). Charlottetown, Prince Edward Island, Canada: gynergy books.

Bart, Pauline. (1993). Prior restraint. In Pauline Bart & Eileen Geil Moran (Eds.), *Violence against women: The bloody footprints* (p. 4). Newbury Park, CA: Sage.

Baris, Mireille. (1991). We don't understand. In Louise Malette & Marie Chalouh (Eds.), *The Montreal massacre* (p. 66). Charlottetown, Prince Edward Island, Canada: gynergy books.

Bricker-Jenkins, Mary, & Hooyman, Nancy. (1987). Feminist pedagogy in education for social change. *Feminist Teacher*, 2(2), 36–42.

Brossard, Nicole. (1991). The killer was no young man. In Louise Malette & Marie Chalouh (Eds.), *The Montreal massacre* (pp. 31–32). Charlottetown, Prince Edward Island, Canada: gynergy books.

Heinzerling, Lisa. (1994). Classifying violent acts against women as hate crimes would be effective. In Karin L. Swisher & Carol Wekesser (Eds.), *Violence against women* (pp. 102–104). San Diego, CA: Greenhaven Press.

Leach, Belinda, Lesink, Ellen, & Morton, Penny A. (1986, Spring). Perception of fear in the urban environment. *Women and Environments*, 10–12.

MacLean, Judy. (1993, March). A not so modest proposal for safer streets. *Funny Times*, 1, 5.

Malette, Louise, & Chalouh, Marie (Eds.). (1991). *The Montreal massacre.* Charlottetown, Prince Edward Island, Canada: gynergy books.

Nemiroff, Greta Holmann. (1991). Where are the 49% when we need them? In Louise Malette & Marie Chalouh (Eds.), *The Montreal massacre* (pp. 145–149). Charlottetown, Prince Edward Island, Canada: gynergy books.

Silverman, Robert, & Kennedy, Leslie. (1993). *Deadly deeds: Murder in Canada.* Scarborough, Ontario: Nelson Canada.

Small, Judy. (1990). Montreal, December '89. *Snapshot*. Fairfield, Australia: Crafty Maid Music.

Trudeau, Mireille. (1991). The common assassination of women. In Louise Malette & Marie Chalouh (Eds.), *The Montreal massacre* (pp. 73–74). Charlottetown, Prince Edward Island, Canada: gynergy books.

ABOUT THE AUTHOR

Jennifer Scanlon is an associate professor and the director of women's studies at SUNY Plattsburgh. She is the author of *Inarticulate Longings: The Ladies' Home Journal, Gender, and the Promises of Consumer Culture* (Routledge, 1995), coauthor of *American Women Historians, 1700s–1990s: A Biographical Dictionary* (Greenwood, 1996), and editor of *Significant Contemporary American Feminists* (Greenwood, forthcoming). She is also the author of many articles on popular culture and feminist pedagogy.

CHAPTER 19

Gender, Race, and Radicalism

TEACHING THE AUTOBIOGRAPHIES OF NATIVE AND AFRICAN AMERICAN WOMEN ACTIVISTS

Joy James

It's been several years since I have taught in women's studies, although I continue to focus on issues of gender, race, and justice. The varied research and teaching environments in which I have found myself have altered my approach, or approaches, to pedagogy. For instance, I no longer consider academe to be singularly depoliticizing or deradicalizing as an environment. So the doubts expressed toward the conclusion of "Gender, Race and Radicalism: Teaching the Autobiographies of Native and African American Women Activists" have been alleviated somewhat. Specifically, can one maintain one's integrity as a dissenting voice, as a progressive voice, in a corporate structure? My response today is yes, as long as you are more than a professional thinker, as long as you have a political life outside of academe that seeps across academic borders. And an ethical drive that calls you to want more than competency or excellence in the classroom. So, I have been criticized for wanting too much from academe, too much from students, and too much from myself. In the essay "Reflections on Teaching: 'Gender, Race, and Class'" (Chapter 7 in this collection) my "exacting" demands are apparent and have been dismissed by some academics as being too political/polemical and unrealistic.

Perhaps I trust myself and my students more. Perhaps I have become more detached. But the urgency that shapes these two essays no longer always appears as a feature in my classes—unless perhaps my students bring this with them.

1992—THE POST-COLUMBUS CLASSROOM: WOMEN'S RESISTANCE TO AMERICAN RACISM

In American society, where indigenous people and African Americans signify the primitive, exotic (often dangerous) "Other," anti-Black and anti-Indian racism coexist within a larger context of political opposition to radicalism. Antiradicalism often appears in reactionary or conservative politics. At other times, radicalism is depoliticized and co-opted into trendy rhetoric and fashion: For instance, TV commercials inform us that the soft drink Mountain Dew is "radical" and that Revlon makes "revolutionary cosmetics for revolutionary women." As in pop culture, within academe, radical and antiracist politics are usually distorted, if not denigrated. With some exceptions, dominant trends in academic studies seem either to denounce radicalism and antiracism as misguided approaches for redressing injustices (that are increasingly denied)—even the liberal remedy of affirmative action is now considered "reverse racism/sexism"—or to reduce radicalism and antiracism to a surrogate liberalism or literary "insurgency." Obviously, there are exceptions: Those who most often go beyond rhetorical antiracism and radicalism are student and faculty activists engaged in social justice organizing. My own student experiences reminded me of how academic sites tend to silence or view radicalism suspiciously.

Since my days as a student organizer, the meanings of *radicalism* have encompassed not only political ideas or rhetoric about political ideas but also practices and strategies for uprooting oppressive structures, rather than assimilating into or reforming them. After several years as a full-time academic in western Massachusetts, estranged from the urban activism I had known in New York City, I was unsure about the nature of progressive politics and race discourse: Most of what I had known as "radical" from my organizing and teaching ethics with religious leaders in New York City was generally received, by more seasoned academics, as inappropriately political (polemical) or academically "uncivilized" in a university setting. As an assistant professor in women's studies engaged in antiracist education, my work focused primarily on marginalized Black and, increasingly, indigenous women. Both groups of women figured prominently in my courses, given that material and "existential" wealth in the United

States/Americas was (is) accumulated through systemic exploitation of these women and their peoples.

While teaching, I often wondered, pessimistically, how students perceive "women of color" whom they encounter as "texts," particularly those activists who critique the U.S. state. I imagined that it was difficult for academics to conceptualize such women as something other than fashionable literary commodities, colorful accessories to Eurocentric as well as trans-ethnic conservative/liberal paradigms. With the ascendancy of post-colonial/postmodern/postracial discourse, I was also curious about whether students considered antiracist, radical activists to be political antiques, cultural throwbacks, or ethnocentric oddities. My pessimism about the academic reception for the worldviews and politics of Native and African Americans confronting genocide was tied to a general reading of dominant, academic politics in which most teaching (conservative, liberal, or postmodern/colonial hybridity) privileges Eurocentric or multicultural paradigms over antiracist frameworks: inviting little critical juxtaposition with radical critiques from nonacademics or nonelites.

The year 1992 was a watershed for education involving the analysis of structural violence and genocide. That fall, community, student, and faculty intellectuals worked to critique the quincentennial and celebrations of the "discovery" of the Americas. In Amherst, at the University of Massachusetts, faculty, staff, and students initiated curriculum changes, held campus forums, and promoted recent publications by Native Americans and others on contemporary indigenous oppression and resistance. This call issued by progressive academics led to various responses. Mine was to develop and teach a first-time course offering at the University of Massachusetts–Amherst the following semester called Gender, Race, and Radicalism: Native and African American Women Activists, which was opened to students in the Five College system (University of Massachusetts and Amherst, Smith, Mt. Holyoke, and Hampshire Colleges). I had taught the autobiographies of Black women active in the civil rights/Black liberation movements of the 1950s, 1960s, and 1970s in other courses. Over several years, Mohawk scholar-activist Donna Goodleaf, who co-lectured in this course, had introduced me to the writings of contemporary Native American women in resistance to state domination or colonization. Gender, Race and Radicalism: Native and African American Women Activists seemed an ideal opportunity to synthesize studies of women in two marginalized ethnic groups into a unique, comparative women's studies class. That the women to be studied were also radical activists brought added significance: to a greater degree than in its marginalization of conservative-liberal "women of color," academe has erased radical women of color.

Often, comparative women's studies focuses on women of European descent as well as liberal or conservative women as normative. Most studies of radicalism emphasize men, as does the comparative literature on Black/Red-Black Indians and Native and African Americans (an estimated one third to one quarter of African Americans have Native ancestry). Departing from those norms, Gender, Race, and Radicalism emphasized writings by Native and African American women radicals from "captive communities" (Spillers, 1987) within nonconventional analytical frameworks. As an upper-level elective, the course brought together approximately 20 students, mostly juniors and seniors interested in not only women of color but also political radicalism in the lives of Native and African American women activists engaged in liberation movements for humane, democratic societies.

CLASSROOM ENCOUNTERS

As an experimental, one-time course offering seeking to expand the context(s) for progressive politics by encouraging the study of women's radical antiracist politics, Gender, Race, and Radicalism was atypical in subject matter, texts, and pedagogy. In this comparative study of American women, which examined the politics of recent indigenous and African American social movements from the perspectives of their women leaders, the assigned texts were by academic or activist Native and African Americans engaged in Red/Black liberation. Course pedagogy incorporated journals for individual reflection, comparative essays, and group presentations on paired autobiographies. Occasionally, students were asked to participate in on-campus cultural and political events organized by women of color (in spring 1993 these events included a performance by the Native American Spiderwoman Theater collective and a conference on women and organizing keynoted by Angela Davis). Exposed to social issues in personal narratives and asked to share their own reflections and experiences, students were confronted with ethical questions. Autobiographical reflections (of student–writers and Native/African American activist–writers) encouraged the class to depart from the explorer–colonizer encounters of contact voyages. (Not every student was willing to engage in such a journey: Some failed to submit the journals that focused on student introspection and reflection on their relationship(s) to text, class, pedagogy, instructor, and women's radical antiracist politics.)

On the first day of teaching, I was pleased to encounter a fairly diverse women's studies class. Two thirds of the students were female, nearly half of the students were of African, Latino, or Asian descent; the remaining half were Euro-American. The students held politically diverse views as well, although all generally considered themselves progressives. A quarter or more of the class identified themselves as community activists. Most of those with extensive organizing within nonacademic/middle-class communities were (upper-) middle-class White women in their 3rd year at Hampshire College, an "alternative" small liberal arts institution. As self-identified activists, these European and Jewish American women had political organizing experience on issues of sexual and racial violence that increased their receptivity to developing critical perspectives on the connections between women's struggles, antiracism, and genocide. A small number of these women activists provided the student comments reprinted below (I thank Rebecca Gould, Joanne Lehrer, and Jenna Magruder for permission to quote from their course papers. The writers are cited by their initials).

The political experiences of student activists shaped their ethnic and gender identities so that they tended to disengage more quickly from self-absorbed reflections or narrow identity politics. During the semester, other students, White and of color, male and female, who had little or no experience in political organizing, more often disassociated introspection from structural analyses to emphasize their personal anxieties and desires over race and acceptance over critiques of racism and genocide. Perhaps because they had a pragmatic approach that connected critiques with practical applications, women student activists tended to advocate classroom attempts to build useful critical analyses:

> Both of us came into "Gender, Race and Radicalism" with a commitment to playing an active role in bringing about social justice in the world, and with experience in attempting to act on this commitment in coalition with other people. We lacked, however, a political analysis which dealt explicitly with genocide and colonialism. Without this analysis, our political actions in the past have often felt incomplete or misguided. (J. M., J. L.)

Not only students felt their past and present political actions to be incomplete. Early on, I had shared with the class my view that the life stories of indigenous and African American women—who survive and resist the most intensive forms of state violence—reveal something of tenacious faith and fierce love in confronting oppression. Suggesting that we encounter these women as conduits for reviewing our own political commitments, rather than as models to be emulated, I did not share with the class my personal search: Working with students to analyze the autobiographies of

Native and African American women activists might help me find my own answers, as an academic, about political integrity and social justice. Teaching from these women's autobiographies for answers to the questions that I silently asked myself, I asked the class: "What does it mean to be a woman in a captive community, in resistance, and what is your relationship to such political actors/actions?" I could not and did not assert what those meanings or relationships were or should be, only that these questions had to be addressed. Throughout that semester, students and teacher struggled with our spoken and unspoken questions. Often, these questions crystallized and collided around the issue of "genocide" in America.

QUESTIONING "GENOCIDE"

During the first class, I lectured on the conditions of Native Americans and African Americans historically devastated by state policies. Today, both peoples suffer greater discrimination and higher infant mortality and mortality rates in the United States than the national average. For decades, African American and Native American activists have organized around U.S. racism and human rights violations. My introductory lecture referred to the African American–led Civil Rights Congress (and to its 1951 petition to the United Nations, *We Charge Genocide: The Crime of Government Against Negro People*) as well as the more recent International Indian Treaty Council's work to interpret and append to U.S. domestic policies the 1948 *UN Convention on the Prevention and Elimination of Genocide*. The *UN Convention* defines genocide as "intent to destroy, *in whole or in part*, a national, racial, ethnic or religious group or kill or inflict serious bodily or mental harm to members of the group" (Patterson, 1951, p. xi).[1] Both African Americans and Native Americans have used the language of human rights and international law to redress destructive state policies.

Stressing that struggles around law and (legal) language also seek to inspire and shape consciousness and activism to counter racism, I raised in our first sessions the role of conventional speech in obscuring critical thinking about genocidal racism in U.S. domestic and foreign policies. For most, U.S./American racism is conceptually severed from genocide. This conceptual estrangement obstructs a national, common language for analyzing genocide against indigenous and African American peoples. I maintained that it was important for the class to engage in critical discussions on contemporary genocide in order to construct a lens for viewing women's autobiographies that refer to cultural or physical genocide or both as byproducts of state racism (James, 1994). For examples of women seeking to build a common language about racism and genocide, I referred to Native American scholar Paula Gunn Allen's (1988) critique of the American moral amnesia concerning the U.S. anti-Indian wars:

> We are horrified by South African apartheid and the removal of millions of indigenous African black natives to what is there called "homelands"—but this is simply a replay of the nineteenth-century U.S. government removal of American Indians to reservations. Nor do many even notice the parallel or fight South African apartheid by demanding an end to its counterpart within the borders of the United States. The American Indian people are in a situation comparable to . . . genocide in many parts of the world today. . . . deliberately, as a matter of national policy, or accidentally as a matter of "fate," every single government, right, left, or centrist in the western hemisphere is consciously or subconsciously dedicated to the extinction of those tribal people who live within its borders. (p. 190)

The familiar, shared context for linking South African apartheid to genocide, or even Nazi anti-Semitism to genocide in Germany, has no counterpart connecting racism to genocide in the United States/Americas. Annette Jaimes's (1992) comparison of U.S. political ideology in historical wars against Native Americans to the campaigns of Nazi Germany was part of course readings that offered a similar argument.

These discussions of language, meaning, and violence were not purely theoretical. The issue of relationships (of student readers to the political struggles of women and oppressed/colonized peoples) and ethics continuously circulated. Exploring the meanings of genocide and of Native and African American women's resistance, I asked the class how our speech about and conceptions of "racism" determine what we say and do about genocide. In their writings, some students expressed that they felt inadequately prepared to analyze genocide as a contemporary phenomenon:

> It is not often in academia (even at oh so liberal [X] college) that we talk about genocide, as a political reality, not off in the past somewhere, but here and now, in attempting to do so, i feel at loss for language. the tools i have been taught to use in writing analytical papers seem insufficient. this seems to be the case more and more as i have made the decision to no longer detach myself from what i write. at the same time, developing a stronger analysis of how systematic oppression/genocide has worked and works in the united states is an incredibly important part of working to end them. (J. M.)

Emphasizing the moral dimensions of speech and acts, students become more engaged in personal reflections. Considering their reflections as their personal responses to the lives of women committed to resisting racist, state oppression, students initially showed discomfort; this dissipated for some but continued throughout the course for others. There was no way around feeling uncomfortable if grappling with ethics was critical to our study of the autobiographies. Ethics, a sense of personal responsibility, moral obligation, or accountability, was central in the autobiographies of the Native and African American women activists. I had incorporated ethical reflections into course pedagogy; reflection summaries concluded each analytical paper; student journals provided the space for less structured reflections; in class and small-group discussions, students were encouraged to explore their relationships to the writings that were studied. Classroom and small-group discussions sparked debates on ethics that developed in student writings. Again, the point was not to dictate to students an appropriate response or reflection but to provide them with the space in which to incorporate those responses or reflections into their institutional education.

FRAMEWORKS

In academic settings where "Whites" study "people of color," where the middle class investigates the lives of poor/working-class peoples, or where conservatives/liberals critique radicals, constructing a critical framework or narrative lens for reading the autobiographies was crucial to deconstructing the "Other." Consequently, the course was divided into two sections. During the first section, students were to quilt an analytical framework for critical reading or literacy in their studies of women struggling against genocide. The class spent the first third of the semester building rudimentary frameworks, which were to be continually reevaluated and refined as later used in papers and oral presentations (in which students would analyze autobiographers' political resistance and vision and include their reflections on these). With references to T. S. Kuhn's *The Structure of Scientific Revolutions* (1963), we discussed paradigmatic shifts, evaluating paradigms (political ideologies) for their ability to address the crises of oppression and to point towards possible strategies or solutions leading to just resolutions.

Building interdisciplinary, analytical frameworks based on course readings and discussions, students outlined key themes to explore—agency, systemic oppression, auto/genocide, ethnic and gender identity—

in the worldviews of the autobiographies as well as in the worldview of the student writer. Most had never been asked to explicate the belief systems or (meta)paradigm shaping their political-social ideas and so found constructing analytical frameworks difficult. Many had naturalized the prevailing framework of their academic experiences, which was largely silent about antiracist radicalism. Pushing the parameters of conventional frameworks in which whiteness or conservatism-liberalism are naturalized, I recalled, as an example of naturalizing whiteness, the commercials of my childhood marketing "flesh-colored" bandages—in one color.

To critique racism in political, economic, and cultural practices, not only as self-contained acts but symptoms of structures (paradigms) of thought and policy, proved very difficult. Students struggled to construct a framework for examining the autobiographies as well as their own political thinking. In an effort to develop these frameworks or paradigms in the course's first section, the class read selections from Manning Marable's *How Capitalism Underdeveloped Black America* (1983b) and Jaimes and Halsey's *The State of Native America* (1992). We also used visual resources: Marlon Riggs's *Ethnic Notions* allowed us to examine U.S. dehumanizing, anti-Black icons and racial-sexual stereotypes of African Americans; and the PBS documentary "In the Image of the White Man" provided historical analysis on the U.S. quest to "de-Indianize" indigenous children through their attendance of residential schools. Through these videos, students examined the images of cultural representations legitimizing violence against Blackness/Africanness and Redness/Indianness. Through the readings of Marable and Jaimes, we examined strategies for resisting dehumanizing images and practices.

During the remaining two thirds of the semester, using their frameworks and selective themes, students wrote comparative papers for each set of autobiographies. I had grouped the texts into pairs of Native and African American women authors. Although the course title identified the autobiographers collectively as radicals, their political ideologies were not monolithic. In fact, I had paired the autobiographies based on possible similarities between Native and African American women's political views. The order in which they were read reflected my perception of increasing radicalism among the women's strategies to counter state domination.[2]

I limited the African American autobiographies to those by activists in the civil rights/Black liberation movements. Given the limited number of autobiographies by U.S. Native American women radicals (Crow Dog lives inside the U.S. domain), I included works by American indigenous activists, Guatemalan Rigoberta Menchu and Bolivian Domitila Chungara, who link their liberation struggles to U.S. foreign policy. Most students knew of Angela Davis and 1992 Nobel Peace Prize laureate Menchu. A few were familiar with Mary Crow Dog through women's studies courses, and some had heard of Anne Moody (whose autobiography is also studied in courses on the civil rights movement); few had heard of Chungara or Assata Shakur.

Through visual resources, students literally saw images of these women in their roles as activists. For the first set of autobiographies, *Lakota Woman* (Crow Dog & Erdoes, 1990) was read alongside the film *Bravehearted Woman: Anna Mae* on Anna Mae Aquash, the assassinated indigenous leader who had organized with Crow Dog at Pine Ridge; the *Eyes on the Prize* segments on the Student Nonviolent Coordinating Committee (SNCC) framed Moody's *Coming of Age in Mississippi* (1968). While reading the second set—Angela Davis's *Autobiography of Angela Davis* (1974/1988) and Rigoberta Menchu's *I, Rigoberta Menchu: An Indian Woman in Guatemala* (1984)—students viewed "A Nation of Law?," the *Eyes on the Prize* segment on Cointelpro and prison conditions, in which Davis is interviewed on the violent suppression of the Attica uprising. Students also screened *When the Mountains Tremble;* this film, narrated by Menchu, examines the Guatemalan war against indigenous Americans in the 1980s and the funding of the Guatemalan military/death squads during the Reagan administration; the film provided, along with the Amnesty International reports on Guatemala, a context for Menchu's *I, Rigoberta.* For the last pair, Assata Shakur's *Assata: An Autobiography* (1978) and Domitila Chungara's *Let Me Speak!* (1978), we watched "Interview with Assata" (1988) and reviewed information on and images of Bolivian workers and peasants.

STUDENT CRITIQUES

As useful as these writers' frameworks proved to be in expanding students' existing paradigms, students were reluctant to critique the writers' racial-ethnic politics and ethnic chauvinism between the two peoples. For instance, they were silent about the absence of Black Indians as either contributors or subject matter, as well as about any discussion of color prejudice among Native Americans in Jaimes's (1992) anthology. When asked about their perceptions of a Crow Dog (Crow Dog & Erdoes, 1990) passage in which she refers to an African American man who assists her as her "slave," they were noncommittal. They were equally noncommittal about Marable's (1983b) distorted portrait of African Americans as the most oppressed ethnic population—these distortions implicit in his disregard of ample documentation that Native Americans suffer the most depressed conditions in the United States. When offered, student criticisms of Black/Indian bias were usually directed at African Americans. Students tended to romanticize and "identify" with Native Americans more than with African Americans. Interestingly, all the non-Black students had personal interactions with African Americans, including those in the class. On the other hand, class members (all non-Native Americans) had virtually no personal interactions with Native Americans, especially those represented in the autobiographies—Native Americans on reservations or in Latin America. Class participants almost uniformly, regardless of their ethnicity, idealized Native Americans as sacrosanct in terms of ethnic-racial politics and attitudes. They were more critical, however, of Native and African American gender politics.

The uneasiness and reluctance with which students addressed classism, (internalized) racism, and the interrelatedness of gender, race, and class issues among Native and African American communities disappeared in their discussions about sexism within those communities. Unsurprisingly, in a women's studies course, students focused on gender; however, in this focus they tended to isolate gender from class and race, ignoring its intersections with other variables. In class, I cited examples of sexism and misogyny among each people, referring to contemporary examples such as the Indigenous Women's Network, which faced criticisms from some Native American men in the International Indian Treaty Council and American Indian Movement (AIM), who argued that women dealing with the specificity of their struggle alienate themselves from "their" men and "community"; and there have been similar accusations used by African American males against African American feminists and women's organizations. Citing examples of patriarchy, though, is not a critique of gender and power relations in antiracist struggles for ethnic sovereignty or independence.

One of the greatest challenges posed by Gender, Race, and Radicalism was that it prodded students to maintain the specificity of gender for a category in critical analysis. It encouraged students to reexamine gender analysis by expanding their concept of gender-progressive to include women who either did not identify as feminists or women who emphasized the concerns of their disenfranchised, ethnic communities. The gender perspectives of these 1960s/1970s Native and African American activists could not be easily dismissed as elements of a "prefeminist" or primitive feminism, although they contradicted feminist ideologies that treat women as a class (a class that often universalizes privileged women). Students were initially inclined to view the activists as gender retrogressive and racially retrograde on the question of nationalism.

Many considered nationalism as uniformly misogynist and counterrevolutionary. Largely ignorant of the works of gender-progressive women (and men) who identified with national liberation struggles, some students considered nationalist women as unenlightened or counterfeminists. In general, most failed to consider the nonessentialism of nationalism; that is, the diversities of nationalism(s) encompass a range of ideologies spanning from the reactionary to the progressive revolutionary.

The women's memoirs highlight a progressive, revolutionary "nationalism." Nearly all of the autobiographers strongly identify with their ethnicity, with some positing their ethnic group as a "nation" (for Native Americans, this nation status is recognized by U.S. law). At the same time, each writer acknowledges the importance of friendships and alliances beyond their own ethnic group. Moody's (1968) and Crow Dog's (Crow Dog & Erdoes, 1990) autobiographies depict how each woman worked with progressive Whites. Other autobiographers explicate their liberation struggles within international politics; for instance, Davis (1974/1988) writes of multiracial transnational struggle:

> [Through] political repression . . . racism, poverty, police brutality . . . Black, Brown, Red, Yellow, and white working people are kept chained to misery and despair. And it was not only within the United States of America, but in countries like Vietnam, with the bombs falling like rain from the U.S. B52's, burning and dismembering innocent children. (p. 382)

For Davis, to address White supremacy one must address capitalism and economic exploitation: "When white people are indiscriminately viewed as the enemy, it is virtually impossible to develop a political solution" (p. 150). Menchu (1984) also asserts the need for the development of oppressed ethnic communities within a just international world order. Shakur (1987), the most "nationalist" of the African American autobiographers, advocates internationalism as a balance to nationalist commitments:

> It was also clear to me that without a truly internationalist component nationalism was reactionary. There was nothing revolutionary about nationalism by itself—Hitler and Mussolini were nationalists. Any community seriously concerned with its own freedom has to be concerned about other people's freedom as well. The victory of oppressed people anywhere in the world is a victory for Black people. . . . Imperialism is an international system of exploitation, and we, as revolutionaries, need to be internationalists to defeat it. (p. 267)

One student wrote that Shakur's autobiography "illustrates the integration of multiple elements: art, music, poetry, history, education, armed struggle, day to day survival, and flexibility, which are necessary for a revolution."

Still others described Chungara's (1978) autobiography as less engaging, partly because of its lack of creative writing, partly because of its silence about racism, ethnicity, and traditional indigenous values. Of the six autobiographies, Chungara's pays the least attention to ethnicity and race. Unlike Crow Dog (Crow Dog & Erdoes, 1990), who emphasizes traditional religions, or Menchu (1984), who seeks a return to ancestral ways and traditional indigenous culture as well as economic justice, Chungara (1978) focuses nearly exclusively on the Bolivian working class. An advocate for exploited miners, she emphasizes the importance of class, socialism, and, especially, internationalism:

> Many other countries suffer persecutions, outrages, murders, massacres, like Bolivia. And how beautiful it is to feel that in other peoples we have brothers and sisters who support us, who are in solidarity with us, and make us understand that our struggles aren't isolated from one another. (p. 37)

It was resistance to international solidarity for workers among some feminists that led to Chungara's strong critique of feminism. *Let Me Speak!* recounts Chungara's disappointment in an international women's conference after participants, most of whom were economically privileged or European/American, rejected her plea for assistance to independence movements and exploited laborers:

> Our position is not like the feminists' position. We think our liberation consists primarily in our country being freed forever from the yoke of imperialism and we want a worker like us to be in power and the laws, education, everything, to be controlled by this person. Then yes, we'll have better conditions for reaching a complete liberation, including our liberation as women. (p. 41)

The autobiographies challenge the construction of monolithic or essentialist approaches to nationalism as universally parochial, chauvinistic, and misogynist. Student generalizations of the Black liberation and Indian movements as uniformly shaped by patriarchal nationalism had led them to dissociate any gender-progressive politics from men or women in national liberation movements within the U.S. in the 1970s. Their assumptions were problematized in an assigned reading, Manning Marable's essay "Groundings With My Sisters" (1983a), which uses a quote from Michelle Wallace's *Black Macho and the Myth of the Superwoman* (1979) to describe patriarchy in the Black liberation movements:

> Every black leader of the 60s accepted and perpetuated the idea of the Black Macho, the notion that all political and social power was somehow sexual and that the possession of a penis was a symbol of revolution. (quoted in Marable, 1983a, p. 100)

Marable is aware that this passage cannot be easily applied to women, who formed a good part of the civil rights leadership. He takes this quote from Wallace's book, in order to critique her reductive depiction of Black leadership as uniformly male. A number of students referred to Wallace's passage (attributing it to Marable) while remaining uncritical of its erasure of women's leadership or of its divergence from the women's own accounts of the complexity of gender struggles within the movements; these accounts by women activists did not erase the sexist and abusive practices of indigenous or African American males. As accurate as the above quote is in regard to tendencies and trends—patriarchy and misogyny obviously existed within the Black movement and the American Indian movement— it is unclear if this machismo can be generalized to all male leaders. For instance, Assata Shakur (1987), a leader in the Black liberation movement, who describes how sexism and elitism led her to leave the Black Panther Party (BPP), writes of her coactivist Zayd Shakur: "I also respected him because he refused to become part of the macho cult that was official in the BPP. He never voted on issues or took a position just to be one of the boys" (p. 223). Despite the constraints of conservative or reactionary gender politics, women's radical independence and interdependency shaped resistance movements and provided national leadership. According to Jaimes's essay, coauthored with Theresa Halsey (1992), on indigenous women and feminism,

> Contrary to those images of meekness, docility and subordination to males with which we women typically have been portrayed by the dominant culture's books and movies, anthropology and political ideologues of both rightist and leftist persuasions, it is women who have formed the very core of resistance to genocide and colonization since the first moment of conflict between Indians and invaders. (p. 311)

Alongside Jaimes's (Jaimes & Halsey, 1992) text, the autobiographical writings exhibit an awareness of gender/sexual oppression coexistent with other injustices and inequalities. Their concepts of liberation pursued *women's equality through the liberation of a people, not a gender within a people.* This of course meant that the goals of liberation could not be set by masculinist standards, a fact that women activists recognized alongside the various constituencies to be freed from oppression. As Rigoberta Menchu (1984) observes: "We have to erase the barriers which exist between ethnic groups, between Indians and *ladinos*, between men and women, between intellectuals and nonintellectuals, and between all the linguistic areas" (p. 223). Erasing barriers and hierarchies in the pursuit of social justice proved extremely dangerous.

REPRESSION AND WOMEN'S RESISTANCE

The autobiographies describe how social-justice organizing was met by a backlash of repression. All the writers were politically targeted for imprisonment, violence, or both. Anne Moody (1968), who was herself placed on a local Klan's hit list because of her civil rights activism, describes the use of lynchings or "terror killings" in the 1960s as a means of intimidating whole communities, to prevent human rights activism. In the 1970s, the Black Panther Party and the American Indian Movement were infiltrated by government informers, some of whom incited violent behavior within the organizations. The FBI and the police were instrumental in assaulting indigenous and African American leaders in the 1970s: incarcerating some as political prisoners, such as Angela Davis, Leonard Peltier (who remains imprisoned), and Assata Shakur (in political exile in Cuba), and intimidating countless other activists in order to destabilize progressive movements.

The autobiographical accounts of violence are grimly shocking for most students unfamiliar with police brutality and police state measures employed during that era: Assata Shakur (1987) recounts New Jersey police actively encouraging her death by repeatedly obstructing her ambulance transport after she was severely wounded by state troopers' gunfire. Crow Dog (Crow Dog & Erdoes, 1990) describes her own violent arrest at Pine Ridge, where from 1973 to 1975, she reports, as many as 25 people out of a population of 8,000 were killed for their political activities or for association with progressives (pp. 193, 195); Crow Dog also links Bureau of Indian Affairs agent/tribal leader Dick Wilson and the FBI to those deaths, including the assassination and mutilation of Anna Mae Aquash (pp. 218–219). Beatings, torture, and the deaths of friends and loved ones have marked and marred the lives of radical women in the United States.

Political violence against indigenous peoples and activists in Latin America, however, was even more brutish and pervasive. Menchu (1984) and Chungara (1978) offer autobiographical accounts of systemic, devastating brutality.[3] Menchu's family was massacred by the military. While pregnant, Chungara, who states that CIA agents were present during her interrogation, was detained in jail and tortured until she gave birth to her dead child.

Despite their experiences of state-directed atrocities, each woman critiques vanguard militarism among activists confronting state violence. Shakur (1987), who argues for political strategies that include large numbers of people, criticizes obsessive, romantic militarism within sections of the BPP. A founder of the Housewives Committee for peasant mining communities, Chungara (1978) maintains that Che Guevara's failure to organize an international liberation movement, and his capture and execution by the Bolivian military, were due in part to the revolutionaries' alienation from poor people who were not necessarily supporters of armed struggle: "It seems to me that that was the mistake these guerrillas made: they didn't get close enough to the people. No one can get anywhere if they aren't in tight with the people" (p. 67).

Not only external violence, but also violence internal to oppressed communities undermined Native and African American communities. In the class's definition, external genocidal violence included systemic poverty; the suppression of traditional cultural practices and languages through religious and educational systems; repression from the police, army, and right-wing vigilantes. Using a term from *The State of Native America* (Jaimes, 1992) the class referred to violence among Native and African Americans as "autogenocide." We understood autogenocidal violence as manifested in community-generated violence. Expanding the definition of auto-genocide to include the failure to resist oppression, assimilation, and working for oppressive conditions, students blurred the distinctions between passivity, opportunism, and complicity, setting very high standards with which to judge Native and African Americans. Paradoxically, they also relied uncritically on a presentation at a women's conference that described "horizontal violence" (autogenocide) as stemming from "vertical violence" (genocide). Some used this construct to absolve oppressed peoples from any responsibility for destructive behavior; this absolution extended to Native and African American men's sexual assaults and domestic violence (autogenocide) whose abuses were excused because the males were oppressed by "vertical" or state violence.

Examples of African or Native American genocide and autogenocide appear in each woman's autobiography. Concerning autogenocide, Angela Davis (1974/1988) writes of her childhood classmates who "fought the meanness of Birmingham while they sliced the air with knives and punched black faces because they could not reach white ones" (p. 94). Anne Moody (1986) describes her father's depression, caused by his inability to provide for the family, and his emotional violence inside the family. In addition, her mother—pregnant with her seventh child by Moody's unemployed stepfather—cried so much, according to Moody, that "she almost drove us all crazy. Every evening I came home from work, she was beating on the children making them cry too" (p. 113). This violence, which Moody describes as based in racial and economic oppression, erupted in the streets as well as in homes:

> Some Negroes would come to town on Saturday night just to pick a fight with another Negro. Once the fight was over, they were satisfied. They beat their frustrations and discontent out on each other. (p. 261)

Drug abuse and domestic violence were also identified as aspects and in-
stigators of autogenocide. In Native American communities, the inability
of Native males to function in untraditional roles as "head of the household" or "breadwinner"

> led to a perpetual spiral of internalized violence in which Indian men engage
> in brutal (and all too often lethal) bar fights with one another, or turn their
> angry attentions on their wives and children. (Jaimes & Halsey, 1992, p. 325)

Jaimes and Halsey write that colonization "has manifested itself in the most
pronounced incidence of alcoholism of any ethnic group in the United
States," resulting in fetal alcohol syndrome, higher death rates from drunk
driving and higher rates of "child abuse and abandonment, [both] unknown
in traditional native societies" (p. 325). "Colonially induced despair" also
created a wave of teen suicide in Native American communities in the 1980s
that was several times higher than the national average (p. 325).

Despite there being violence, betrayal, and massive fissures in community foundations, the autobiographers portray their ethnic groups as a
people with shared interests, values, and culture; that is, as a community.
The women's affirmation of the ability to build community irrespective of
genocidal and autogenocidal violence challenged students' perceptions of
agency and power that focused on the isolated individual.

Students found commonalities in the women's resistance to violence
and abuse. For instance, Shakur (1987) and Moody (1968) both write about
their experiences as teenagers with sexual violence and harassment inside
the African American community: Moody is sexually harassed by her stepfather and forced to leave home; Shakur, a runaway, escapes a "train" or
gang rape by Black male teens. Moody's accounts of sexual abuse, family
rejection, extreme poverty as a girl and young adult resonated with women
students. Although overwhelmed by racist violence, political repression,
nonsupportive family, the financial burdens of attending and graduating
from college, Moody continued to grow as a woman in the movement,
through her struggles and in "the struggle." Several student papers quoted
Moody's passage: "Something happened to me as I got more and more
involved in the Movement. . . . It no longer seemed important to prove anything. I had found something outside myself that gave meaning to my life"
(p. 263).

Moody's (1968) and Crow Dog's (Crow Dog & Erdoes, 1990) "coming-
of-age" stories, detailing adolescent alienation and abuse, were especially
compelling for students who were in their late teens or early to mid 20s.
Young people struggling with racial identity, some with "mixed" parent-
age, noted how both autobiographies refer to racism and colorism, reveal-

ing painful, personal experiences of rejection or acceptance in which "light-skin" or "high-yellow" were constructed in opposition to "dark-skin" Blacks or "full-blood" in opposition to "half-breed" Indians. Observing that in the residential schools, White teachers/administrators favored lighter-skinned Indians, some students compared the attempts to de-Indianize indigenous peoples with the dependence fostered in African American schools/education. However, the cultural genocide and violence of residential schools is unique to Native Americans. *Lakota Woman* (Crow Dog & Erdoes, 1990) describes this particularly violent assimilation through institutional education:

> The kids were taken away from their villages and pueblos, in their blankets and moccasins, kept completely isolated from their families—sometimes for as long as ten years—suddenly coming back, their short hair slick with pomade, their necks raw from stiff, high collars, their thick jackets always short in the sleeves and pinching them under the arms, their tight patent leather shoes giving them corns, the girls in starched blouses and clumsy, high buttoned boots—caricatures of white people. When they found out—and they found out quickly—that they were neither wanted by whites nor by Indians—they got good and drunk, many of them staying drunk for the rest of their lives. (p. 30)

Regardless of violent repression and internal, domestic violence, Native and African American women activists consistently advocated a democratic concept of power. In these writings, power stemmed from the people as a collective: It was not reducible to military or intellectual vanguards and elites. The autobiographers criticize centralized, autocratic leadership, advocating a concept of shared, nonhierarchical leadership. Rigoberta Menchu (1984) maintains:

> [W]e have understood that each one of us is responsible for the struggle and we don't need leaders who only shuffle paper. We need leaders who are in danger, who run the same risks as the people. When there are many companeros with equal abilities, they must all have the opportunity to lead their struggle. (p. 228)

Nonelitist notions of leadership coexist with recognition of the role of culture in community identity, spirituality, and resistance. Moody (1968) describes the inspirational role of music in Black liberation movements: "Listening to those old negroes sing freedom songs was like listening to music from heaven. They sang as though they were singing away the chains of slavery" (p. 303). Traditional forms of singing and dancing by enslaved Africans and African Americans were banned just as the religious singing and dancing of Native Americans had been: In *Lakota Woman*, Crow Dog (1990) recounts indigenous efforts to revive the sun dance (p. 253). Collective leadership and culture, tenaciously shared and renewed, were cementing bonds for women and communities in crisis and resistance.

RADICAL VISIONARIES

The concept of "community" was the most problematic and contentious for the class. Students frequently used the existence of violence within groups or in intraethnic relations to argue the nonexistence of community. Interestingly, student alienation caused by emotional, physical, and sexual abuse within their families and society (some students volunteered accounts of surviving rape and other abuse) did not lead them to assert the nonexistence of family or society. Somehow community in its ideal form supplanted communities in their imperfect forms. Using its imperfect manifestations as a reason to negate the possibility of community, class members courted nihilism. With the perfection of an idealized community unavailable, they argued that in the absence of a "realizable" ideal, there was nothing for which to strive; struggling to transform flawed communities became unrealistic. Using this line of argument, students resigned themselves to the given social injustices as unchangeable reality. Without the courageous optimism of Moody's (1968) struggles, they echoed the pessimism of *Coming of Age in Mississippi*'s concluding paragraphs, which question the efficacy of communal power in the face of social/state violence and family betrayal.

When students stated that they had no community, belonged to and identified with none, their understanding of past, present, and future relationships were shaped by personal experiences of isolation as well as by a social ideology of individualism. Detailing violence and betrayal in community, the autobiographies also presented communal, democratic society as the fundamental enterprise, describing it not only as objective but also as a vehicle for social transformation: Liberation emerged from the unified efforts of people with common, progressive goals. When students reflected on the Native and African American women's perceptions of liberation as a collective enterprise, they strove to comprehend the claims made by Davis (1974/1988) (and others) that "individual activity—sporadic and disconnected—is not revolutionary work" (p. 162). In the process, class members began to reexamine their personal individualism as neither universally applicable to the women activists, nor even uniformly applicable to their own lives:

> Many of my attempts to understand and name my community have been frustrated by my individualist education. My tendency has

been to try and "figure out" where i "fit in," rather than recognizing that i am already a part of a community, and in actuality, many communities. (J. M.)

The concept of *many communities* rather than of one exclusive community is found within the autobiographies. As members of multiethnic political groups, most of the writers present community as expansive and internationalist. At times their political affiliations, such as Davis's (former) membership in the Communist Party USA and Menchu's affiliation with *Comité de Unidad Campesina*, did not necessarily embody the cultural and spiritual values of the cultures of their youths. Davis (1974/1988) describes an "overwhelming sense of belonging to a community of humans—a community of struggle against poverty and racism" (p. 2). Menchu (1984) writes: "The important thing is that what has happened to me has happened to many other people too: my story is the story of all poor Guatemalans. My personal experience is the reality of a whole people" (p. 1). For the autobiographers, community is transcendent, unrestricted by color, language, gender, or even conventional time and space. For some, such as Davis (1974/1988), it includes ancestors:

> There were visions in my head of my grandmother going to join Harriet Tubman, where she would look down peacefully upon the happenings in this world. Wasn't she being lowered into the same soil where our ancestors had fought so passionately for freedom? After her burial the old country lands took on for me an ineffable, awe-inspiring dimension: they became the stage on which the history of my people had been acted out. And my grandmother, in death, became more heroic. I felt a strange kind of unbreakable bond, vaguely religious, with her in that new world that she entered. (p. 82)

A sense of community, independent of oppression, is reflected in Menchu's (1984) writings on her traditional customs:

> So, a mother on her first day of pregnancy goes with her husband to tell these elected leaders that she's going to have a child, because the child will not only belong to them, but to the whole community, and must follow as far as he can in our ancestors' traditions. The leaders then pledge the support of the community and say: "We will help you, we will be the child's second parents." (p. 7)

These understandings of community, as well as women's sense of accountability to community, called women to, and sustained them in, political activism. They became the conduit for students rethinking their own perceptions of communal relations.

RADICALISM DEMYSTIFIED

In Gender, Race, and Radicalism, the initial student confusion and frustration with unconventional topic, texts, and pedagogy were predictable. However, for some students, classroom frustrations and uneasiness gave way to introspection and insight in papers and journal entries. Only that summer, though, while reading anonymous course evaluations, did I find out that most students were deeply affected by our study of the autobiographies of Red/Black women activists.

Many students were/are survivors of racism, sexism, homophobia, anti-Semitism, and classism. Social violence, family abuse, or both had led them to see and represent themselves as victims powerless to effect social change. Initially, students were baffled at how women activists kept faith and agency amid oppression. Gradually, through their reflections on the political–spiritual values and collective struggles revealed in the autobiographies, students began to respond to narratives of resistance. Relatively privileged ones had been moved to write:

> Reflecting on the tremendous fears that festered in these communities and served as a constant barrier to [unified resistance] . . . I began to analyze my own fears which keep me from truly dedicating myself to the struggle against racism. . . . There are two primary fears which I find myself faced with as I work through and analyze my own racism and white privilege. The first is the fear of isolation, of losing support from family and friends for having ideas which are "too radical." The second, the fear of moving down the class system. . . . All my life I have been prepared by my family, friends, and a white education system, to stay in the same class level or move up through individual achievement in high school and college in order to *succeed* in a well-paying job. (R. G.)

Using the course as a channel for examining the political commitments that they felt socially marginalized them, class members who sought to see themselves as engagees were empowered by Native and African American women radicals. Without sharing the experiences or political ideologies of the autobiographers, students reaffirmed their commitments *actively* to counter racism, (hetero)sexism, and economic poverty, irrespective of the (un)popularity of these politics in the general society. Displaying a resilience for critical inquiry and self-reflection, some confronted their fears with a resolve to continue their investigations and commitments:

> so severe is the reality of political repression, that we at times find ourselves paralyzed by fear and overwhelmed by feelings of hope-

lessness and grief. the emphasis so often placed on the realities of the oppressions we act to counter can sometimes obscure the fact that the history of oppression is also a history of resistance. it is our connection to this history of resistance, to this history of pain, joy, struggle, strength and freedom, which brings guidance and sustenance to our work. (J. M.)

Not only students found at least partial answers to spoken and unspoken questions. Over the years, I had repeatedly read the autobiographies as well as taught the African American autobiographers in other classes.[4] In the past, I had found these texts to be the most thought provoking component in courses. In Gender, Race, and Radicalism, rather than the literature itself, it was students' use of the autobiographies to decipher their own life stories and strengthen a resolve for ethical practice that called me closer to my own beliefs about radicalism. Focusing on the developing critical consciousness of my students, my own vision and paradigm became less cloudy. I was better able to see that in a one-semester journey, student struggles for self and community transformation radicalized the course and shaped our relationships in an academic site. Although students had repoliticized the classroom, critical questions about radicalism and academic intellectuals remained.

Earlier in the semester, when I had encouraged students to differentiate between the radicalisms of the women's autobiographies, they responded by pressing me to give my own political identification: Was I a "radical"? A "revolutionary"? If so, in what ways? These "naming questions"—which I had never put to them—I was unable and unwilling to answer at the time. In one of our last classes, I finally stated that an academic, such as myself, had self-selected out of a revolutionary praxis to work within a corporate setting that modifies radical notions of social transformation. Several of my students, disagreeing with my refusal to name myself—*as a teacher*—on a radical continuum, offered their own assessment of teachers and students struggling in academic sites:

There needs to be some criteria for the evaluation of political action that claims to be revolutionary. . . . A revolutionary agenda is one which is able to adequately confront colonialism and genocide [one] which can not be co-opted by the oppressive dominant society. We feel however that actions in themselves are not inherently "revolutionary" or "nonrevolutionary"; it is the context in which they occur and their connection to a larger movement for change that determines their revolutionary status. In order for one's action[s] to be revolutionary, they must be consciously connected to a larger movement for revolutionary change. Under this definition, it is possible for even the University professor who makes concessions in order to remain in an academic institution to be contributing to a revolutionary process. (J. M./J. L.)

COURSE TEXTS/VISUAL RESOURCES

Historical/Analytical Readings

Jaimes, Annette (Ed.). (1992). *The State of Native America.* Boston: South End Press.
Marable, Manning. (1983). *How Capitalism Underdeveloped Black America.* Boston: South End Press.

Autobiographies

Chungara, Domitila. (1978). *Let me speak!* New York: Monthly Review.
Crow Dog, Mary, & Erdoes, Richard. (1990). *Lakota Woman.* New York: Grove.
Davis, Angela. (1988). *The autobiography of Angela Davis.* New York: International Publishers. (Original work published 1974)
Menchu, Rigoberta. (1984). *I, Rigoberta Menchu: An Indian woman in Guatemala.* London: Verso.
Moody, Ann. (1968). *Coming of age in Mississippi.* New York: Dell.
Shakur, Assata. (1987). *Assata: An autobiography.* London: Zed.

Videos/Films

Bravehearted woman: Anna Mae. Brown Bird Productions. 1980. [Video]. (Film on Anna Mae Aquash and Pine Ridge occupation and police/FBI repression in 1973)
Ethnic Notions. Marlon Riggs (Director). California Newsreel, 1987. [Video]. (Documentary of anti-Black racism in popular culture and entertainment from 19th to 20th centuries)
In the image of the white man. Public Broadcasting Service. (Documentary on the forced relocation of indigenous children into U.S. residential schools)
Interview with Assata. Gil Noble (Director). *Like It Is.* 1988. (African American, New York City–based television talk show)
Eyes on the prize II: Nation of law? Michael Chin & Robert Shepard (Directors). Blackside Productions. 1989. [Video]. (This segment of the series, focusing on FBI Cointelpro and Attica rebellion, includes an interview with Angela Davis on prisons and human rights)
When the mountains tremble. Pamela Yates & Thomas Sigel (Directors). New Yorker Films. 1983. [Video]. (Film on the U.S. funding of the Guatemalan military and human rights abuses against Native Americans, narrated by Rigoberta Menchu)

Supplemental Readings

Churchill, W., & VanderWall, J. (1989). *Agents of repression: The FBI's war against the Black Panther Party (BPP) and the American Indian Movement (AIM)*. Boston: South End Press.
Churchill, W., & VanderWall, J. (1992). *Struggle for the land*. Maine: Common Courage Press.
Katz, W. L. (1986). *Black Indians: A hidden heritage*. New York: Atheneum.
National Urban League. (1988). *The state of Black America*. New York: National Urban League.

NOTES

1. According to Francis Boyle (1988), the U.S. Senate's 1986 ratification of the *UN Convention on Genocide*, with its crippling amendments, was an attempt to prevent Native Americans and African Americans from petitioning the government under the Genocide Convention.

2. Curious to see if students identified variations of radicalism, I asked about the differences between revolutionary, radical, liberal, and conservative politics. Our imprecise definitions (I refused to provide a "definitive" definition) reflected the general imprecision of political references and labels for political phenomena. Students who felt confident enough to distinguish, even if with some imprecision, between conservatism, liberalism, and radicalism were nonplussed when asked to differentiate between *radical* and *revolutionary*; revolutionary was either indistinguishable from radical or, as irrelevant terminology, was absent from the political continuum.

3. Distinguishing assimilation from acculturation, Menchu's autobiography presents ladinized Indians who joined the Guatemalan army and killed indigenous people as having assimilated or adopted the "genocidal" values of the dominant culture: She describes as acculturated those who learn the language, trades, and technology of Guatemalans in a process of adaptation of methods or resources of the dominant culture, with the aim of serving oppressed people.

4. I examine the autobiographical writings of African American women as a form of theorizing in "African Philosophy, Theory, and 'Living Thinkers'" and in "Teaching Theory, Talking Community," both in *Spirit, Space and Survival*.

REFERENCES

Allen, Paula Gunn. (1988). *The sacred hoop: Recovering the feminine in American Indian traditions*. Boston: Beacon Press.
Boyle, Francis. (1989). The hypocrisy and racism behind the formulation of U.S. human rights foreign policy. *Social Justice*, (16)1, 71–93.
Chungara, Domitila. (1978). *Let me speak!* New York: Monthly Review.

Crow Dog, Mary, & Erdoes, Richard. (1990). *Lakota woman*. New York: Grove.

Davis, Angela. (1988). *The autobiography of Angela Davis*. New York: International. (Original work published 1974)

Jaimes, Annette. (Ed.). (1992). *The state of native America*. Boston: South End Press.

Jaimes, Annette, & Halsey, T. (1992). American Indian women: At the center of indigenous resistance in North America. In A. Jaimes, *The state of Native America* (pp. 311–344).

James, Joy. (1993a). African philosophy, theory, and "Living Thinkers". In J. James & R. Farmer (Eds.), *Spirit, space and survival: African American women in (white) academe* (pp. 31–46). New York: Routledge.

James, Joy. (1993b). Teaching theory, talking community. In J. James & R. Farmer (Eds.), *Spirit, space and survival* (pp. 118–135).

James, Joy. (1994). The politics of language and of law: Racism, resistance and the UN Treaty on Genocide. In A. Callari, C. Biewener, & S. Cullenberg (Eds.), *Marxism in the new world order: Crises and possibilities* (pp. 115–125). New York: Guilford.

Kuhn, Thomas. S. (1962). *The structure of scientific revolutions*. Chicago: University of Chicago Press.

Marable, Manning. (1983a). Groundings with my sisters. In M. Marable, *How capitalism underdeveloped Black America* (pp. 69–104). Boston: South End Press.

Marable, Manning. (1983b). *How capitalism underdeveloped Black America*. Boston: South End Press.

Menchu, Rigoberta. (1984). *I, Rigoberta Menchu: An Indian woman in Guatemala*. London: Verso.

Moody, Anne. (1968). *Coming of age in Mississippi*. New York: Dell.

Patterson, William. (Ed.). (1951). *We charge genocide: The crime of government against the Negro people. A petition to the United Nations*. New York: Civil Rights Congress.

Shakur, Assata. (1987). *Assata: An autobiography*. London: Zed.

Spillers, Hortense. (1987). Mama's Baby, Papa's Maybe: An American Grammar Book. *Diacritics, 17*(2), 65–81.

ABOUT THE AUTHOR

Joy James teaches feminist and political theory in the Department of Ethnic Studies at the University of Colorado at Boulder. She coedited *Spirit, Space and Survival: African-American Women in (White) Academe* (Routledge, 1993), which won the Gustavus Myers Human Rights Award, and is the author of *Resisting State Violence: Radicalism, Gender and Race in U.S. Culture* (University of Minnesota Press, 1996). James's most recent work is *The Angela Y. Davis Reader* (Blackwell). She is currently working on issues of prisoners' rights.

Index

Abbott, Franklin, 57
Action, consciousness-raising and, 109–110
Adaptive approach, 77–78
Adler, Elizabeth, 74
Administrators, feminist, 6, 178–183
Advertising, 90–91
African Americans. *See* Blacks
African Religions and Philosophies (Mbiti), 80
Ageism, humanism versus, 51
AIDS, 155, 156
Allen, Pamela, 112, 112
Allen, Paula Gunn, 80, 240
American Association of University Women, 31
American Dream/Myth of Success and, 138–139, 141
American Indian Movement (AIM), 244, 248
Amherst College, 236
Amnesty International, 243
Andersen, Margaret L., 68
Antifeminism, 2
Antiracism, 76–77, 135, 235
Apple, Michael W., 216
Aquash, Anna Mae, 243, 248
Arbeiter, Joan, 111
Arendt, H., 80
Arnold, Matthew, 188
Association of American Colleges, 4–5, 31–42
Atlas Shrugged (Rand), 83
Attendance, 28–29

Audet, Elaine, 229
August, Eugene R., 57
Authentic relationships, 194–195
Authority
    attendance by students and, 28–29
    concept of, 25
    in selection of course content, 27–28, 29
    of teachers, 4, 25–30
    use of teacher's paper and, 29
Autobiography of Angela Davis (Davis), 243
Autogenocide, 249
Averages, generalizations and, 65

Backlash
    to feminism, 2
    to gay/lesbian coming out, 200–201
    of repression, 248–252
Bakhtin, M., 120
Banking concept of education (Freire), 117, 121, 125, 194
Bardige, Betty, 58
Baris, Mireille, 228
Bart, Pauline, 229–230
Baudino, Gael, 218
Beecher, Catharine, 210
Being and Time (Heidegger), 185
Belenky, Mary Field, 85, 193–194, 197
Belknap, Joanne, 74
Benke, Timothy, 57
Berg, Allison, 6, 7, 168–177, 170
Berger, P. L., 79
Bernard, Jessie, 142

2430